Entrepreneurship in India

Entrepreneurship in India

Dr. Deependra Sharma

Dean & Professor
Unitedworld School of Business
Karnavati University, Gandhinagar
Gujarat, India.

Routledge
Taylor & Francis Group

LONDON AND NEW YORK

Manakin
PRESS

First published 2023
by Routledge
4 Park Square, Milton Park, Abingdon, Oxon OX14 4RN

and by Routledge
605 Third Avenue, New York, NY 10017

Routledge is an imprint of the Taylor & Francis Group, an informa business

© 2023 Contributors and Manakin Press

Print edition not for sale in South Asia (India, Sri Lanka, Nepal, Bangladesh, Pakistan or Bhutan)

British Library Cataloguing-in-Publication Data
A catalogue record for this book is available from the British Library

Library of Congress Cataloging-in-Publication Data
A catalog record for this book has been requested

ISBN 13: 978-1-03-237858-9 (hbk)
ISBN 13: 978-1-03-237860-2 (pbk)
ISBN 13: 978-1-00-334228-1 (ebk)

DOI: 10.4324/9781003342281

Typeset in Times New Roman
by Manakin Press, Delhi

Manakin
PRESS

Foreword

"Entrepreneurship" has been a buzzword for quite some time but it has not yet been able to assume the shape of a mass movement, especially in India. There has also emerged a good amount of literature on this subject but even this too has failed to evoke the desired response. To say this is not to say that entrepreneurs are not there in our country, they are there but not to the desired extent. India is rich in natural resources and further that today it has the largest number of young people - a good number of whom are engineering and management graduates - and is likely to be so in the near future as well. Though many of them are talented but the spirit of entrepreneurship is, by and large, missing. There may be a number of factors that may give rise to this sort of spirit but one such vital factor is the availability of a good book that presents a vivid picture of the concept of entrepreneurship and all other relevant issues that may prompt the youth, especially the budding managers, not only to take a dip into the ocean of entrepreneurship but also to swim effectively and successfully to undertake the journey of entrepreneurship to its logical ends. It is here that the book entitled, 'Entrepreneurship in India', comes into vogue.

It is my pleasure to state here that the book in question is a beautiful and meaningful exercise in presenting the complete anatomy of entrepreneurship in a packed volume as it is before the readers. Besides explaining the concept and meaning of entrepreneurship initially, the author endeavours to spell out the process of entrepreneurship and identifies opportunities available, in addition to presenting feasibility analysis. Going further and having explained the intricacies of a business plan, the author ventures into presenting industry and competition analysis. How to build a new venture, especially the financial, funding and marketing issues involved, the importance of intellectual property rights, challenges of business growth and how to tackle them, are some of the other issues that are dealt with in the right perspective. A very important factor rarely touched upon by others,

v

pertains to the ethical aspect being faced by the new ventures, in addition to social entrepreneurship, has been given a fairly good treatment.

I deem it my privilege to write a foreword for the present treatises on entrepreneurship which is written in a good mix of lucid and ostentatious style and gives readers a whole gamut of exposure to an interesting subject of entrepreneurship.

Prof (Dr) RC Sharma
(Ex-Professor Emeritus)
Amity Business School, AUG)
Founder Vice Chancellor
Amity University, Gurugram

Preface

Studying and practising entrepreneurship is gaining importance across the world including India. It is acknowledged as a highly beneficial activity not only for the entrepreneurs but also for the economies in which they start their ventures and conduct their operations. I am thrilled about this book because it has been observed that even during challenging economic conditions, currently because of COVID-19, start-ups are conceptualizing and offering new products and services that make lives easier, more productive and healthier for the world citizens.

In this book, while discussing the characteristics of an entrepreneur, readers will recognise that entrepreneurs are some of the most zealous and inspirational people they would ever meet. It is evident by the fact that Infosys was found in garage or in a hostel room like Facebook. Further, passion an entrepreneur has about a business idea is more critical than posh offices for the success of any new venture. But, it should be noted that only passion and motivation alone are not sufficient. One needs to have right information at the right time, a feasible business idea, and the knowledge to execute the business plan effectively and efficiently to ensure success.

This book will offer practical guidance as how to launch a successful and growth oriented entrepreneurial venture by following the entrepreneurial process. The process includes opportunity recognition and conducting feasibility analysis. It is critical for the success because many a time the idea entrepreneur tries to bring to the marketplace is not representing the right opportunity. The entrepreneur needs to understand the difference between idea and opportunity.

Therefore, the main objective of this book is to sensitize the reader about the various steps involved in the entrepreneurial journey of setting up a new venture. It will enhance the success probability of the start-up as the entrepreneur would be able to appreciate thoroughly not only the various steps involved in the entrepreneurial process but also will learn how to effectively and efficiently follow those steps to bring desirable results.

Editor

Contributors List

1. **Amit Kumar Marwah,** Professor, Acropolis Institute of Technology and Research, Indore (MP).

2. **Amruta Desai,** Freelancer, Marketing & Creative Ventures.

3. **Bhavesh P. Joshi,** Professor, Manav Rachna International Institute of Research and Studies, Faridabad (India).

4. **Himani Singhal,** Assistant Professor, DPGITM, Sector 34, Gurugram.

5. **Kumar Abhishek,** Assistant Professor (MBA Dept.) & Assistant Registrar (Academic), Dr. Abdul Kalam Technical University, Lucknow.

6. **Manisha Gaur,** Assistant Professor, Swami Vivekanand College of Engineering, Indore (MP).

7. **Manisha Gupta,** Assistant Professor, Associate-Professor School of Business Studies, Sharda University, Greater Noida.

8. **N K Sharma,** Principal, Vivek College of Management and Technology, UP.

9. **Nandita Mishra,** Dean & Professor, MITCON Institute of Management Pune.

10. **Rajesh Kumar Pandey,** Associate Professor, SSR IMR, Silvassa Affiliated to SPPU, Pune.

11. **S Anjani Devi,** Assistant Professor, GITAM Institute of Management, GITAM (Deemed to be University), Visakhapatnam.

12. **Sakha Gangadhara Rama Rao,** Assistant Professor, GITAM Institute of Management, GITAM (Deemed to be University), Visakhapatnam.

13. **Sanjeev Malaviya,** Assistant Professor & Faculty Coordinator, ICFAI Business School, ICFAI University Dehradun.

14. **Soni Sharma,** Assistant Professor, Birla Institute of Management Technology.

Brief Contents

Detailed Contents

1

What is Entrepreneurship?

Dr. Soni Sharma
(Assistant Professor, Birla Institute of Management Technology)
Dr. N K Sharma
(Principal, Vivek College of Management and Technology, UP)

LEARNING OBJECTIVES

After reading this chapter, the reader should be able to:

1. Develop the understanding about entrepreneurship and its importance.
2. Appreciate the concept of corporate entrepreneurship and its importance in established firms.
3. Identify factors that make an individual a successful entrepreneur.
4. Bust the myths on entrepreneurship.
5. Understand the impact of entrepreneurial firms on economies and societies.

Entrepreneurship has created tremendous interest and attention around the world. Nevertheless, this statement might sound bold, there are enough examples to prove it. Some of which are itself authenticated by the Global Entrepreneurship Monitor (GEM). It is a joint research initiative by Babson College, London Business School, and Universided del Desarrollo, Santiago, Chile. GEM is mainly focused on the research of those businesses which are in the initial stage of entrepreneurial activity, and businesses that have been running for less than three and half years. The 2010 survey showed that nearly 110 million people between 18 and 64 years old were just starting businesses, and another 140 million were running businesses they started less than three and one-half years ago. As survey suggested around 250 million people were found engaged in primary entrepreneurial activity in the 59 countries included in the study. A sample of the rate of early-stage entrepreneurial activity in countries included in the GEM study is shown in Table 1.1.

Table 1.1: Rates of early-stage entrepreneurial activity (ages 18 to 64)

Country	Percent of Population Starting a New Business
Argentina	14.2%
Brazil	17.5%
China	14.4%
France	5.8%
Germany	4.2%
Peru	27.2%
Russia	3.9%
Turkey	8.6%
United Kingdom	6.4%
United States	7.6%

Source: Based on D. Kelley, N. Bosma, and J. E. Amoros, Global Entrepreneurship Monitor 2010 Global Report (Babson College and Universidad del Desarrollo, 2010).

Entrepreneurial start-up activities were found quite high and frequent in low-income countries, where good jobs were not sufficient, however, the rates were also satisfactory in high-income countries like France (5.8 percent), United Kingdom (6.4 percent), and the United States (7.6 percent). What the 7.6 percent means for the United States is that almost 1 out of every 13 American adults is actively engaged in starting a business or is the owner/manager of a business that is less than three and one-half years old.

The research found that the majority of people in high-income countries were attracted to entrepreneurship to take advantage of attractive opportunities provided by government. On the contrary, people in low-income countries, were involved in entrepreneurship primarily because of necessity or due to lack of employment. One negative side of entrepreneurship, which is mentioned frequently, is that the majority of new businesses fail. It merely is not true. The often used statistic that 9 out of 10 businesses fail in their first few years might be a myth or an exaggeration. Brian Head, a famous economist of the U.S. Small Business Administration concluded that after four years, 50 percent of new businesses were in the running position, 33 percent failed, and 17 percent were closed but were considered to be successful by their owners.

While overall these figures are heartening, the 33 percent of start-ups that fail show that a motivation to start and run a business isn't enough; it must be coupled with a solid business idea, good financial management, and effective execution to improve the chances for success. In this chapter, we will try to discuss and break the myth of failure through many examples of successful entrepreneurial firms.

1.1 What is Entrepreneurship?

The word entrepreneur has been derived from the French words entre, meaning 'between' and prendre; meaning 'to take'. The word was originally used to describe people who were able to take risk between buyers and sellers or who were able to handle such activities or task such as starting a new venture. Inventors and entrepreneurs are different from each other. An inventor or innovator creates something new. An entrepreneur collects and then assimilates all the resources needed—the money, the people, the business model, the strategy, and also the risk. He puts all the efforts to transform the invention into a workable business. Entrepreneurship is also a process in which an individual chases opportunities without being perturbed about the resources he needs to run business. Venture capitalist Fred Wilson defines it more simply, seeing entrepreneurship as the art of turning an idea into a business. The tasks called for by this behavior can be accomplished by either an individual or a group and typically require creativity, drive, and a willingness to take risks.

For instance, Sam Hogg, the cofounder of GiftZip.com, exemplifies all these qualities. Hogg saw an opportunity to create a single place for people to shop for electronic gift cards, he risked his career by giving up alternatives to work on GiftZip.com full-time, and he's now working hard to put GiftZip.com in a position to deliver a creative and useful service to its customers.

An entrepreneur or teams of entrepreneurs travel a journey after launching a new business. How ever, existing or running firms can also behave entrepreneurially. Established firms with an entrepreneurial emphasis are quite proactive, innovative, and risk-taking. It widely depends on the kind of success journey the business owner or a business had.

For example, Apple Inc. is widely recognized as a firm in which entrepreneurial behaviors are clearly evident. Steve Jobs was at the heart of Apple's entrepreneurial culture. He had the ability to persuade and motivate other's imaginations, He always inspired Apple's employees to develop innovative product. To consider the penetration Apple has with some of its innovations, think of how many of your friends own an iPhone, iPad, or Macintosh computer. Similarly, studying Facebook or Zynga's ability to grow and succeed reveals a history of entrepreneurial behavior at multiple levels within the firms. In addition, many of the firms that traded on the NASDAQ, such as Intuit, Amazon.com, Google, and Research in Motion are commonly thought of as entrepreneurial firms. The NASDAQ is the largest U.S. electronic stock market, with over 2,850 companies listed on the exchange. Established firms with an orientation to behave entrepreneurially practice corporate entrepreneurship. All firms fall along a conceptual continuum that ranges from highly conservative to highly entrepreneurial. The position of a firm on this continuum is referred to as its entrepreneurial intensity. As mentioned earlier, entrepreneurial firms are typically proactive innovators and are not averse to taking calculated risks. In contrast, conservative firms take a more "wait and see" posture, are less innovative, and are risk averse. One of the most persuasive indications of entrepreneurship's importance to an individual or to a firm is the degree of effort undertake to behave in an entrepreneurial manner.

Firms with higher entrepreneurial intensity regularly look for ways to cut bureaucracy.

1.2 Why to Become an Entrepreneur?

There may be various reasons to be an entrepreneur. But three primary reasons why people want to be entrepreneurs and start their own firms are to be their own boss, pursue their own ideas, and gain financial benefits.

1.2.1 Be Their Own Boss

The reason to be one's own boss—can be common. This doesn't mean, however, that it is difficult to work with them or that they feel uncomfortable accepting authority. Instead, many entrepreneurs want to be their own boss because either they have had a long aspirations to own their own firms or because they might be frustrated working in traditional jobs. The desire to be their own boss results from a realization that the only way they will achieve an important personal or professional goals is to start their own businesses.

For example, Christopher Jones, David LaBat, and Mary McGrath started a business for this reason. The three, who are educational psychologists, had secured jobs at a public school in the Santa Clarita Valley, north of Los Angeles. Over the time, they felt subdued by the limited range of services they were able to provide students in a school setting, so they left their jobs to start Dynamic Interventions, a more full-service educational psychology and counseling center. Jones felt that the idea came from some general frustrations with not being able to practice the breadth of service that they wanted to, and instead of going to work and being angry about it for the next 30 years, they decided to do something about it. With Dynamic Interventions, their services would not stop at the end of the school day. They can go more in-depth and be more beneficial to the whole family.

1.2.2 Pursue Their Own Ideas

The second reason people start their own firms is to pursue their own ideas. Some people are naturally alert, and when they recognize opportunities for new products or services, they have a desire to see those ideas realized. Corporate entrepreneurs who innovate within the context of an existing firm typically have a mechanism for their ideas to become known. Established firms, however, often resist innovation. When this happens, employees are left with good ideas that go unfulfilled. Because of their passion and commitment; some employees choose to leave the firms employing them in order to start their own businesses as the means to nurture their own ideas. This chain of events can take place in non-corporate settings, too. For example, some people, through a hobby, leisure activity, or just everyday life, recognize the need for a product or service that is not available in the marketplace. If the idea is viable enough to support a business, they commit tremendous time and energy to convert the idea into a part-time or full-time firm.

An example of a person who left a job to pursue an idea is Kevin Mann, the founder of Graphically, a social digital distribution platform for comic book publishers and fans. Mann became discouraged when he couldn't find a comic book in which he was interested. He even took a 100 mile train ride to search for it in a neighboring city. His frustration boiled over on the train ride home. He kept thinking that there had to be a better way of buying comics; and then it dawned on him. That morning he had purchased a movie from iTunes, which he was watching right there on the train. Why shouldn't buying comics be just as easy? Why did he has to travel over a 100 miles and waste the better part of day for no use. He realized he had two options. He could quit buying comics or he could quit his job and build the iTunes of comics. This revelation led to the launch of Graphically in the fall of 2009. Today, Graphically is both a robust platform for the sale of digital comics and a social network for people who enjoy discussing the comics they're reading.

1.2.3 Pursue Financial Rewards

People start their own firms to pursue financial rewards. This motivation, however, is typically secondary to the first two and often fails to live up to its hype. The average entrepreneur does not make more money than someone with a similar amount of responsibility in a traditional job. The financial lure of entrepreneurship is its upside potential. People such as Jeff Bezos of Amazon.com, Mark Zuckerberg of Facebook, and Larry Page and Sergey Brin of Google made hundreds of millions of dollars building their firms. Money is also a unifier. Making a profit and increasing the value of a company is a solidifying goal that people can rally around. But money is rarely the primary motivation behind the launch of an entrepreneurial firm. Some entrepreneurs even report that the financial rewards associated with entrepreneurship can be bittersweet if they are accompanied by losing control of their firm.

1.3 Characteristics of Successful Entrepreneurs

Although many behaviors have been ascribed to entrepreneurs, several are common to those who are successful. Those in new ventures and those who are already part of an entrepreneurial firm share these qualities.

1.3.1 Passion for the Business

The number one characteristic shared by successful entrepreneurs is a passion for their business, whether it is in the context of a new firm or an existing business. This passion typically stems from the entrepreneur's belief that the business will positively influence people's lives. For example "A" is a company that allows people with life-changing diseases to converse with one another, share their experiences, and learn techniques from one another that help them better cope with their diseases. Making a difference in people's lives is also the primary motivator behind many social enterprises, which are often started by people who set aside promising careers to pursue a social goal. Passion is particularly important for both for-profit and not-for-profit entrepreneurial organizations because, although rewarding, the process of starting a firm or building a social enterprise is demanding. There are five primary reasons why passion is important, as reflected in Table 1.2. Each of these reasons reflects a personal attribute that passion engenders. Removing just one of these qualities would make it much more difficult to launch and sustain a successful entrepreneurial organization.

Table 1.2   Five primary reasons of passions are important for the launch of a successful entrepreneurial organization

1. The ability to learn and iterate. Founders don't have all the answers. It takes passion and drive to solicit feedback, make necessary changes, and move forward.
2. A willingness to work hard for an extended period of time. Commonly, entrepreneurs work longer hours than people with traditional jobs. You can only do that, on a sustained basis, if you're passionate about what you're doing.
3. Ability to overcome setbacks and "no's" It's rare that an entrepreneur doesn't experience setbacks and hear many "no's" from potential customers, investors, and others while building an entrepreneurial business or social enterprise. The energy to continue comes from passion for an idea.
4. The ability to listen to feedback on the limitations of your organization and yourself. You'll meet plenty of people along the way—some with good intentions and some without—who will tell you how to improve your organization and how to improve yourself. You have to be willing to listen to the people with good intentions and make changes if it helps. You have to be able to brush aside feedback from people with bad intentions without letting them get you down.
5. Perseverance and persistence when the going gets tough .Perseverance and persistence come from passion. As an entrepreneur, you'll have down days. Building an entrepreneurial organization is fraught with challenges. Passion is what provides an entrepreneur the motivation to get through tough times

An entrepreneur should be always careful of this thought that entrepreneurs should not have only passion, they should not carry rose-colored glasses or live in fancy world. It would be a mistake to believe that all one needs is passion and anything is possible. It is important to be enthusiastic about a business idea, but it is also important to understand its potential flaws and risks. In addition, entrepreneurs should understand that the most effective business ideas take hold when their passion is consistent with their skills and is in an area that represents a legitimate business opportunity.

1.3.2 Product/Customer Focus

A second defining characteristic of successful entrepreneurs is a product/ customer focus. This quality is exemplified by Steven Jobs, the cofounder of Apple Inc., who commented the computer is the most remarkable tool which is ever built, but the most important thing is to get them in the hands of as many people as possible. This sentiment underscores an understanding of the two most important elements in any business—

products and customers. While it's important to think about management, marketing, finance, and the like, none of those functions makes any difference if a firm does not have good products with the capability to satisfy customers. It's also important to focus on the right things. For example, JibJab is a digital entertainment company, which was founded in 1999 by Evan and Gregg Spiridellis. It gained attention during the 2004 presidential election when its animated video of George W. Bush and John Kerry singing "This Land Is Your Land" became a hit. (It's been viewed on YouTube over 2.1 million times.) The goal of the company, from the start, was to build a scalable platform for creating and distributing digital entertainment products. A problem the founders had was they were really good animated content creators, so would get offers to do side jobs while working on their core business. They learned that they needed to be disciplined and quit doing this because it took time away from their real passion: You need to be disciplined. You need to turn down jobs. An entrepreneur needs to say that he could really use that $50,000 gig, but if they do that, they are going to be locked down for three months and they are not going to be able to do these other projects. So, its does require discipline and passing on opportunities. Knowing what to pass on is a really important skill which is important to be developed. A product/customer focus also involves the diligence to spot product opportunities and to see them through to completion. The idea for the Apple Macintosh, for example, originated in the early 1980s when Steve Jobs and several other Apple employees took a tour of a Xerox research facility. They were astounded to see computers that displayed graphical icons and pull-down menus. The computers also allowed users to navigate desktops using a small, wheeled device called a mouse. Jobs decided to use these innovations to create the Macintosh, the first user-friendly computer. Throughout the two and one-half years the Macintosh team developed this new product, it maintained an intense product/customer focus, creating a high-quality computer that is easy to learn, is fun to use, and meets the needs of a wide audience of potential users.

1.3.3 Tenacity Despite Failure

Because entrepreneurs are typically trying something new, the failure rate associated with their efforts is naturally high. In addition, the process of developing a new business is somewhat similar to what is an example of the degree of tenacity. There is a small story about the entrepreneur Kyle Smitley the founder of 'barley & birch', a business that sold organic children's clothing. Smitley launched barley & birch in January 2009, at the age of 22, with the goal of giving parents and children the most environmentally friendly clothing possible. Despite having flawless credit, she was turned down at every bank wherever she approached. She finally received a $10,000 loan from ACCION, a microfinance organization. She next embarked on a major marketing campaign, sending 500 hand-signed letters with literature about her products to environmentally friendly stores. That effort fell flat. She finally reached out to mom bloggers, who spread the word about her company, and motivated their readers to start asking about barley & birch products at children's clothing stores. By the end of 2009, Smitley's products were in 30 stores. With the help of sheer tenacity which prevented Smitley from giving up before she reached this critical milestone.

1.3.4 Execution Intelligence

Executing Intelligence (that allows him to convert an idea into a viable business is one of the key characteristic of successful entrepreneurs). In most of the instances, execution of intelligence is a determining factor of failed or successful startups. According to an ancient Chinese saying, "To open a business is very easy; to keep it open is very difficult." Effective execution of a business idea means to develop a business model, putting together a new venture team, raising money, establishing partnerships, managing finances, leading and motivating employees, and so on. It also demands the ability to translate thought, creativity, and imagination into action and measurable results. Jeff Bezos who is the founder of Amazon. com once said, "Ideas are easy. It's execution is hard." The biggest challenge before entrepreneurs is the hardest time is shortly after they launch their firm. Jodi Gallaer who is the founder of a lingerie company has found the entreprenurship as most challenging because in business you do every thing first time. To illustrate solid execution, let's look at Starbucks. Although Starbucks is not growing as fast and profitably as it once did, it is still a remarkable success story. The business idea of Howard Schultz, the entrepreneur who purchased Starbucks in 1987, was his recognition of the fact that most Americans didn't have a place to enjoy coffee in a comfortable, quiet setting. Seeing a great opportunity to satisfy customers' needs, Schultz attacked the marketplace aggressively to make Starbucks the industry leader and to establish a national brand. First, he hired a seasoned management team, constructed a world-class roasting facility to supply his outlets with premium coffee beans, and focused on building an effective organizational infrastructure. Then Schultz recruited a management information systems expert from McDonald's to design a point-of-sale system capable of tracking consumer purchases across 300 outlets. This decision was crucial to the firm's ability to sustain rapid growth over the next several years. Starbucks succeeded because Howard Schultz knew how to execute a business idea. He built a seasoned management team, implemented an effective strategy, and used information technology wisely to make his business thrive. These fundamental aspects of execution excellence should serve Schultz and Starbucks when it comes to dealing with the competitive challenges in future.

1.4 Common Myths about Entrepreneurs

There are many misconceptions about who entrepreneurs are and what motivates them to launch firms. Some misconceptions are because of the media covering atypical entrepreneurs, such as a couple of college students who obtain venture capital to fund a small business that they grow into a multimillion-dollar company. Such articles rarely state that these entrepreneurs are the exception rather than the norm and that their success is a result of carefully executing an appropriate plan to commercialize what inherently is a solid business idea. Let's look at the most common myths and the realities about entrepreneurs.

Myth 1: Entrepreneurs are Born, not Made

This myth is based on the mistaken belief that some people are genetically predisposed to be entrepreneurs. The consensus of many hundreds of studies on the psychological and sociological makeup of entrepreneurs is that entrepreneurs are not genetically different from other people. This evidence can be interpreted as meaning that no one is "born" to be an entrepreneur and that everyone has the potential to become one. Whether someone becomes an entrepreneur or doesn't is a function of environment, life experiences, and personal choices. However, there are personality traits and characteristics commonly associated with entrepreneurs; these are listed below:

Common traits and characteristic of Entrepreneurs:

- A moderate risk taker
- A networker
- Achievement motivated
- Alert to opportunities
- Creative
- Decisive
- Energetic
- A strong work ethic
- Lengthy attention span

These traits are developed over a period and evolve from an individual's social context. For example, studies show that people with parents who were self-employed are more likely to become entrepreneurs. After witnessing a father's or mother's independence in the workplace, an individual is more likely to find independence appealing. Similarly, people who personally know an entrepreneur are more than twice as likely to be involved in starting a new firm as those with no entrepreneur acquaintances or role models. The positive impact of knowing an entrepreneur is explained by the fact that direct observation of other entrepreneurs reduces the ambiguity and uncertainty associated with the entrepreneurial process.

Myth 2: Entrepreneurs are Gamblers

Another myth about entrepreneurs is that they are gamblers and take big risks. The truth is, entrepreneurs are usually moderate risk takers, as are most people. The idea that entrepreneurs are gamblers originates from two sources. First, entrepreneurs typically have jobs that are less structured, and so they face a more uncertain set of possibilities than managers or rank-and-file employees. For example, an entrepreneur who starts a social network consulting service has a less stable job than one working for a state governmental agency. Second, many entrepreneurs have a strong need to achieve and often set challenging goals, a behavior that is sometimes equated with risk taking.

Myth 3: Entrepreneurs are Motivated Primarily by Money

It is naïve to think that entrepreneurs don't seek financial rewards. As discussed previously, however, money is rarely the primary reason entrepreneurs start new firms. The importance and role of money in a start-up is put in perspective by Colin Angle, the founder and CEO of iRobot, the maker of the popular Roomba robotic vacuum cleaner. He commented on his company's mission statement to produce "iCool Stuff, Deliver Great Products, Have Fun, Make Money ,Change the World (mission statement)" unified them with a common purpose. It reminded them that their goal was to have fun and make money. Most importantly, it reminded its employee that their mission was not only to make money, but to change the world in the process.

Myth 4: Entrepreneurs should be Young and Energetic

Entrepreneurial activity is fairly evenly spread out over age ranges. According to an Index of Entrepreneurial Activity maintained by the Kauffman Foundation, 26 percent of entrepreneurs are ages 20 to 34, 25 percent are of ages between 35 to 44 years, 25 percent are of ages between 45 to 54 years, and 24 percent are between ages 55 to 64 years. The biggest jump, by far, from 1996 to 2010, which is the period the Kauffman date covers, is the 55 to 64 age bracket. A total of 14 percent of entrepreneurs were 55 to 64 years old in 1996, compared to 23 percent in 2010. The increasing number of older-aged entrepreneurs is a big change in the entrepreneurial landscape in the United States. Although it is important to be energetic, investors often cite the strength of the entrepreneur (or team of entrepreneurs) as their most important criterion in the decision to fund new ventures. In fact, a sentiment that venture capitalists often express is that they would rather fund a strong entrepreneur with a mediocre business idea than fund a strong business idea and a mediocre entrepreneur. What are the factors that makes an entrepreneur "strong" in the eyes of an investor is experience in the area of the proposed business, skills and abilities that will help the business, a solid reputation, a track record of success, and passion about the business idea. The first four of these five qualities favor older rather than younger entrepreneurs.

Myth 5: Entrepreneurs Love the Spotlight

Indeed, some entrepreneurs are flamboyant; however, the vast majority of them do not attract public attention. In fact, many entrepreneurs, because they are working on proprietary products or services, avoid public notice. Consider that entrepreneurs are the source of the launch of many of the 2,850 companies listed on the NASDAQ, and many of these entrepreneurs are still actively involved with their firms. But how many of these entrepreneurs can you name? Perhaps a half dozen? Most of us could come up with Bill Gates of Microsoft, Jeff Bezos of Amazon.com, Steve Jobs of Apple Inc., Mark Zuckerberg of Facebook and maybe Larry Page and Sergey Brin of Google. Whether or not they sought attention, these are the entrepreneurs who are often in the news. But few of us could name the founders of Netflix, Twitter, or GAP even though these firms' products and services are used frequently. These entrepreneurs, like most, have either avoided attention or been passed over by the popular press. They defy the myth that entrepreneurs, more so than other groups in our society, love the spotlight.

1.5 Entrepreneurship's Importance

Entrepreneurship's importance to an economy and the society in which he resides was first articulated in 1934 by Joseph Schumpeter an Austrian economist who did the majority of his work at Harvard University. In his book, The Theory of Economic Development, Schumpeter argued that entrepreneurs develop new products and technologies that over time make current products and technologies obsolete. Schumpeter called this process 'creative destruction'. Because new products and technologies are typically better than those they replace and the availability of improved products and technologies increases consumer demand, creative destruction stimulates economic activity. The new products and technologies may also increase the productivity of all elements of a society. The creative destruction process is initiated most effectively by start-up ventures that improve on what is currently available. Small firms that practice this art are often called "innovators" or "agents of change." The process of creative destruction is not limited to new products and technologies; it can include new pricing strategies (e.g., Netflix in DVDs), new distribution channels (such as e-books for books), or new retail formats (such as IKEA in furniture and Whole Foods Market in groceries).

1.6 Economic Impact of Entrepreneurial Firms on a Society and Country

Entrepreneurial behavior has a strong impact on any country's economy's strength and stability. Innovation is the process of creating something new, which is quite prominent to the entrepreneurial process. The entreprenurship ecosystem is often considered as young, innovative, aspirant and futuristic. According to a report, small firms (less than 500 employees) are providers of a significant share of the innovations that take place in any country. Several researches found that small businesses outperform their larger counterparts in terms of patent activity (issuance). Small businesses are the creators of most new jobs , and employ more than half of all private sector employees. Small business is held in high regard in this area. The entrepreneurs are considered 'change agents' in the process of industrial and economic development of an economy. The premium mobile role that entrepreneurs play in promoting industrial and economic development of an economy is well adduced across the countries.

Some of the key factors,that show the positive impact of the Entrepreneurship industry on the economy are:

- Growth drivers like access to capital/mentors, whitespace opportunities and increased M&A activity are accelerating the start-ups growth which in turn helps the economy to safeguard against economic downturns. Indian start- ups, with their unique solutions, are witnessing increased traction in global whitespace opportunities such as internet of things, augmented reality, smart hardware, big data & analytics, cloud computing, etc.
- Domain solutions emerging – Ad-Tech, Edu- Tech and Health-Tech and other niche solutions emerging for healthcare, agriculture, etc.
- Young entrepreneurs dominate the start-up landscape with over 73 per cent of founders in the age bracket of less than 36 years. Most of these founders with a strong consumer-centric approach, have come up with some of the best-in- class B2C start-ups. Women entrepreneurs have also started to leverage the innovation economy.

In a sense, entrepreneurs are the 'spark plug' who transform the economic scene of an economy. For example, Japan and United States are developed because of their entrepreneurial development and Bangladesh and Nepal are underdeveloped because of lack of their entrepreneurial development. Within India itself, Gujarat and Punjab are developed because of their entrepreneurial development and Bihar and Odisha are backward or underdeveloped because of the lack of entrepreneurial development. Thus, with entrepreneurs societies prosper, without them they are poorer.

Review Questions based on Chapter

1. Entrepreneurship is now a buzz in countries throughout the world. Do you think entrepreneurship will continue to spread throughout the world, or do you think its appeal or attraction might subside over time?

2. What is entrepreneurship? How can one differentiate an entrepreneurial firm from any other type of firm? In what ways is an entrepreneur who just launched a super store different from someone who just took a job as the general manager of an established super store owned by a major store chain?

3. What are the three primary reasons people become entrepreneurs? Which reason best describes why one may choose to become an entrepreneur?

4. What are the four primary traits and characteristics of successful entrepreneurs?

5. What are the five common myths of entrepreneurship? What evidence we debunks the myth that entrepreneurs are born, not made?

Applied Questions

1. Karan grover has a good job working for a reputed firm, but is weary of 2 percent (or less) per year pay raises. Because he has read magazine articles about young entrepreneurs becoming extremely wealthy, he decides to start his own firm. Do you think Karan is starting a firm for the right reason? Do you think the money he likely will earn will disappoint him? Do you think Karan's reason for starting a firm will contribute in a positive manner or a negative manner to the tenacity that is required to successfully launch and run an entrepreneurial venture?

2. Monika, a friend of yours, has always had a nagging desire to be her own boss. She has a good job with AT&T but has several ideas for new products that she can't get AT&T interested in. Monika has done a good job saving money over the years and has over $100,000 in the bank. She asks you, "Am crazy for wanting to leave AT&T to start my own businesses? How do know that have what it takes to be a successful entrepreneur?" What would you tell her?

3. Make a list of 10 prominent entrepreneurs who are women, minorities, or seniors (55 years or older when their firms were started). Single out one of these entrepreneurs and provide a brief overview of her or his entrepreneurial story. What did you learn about entrepreneurship by familiarizing yourself with this person's story?

4. Identify a successful entrepreneur that you admire and respect. (It can be someone that is nationally prominent or someone you know personally, such as a family member or a friend.) Briefly describe the person you identified, the company that he or she started, and the manner in which the individual exemplifies one or more of the four characteristics of a successful entrepreneur.

References

1. R. Duane as per APA Ireland, Bruce R. Barringer (2012) Entrepreneurship, Successfully Launching New Ventures, 4th edition, Pearson Education, inc., publishing as Prentice Hall.

2. Robert D. Hisrich, Michael P. Peters. Dean A. Shepherd, 2020, Entrepreneurship 11th Edition, Mcgraw hill.

2

Entrepreneurship Process and Identifying Opportunities

Dr. Sakha Gangadhar Rama Rao
(Assistant Professor, GITAM Institute of Management, Visakhapatnam)
Dr. S Anjani Devi
(Assistant Professor, GITAM Institute of Management, Visakhapatnam)

Dr. Sakha Gangadhar Rama Rao
(Assistant Professor, GITAM Institute of Management, Visakhapatnam)
Dr. S Anjani Devi
(Assistant Professor, GITAM Institute of Management, Visakhapatnam)

LEARNING OBJECTIVES

After reading this chapter, the reader should be able to:

1. Understand and identify opportunities for new business
2. Identify the sources and techniques for generating ideas
3. Recognize the gaps in the marketplace
4. Know about protecting new ideas
5. Understand the process of encouraging creativity at the firm level

2.1 Introduction

This chapter deals with an important area of entrepreneurship which identifies and recognises, opportunities for new businesses. How can one discover opportunities and others do not, how are the opportunities recognised, how to solve the problems, finding gaps in the market place and to generate ideas for budding new ventures will be covered in this chapter. Also, this chapter concentrates on brainstorming, focus groups, creativity and protecting ideas from being lost or stolen. The sustainability of an enterprise depends on identifying right opportunity at the right time and implementing the same with commitment.

2.2 Entrepreneurship Process for New Business

2.2.1 Identifying and Recognizing Opportunities

Success of an enterprise depends on identifying and recognizing best opportunities. Five forms of entrepreneurial opportunities identified by Schumpeter (1934) are "introduction of new goods, introduction of new method of production or service, opening of a new market, control on a new source of raw materials or semi-manufactured goods, and creation of new type of industrial organization." Opportunities to create new businesses or improve the current business result in high profits (Hills, Lumpkin, & Singh, 1997). There are three ways to identify opportunities. **Observing the trend** is the first approach to identifying opportunities. *Trend* is a change or a universal progress. It is better to pay attention on continuous development or changes over a period of time on a particular field or area to understand better about the opportunities. *Careful study* and *evaluation* are the other two ways that entrepreneurs can adopt to change with the changing environmental trends. Most of the entrepreneurs depend on research agencies for customized ideas and market analysis. As a potential entrepreneur, it is vital to be aware about changes and developments in these areas. Environmental trends like economic factors, social factors, political and regulatory issues, opportunity gaps in business or product/services, and advances in technology are the key important trends to observe.

The entrepreneur must study and understand the environmental trends than pay to independent research firms for customized trend forecasts and market analysis. If the entrepreneur pays attention on these areas, he has hands on experience in the specified field or area, and his further decisions are better than customized data. Furthermore, looking at economic factors, if entrepreneur depends on customized data, may be similar data is purchased by another entrepreneur for the same purpose. With this reason he/she invites the competition by spending lot of money and energy. Entrepreneur has to evaluate the trends on his own and the one who has money to invest in the area that they are liking the most for their business start-ups. Entrepreneur has to put the efforts on minimizing the risk by targeting few focus groups. If people have more than sufficient income or there is plenty of money available, they buy the products and services that enrich their lives. For example, the kids and teenage group (age between 10 years to 19 years) market, when they have money and they wish to buy stuff. The preferred products and services are fashionable clothing, music services from online, smart phones and all other items as these age groups can create a big market. Therefore, companies have opportunistic possibilities to attract these markets. There are few types that can offer opportunities associated to social factors. They are family and working environment, population's age (generation X, Y, Z, etc.), workplace diversity, healthcare and fitness concerns, impact on electronic gadgets, advances in technology, together with social and economic factors to provide opportunities.

Innovation is the key factor to encash opportunities for generating new technologies and methods to simplify the processes. The combination of existing method, knowledge, information and innovative idea creates an opportunity. Technological improvements always provide better opportunities to fulfil the basic needs and wants in a better way. When new technology comes into force, new products or services advancements are generally not far behind. Changes in politics and legal framework also creates opportunities for the organizations. New and modified laws, cyber-attacks, global terrorism, global warming and political instability have all created business opportunities. For example, governments and companies are investing huge amount on protect their physical as well as intellectual property from the attacks.

Now-a-days, smartphone is a need for many people because it provides many benefits, from many trends converging at the same time, containing an increasingly mobile population (social trend), the continuous consumption of e-services (technological trend), and their ability to help consumers in managing their monetary resources via electronic banking and comparison shopping on online (economic trend). If all these trends were not existing, the success of smartphones would not have been be the same as it is today. There are four trends (Fig. 2.1) that really influence entrepreneurs to think differently to start their businesses.

Trend 1: Economic Forces

Understanding economic forces are useful in identifying suitable areas for developing new and innovative business ideas. If the country's economy is strong and stable then public has sufficient money to buy, their purchasing power increases, and their chances to select the products as per their discretion also increases. If the economy's condition is in doldrums, people would not have purchasing power, they usually would be reluctant to spend money that they have. If the economy is in recession stage, people might lose their employment because of the weak economy. In some cases, a low or weak economy may offer business opportunities for entrepreneurs that lead to consumer savings. For example, Gas Buddy and GasPriceWatch.com are two companies helping consumers to save money on gasoline. The company is offering its products as low as $1.00. It is not only aiming high and medium economy people but also targeting poor or weak economy to sell large-scale and needy items on a 'discount' basis.

Other examples are Groupon and Living Social daily deal sites. The two companies experienced rapid growth when they offered deep discounts on their products and services like trips to museum, high-end restaurants and consumers' access to local providers. Similarly, Gilt Groupe is selling premium products at a discount on limited period. In recession period, many of the people buy products from the street vendors instead of it from the grocery stores. The reason is to bargain the products at street vendor but there is no chance at grocery store. It is also required to understand how economic factors influence people's behavior considering for high discounts and worth for their money. When the economy is slow or weak, majority of the people are forced to acquire new skills to retain their present job. This situation not only provides opportunity to traditional and online institutes but also to businesses that develop products to support them. An example is BenchPrep, the business was developed by two students who were preparing for GMAT. BenchPrep, is a business which sells apps to the students who are preparing for college admission tests. The idea of this business is students need not carry any books and they have electronic gadget which supports the app. These kind of apps are environmental friendly and low cost. When the economy is poor, these kind of businesses (ideas) will get advantage.

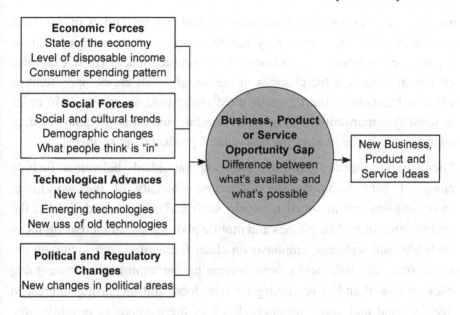

Fig 2.1: Business or Product Opportunity Gaps

Source: Bruce R. Barringer R. Duane Ireland (2008). Entrepreneurship: Successfully Launching New Ventures, 2/e. Prentice Hall.

A thorough analysis and understanding of economic changes can also help to identify the type of areas to avoid. If the fuel prices are continuously growing, it is not a right time to start a new business which is depending on fuel. For example, cab services, transportation related companies, etc. are mainly depending on fuel to run the business. Understanding and careful observation on market conditions are required to avoid the situational unsuccessful businesses. There are some businesses that started at wrong time and were wiped out from the markets at faster rate.

Trend 2: Social Forces

Social forces play key role in understanding the trends and its impact on new products, services, and innovative ideas to recognize an opportunity. For example, the spread of fast-food restaurants is not because of people's interest but because of the reason that people are busy, and they can't spend much time on preparation of their own food. In the same way, social networking websites like Facebook and Twitter are popular because these sites permit people to stay connected and share their information with each other, not because of just posting the photos. Swiggy and Zomato are the other examples where people need not go and wait for food parcels at restaurants, once they use these apps the selected items from the selected restaurant are delivered to a specified place. These examples clearly indicate that the changes in the social trends create opportunities for new businesses. Entrepreneur must understand social trends in order to identify opportunities. Clear understanding and thorough analysis may create space in the market for newly built products and services.

Social trends that are currently affecting individuals behaviour include aging of baby boomers, the increasing diversity of the workforce, increasing interest in social networks such as Facebook and Twitter, the proliferation of mobile phones and mobile phone apps, an increasing focus on health and wellness, emphasis on clean forms of energy including the wind, solar, biofuels, and others, increasing the number of people going back to school and/or retraining for new jobs, and increasing interest in healthy food and green products. Each of these trends is providing the impetus for new business ideas.

An increasing emphasis on another forms of energy is spawning business ideas ranging from solar power to biofuels. The aging of the baby boomers is creating business opportunities from vision care to tech assistance to senior dating sites. An example is Glaukos, a company that's developing new approaches for treating glaucoma, which is an age-related eye disorder. There are now 76 million baby boomers (people born between 1946 and 1964) in the United States. Many baby boomers will develop glaucoma and similar age-related ailments. The fact that roughly 10,000 baby boomers in the United States are now retiring on a daily basis also creates entrepreneurial chances related to social trends associated with this population of senior citizens.

The faster rate of explosion of smart phones and its apps are creating new business opportunities for entrepreneurs on the globe. Nearly 131 per cent of the growth has been registered in penetration of smart phone in the worldwide for the last 10 years. One company, Pharma Secure is leveraging this trend to save lives in developing countries. It's estimated that 10 per cent of medications sold worldwide are counterfeit. In India alone, 1 million people a year die from ingesting counterfeit drugs. Pharma Secure provides drug companies the ability to place a nine-digit alphanumeric code directly on the blister pack, medicine bottle or vial, or on the product's label, along with a phone number.

Consumers can verify the code and by extension make sure the drug they have purchased isn't counterfeit by texting it to the accompanying phone number. In India, 55 per cent of the population has a mobile phone, and it's the fastest-growing market for mobile phones in the world. If it weren't for the proliferation of smart phones in India and elsewhere, Pharma Secure's business wouldn't be possible.

The faster growth rate of social networking websites such as Facebook, Twitter and Whatsapp provides opportunities for the people to connect and share the information and it also creates platform for other businesses to build on. Farmville and Scramble online games were developed by Zynga. Basically these games are popularly browser-based games and worked as application widgets on My Space and Facebook. Similarly, entrepreneurs have developed businesses for the tenacity of beginning social networks that provide to precise niches. An example is Patients Like Me, which is a social networking site for people with serious diseases.

Trend 3: Advancement in Technology

The recent trends in the micro and macro environment are creating opportunities in the business along with the changing technology advancement. Because of the current generation lifestyle everyone is facing the health issues. The eating habits and the work culture at the odd hours is creating the problems to the health. In order to overcome the stress and lack of time to take care of oneself, most of us are depending on the electronic gadgets and the technologies which give us the alerts to monitor one self. The young and enthusiastic entrepreneur came up with an online start-up Airstrip Technologies which allows us to approach doctors online. Recently many apps have come down to track the health and remind us timely what to eat and the intake of the calories to make the people fit.

Many of us approach the medical stores for the basic illness and continue the medicine for a short while as directed by the medical store executive. This is the common practice in India because of various reasons. The economic conditions of the middle-income group to consult the doctor in the rural areas and the time taking process because of the prevailing traffic issues in the urban areas. To overcome this, brainstorming was done to make the doctor approachable online. Initially the patient can contact doctor online, take the medication for the immediate relief in case of unavailability of the doctor especially in the rural areas as most of the doctors would not like to stay in the remote areas. In case the patient was not cured with the treatment given, then they will approach doctor physically. Online medical treatment is the most encouraging sector for the business opportunities in the recent days.

Technology is bringing vast changes in the every step of an individual. It is helping the human in getting the things done faster and easier. To quote an example, Airstrip Technologies developed an app for the doctors to monitor their patients by linking up the treatment procedure to the mobile application. The doctor can view the patient condition through the mobile and respond accordingly by giving instructions online. Robotics is the new area of medical science where the doctor will do the surgery with the help of the Robo. One more example, Swiggy and other online food delivery services are playing major role in providing door delivery service to the customer.

Make my Trip (MMT) or Yatra.com are the other examples where an individual who is planning for a vacation can take the feedback regarding the hotel accommodation, transportation and the travel facilities available at part of the globe. They also provide special concession if the services are registered from their websites. They also provide ratings and comparison of the competitors who are rendering the similar type of service. Opentable.com is the other website that aptly provide the information to the customer in making the reservation for the table at a restaurant etc.

Changing technologies and the updating of the technologies timely is the biggest challenge for the service provider. The creation of the smart phones and the android mobiles brought major revolution in the mobile markets. The life span of the mobile became very short. Timely changing applications bring the liveliness to the invention and the best example for this will be iPhone which made life easier and created an image that everything happens in your hands with the help of the applications designed for the same.

Even during swimming, surfing or any other activity where there is a change that the mobile can get wet, the iPhone came up with the water proof technology which will not let cause the damage to the smart phones. With the growing smart devices the app market is also growing. Anyone can design an app and can make available for the usage of the customer. In case the app gets the overwhelming response from the users, service providers like google etc. would like to takeover. WhatsApp is one amongst them where the marketers have seen the potentiality and poured money for procuring it because of the customer base and the usability.

Trend 4: Political Action and Regulatory Changes

The concept of Entrepreneurship is the emerging trend as the changes in regulations and the political actions are providing the platform for the start-ups with the support extended by the organizations, students and the government institutions. GST in India is the other issue as many of the companies needs to change their regular calculation of tax to GST based calculation. Because of this regulatory change many Chartered Accountants and accounting professionals were gaining advantage to build up their own consultancy companies.

According to the 'No Child Left Behind Act of 2002', which provides activity-based education and assessment in basic skills to the students' states that the grading should be done frequently to create opportunity of learning. The two high school teachers named Jay Kleeman and Kim, initiated an organization Shakespeare Squared that produces material which is required by the schools. Under the changing situations, and the government regulations it is encouraging the business firms to come with the start-ups. Eco friendly products or the organic products for the babies is the business thought that was lucrative to mint money by the industries based on the emotional appeal of the customers. Everyone is ready to pay extra for the organic products because of the lifestyle and the increasing consciousness for the healthy diet. The government is also monitoring by setting the standards to the organizations.

There is lot of threat for any organization as survival for the fittest is the challenge that the organizations are facing through. To quote an example the competition faced by the hospitals is creating new scope of opportunity i.e. nursing care at home. Many hospitals are coming up with concept of nursing care services as the concept of nuclear families is increasing and at the same time there is no one to take care of the old at home. In these situations the nursing assistants will provide the facilities like one among their family members. Because of the innovativeness in the concept and services are provided at the home itself, the demand is increasing and the profitability also has enhanced with the current trends of start-ups culture.

The concept of FDI in the Indian market has paved the way for majority of the MNC's to look at the industrial development through the entrepreneurial development. Research and Development is also playing a role in designing new product or service to the customers. The innovations can be patented so that others will not copy the original formulae of the products or the services.

The emerging concepts like Data analytics or the business analytics made the life easier for the marketers. Earlier segregation of the markets was missing and the entire range of markets was treated as a single unit. Data mining takes an attempt to get the relevant data which is useful for the marketers to segment the customers. E commerce and M commerce are the innovative technologies where the share data would reach to the appropriate segmented markets.

2.2.2 Solving a Problem

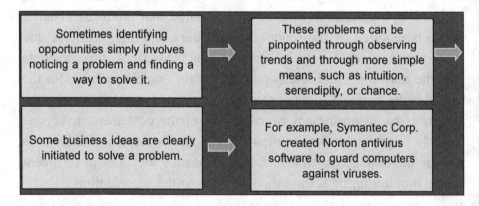

Source: Bruce R. Barringer R. Duane Ireland (2008). Entrepreneurship: Successfully Launching New Ventures, 2/e. Prentice Hall.

For someone who is interested to come up with the concept of entrepreneurship, in case if they can approach the achievers in the respective fields, then majority of the apprehensions will be lost. It's like a day wise challenging situation to the marketers as they need to overcome the hurdles that they come across in the process of the initiation of the proposals. The profession of being an entrepreneur is not a fashionable job. They need to face a lot of challenges that will come across in day to day interaction with many clients. Slowly the learning of being patience to resolve the problems will be adopted, so that the practice of being dynamic can be the learning for the individuals.

2.3 Finding Gaps in the Marketplace

Identification of Gap in the market place is the biggest challenge for the marketers. Generally gap occurs because of four major reasons i.e. Quality gap, knowledge gap, delivery gap and the communication gap. It occurs when there is difference between the perception and the expectation of the customer. Meeting the requirements of the customer is the biggest challenge to the entrepreneurs. Customers will be rewarded in case if they found any gaps. That's how the marketers are trying to create niche market for their business in the competitive world.

Because of the competition prevailing in the retail markets, retailers are focusing on the niche segment within the wide scope of markets that are available for them. D Mart is the best example for narrowing the group as it targets with the concept of starting of outlets in the residential areas and that too in their own retail space. The products that are available in their mart are positioned for the middle income group and the price will be comparatively lower from the other retailers.

Being an entrepreneur one should grab the opportunities that knock at their doors. Earlier the concept was 'earn while you learn'. Now the concept is be an entrepreneur and provide employment to others or at least be a self-employed. The entire world is looking at the trend that goes in USA for the entrepreneurial changes happening but USA is concentrating on China and Japan where both the countries are competing with each other to be the global leader.

2.4 Sources of Generating Ideas

2.4.1 Existing Products and Services

Brainstorming of an idea is the key element in the entire process of the invention. The idea that is generated should be screened to know the feasibility of the markets. Identification of the strategies and the business analysis will help in the development of the concept by the organizations. Many of them will test their concepts to take the feedback from the consumers to provide products or services accordingly. Ultimately enterprises will look at the commercialization of the process and generation of the revenue from the markets in the cut throat competition.

2.4.2 Distribution Channels

The intermediaries of distribution channel i.e. the distributors, wholesalers and retailers may share the feedback for the new product development or the modification of the existing products when they are in the saturation stage. For example, an entrepreneur was informed by the departmental salesman that even though there was lot of demand for the hosiery in the market but the departmental store was not able to leverage it as the young customers are not preferring the dark shade and they prefer the light shade. The stock which was there in the store was dark colour and the entrepreneur accepted the suggestions of the sales man and replaced the stock with the light shade. Then they observed the drastic change in the increasing demand for the same stock in a short span and able to do ample business.

2.4.3 Government

For generating the new product concepts, the government is also encouraging the current generation in various ways. For example, government from time to time comes out with regulations on products, production and consumption. Many a times, these regulations become excellent sources of generating entrepreneurial thoughts.

For example, the ban on polythene bags of certain micron thickness has aroused thought process of the jute bag, paper bags manufacturing etc. and also had encouraging market for both the sellers and buyers of these innovative products. The awareness created by the government on patent and licensing will provoke the entrepreneurs to think innovatively and to provide the customers with the products which are not already available in the market. The government is also encouraging the entrepreneurs to associate with the academic institutions and the agencies like NABARD, FICCI, CII, etc. to share information on the common platform and also the basis for the development of the young entrepreneurs.

2.4.4 Research and Development

The main source of new idea generation is through Research and Development (R&D) activity. R&D can be carried out in-house or outside the organization. Without R&D the organizations may not sustain for the long-time. R&D activity suggests that the new or modified product can be produced to meet the customers' requirements. In case the organization could not contribute to the R&D, even though it is a top MNC, chances are there that the competitors will grab its market as they are late into the market through innovations. Many examples like Nokia, once a market leader was late in R & D and in launching the touch screen resulting in its ouster from the market and allowing the competitors to grab the market.

R & D initiated by the institutions is the root for the product extension or the diversifications either in length, depth and breadth of the product, techniques for generating ideas. In general, to attract new markets, new segments and reaching the unreached markets or the untapped markets as they are looking for the market expansion. Several techniques are utilized for stimulating and facilitate the generation of new ideas for products, services, and businesses.

2.5 Techniques for Generating Ideas

Earlier the concept was seeking the job but now the concept shifting to generating the jobs. Even the students at IIM's and other B-schools are coming up with their thoughts to prove them to be entrepreneurs. Few years back, it was difficult to start up a firm but now if there is a feasible idea, the investors are ready to give monetary support in the establishment of the firm. Once the ideas are successful at the launching stage then the competitors or the MNC's are ready to grab the opportunity of attracting the new generation entrepreneurs. For idea generation focused group discussions, brainstorming, and problem inventory analysis are the most common methods used among the clientele interested in being entrepreneurs to generate new thought process.

2.5.1 Focus Groups

Focus group discussion happens among the participants ranging from six to ten in number, belonging to different genders, socio economic background. It happens within the purview of the moderator who makes the participants to come with understanding and discuss the practical issues that they come across while taking up the concept.

The mode of discussion of the group can be either in a directive or a non-directive manner. This will create platform for the idea generation, screening of the idea, concept development, market analysis, concept testing and launching of the concept to pursue as a venture. The reason for adopting this concept is to storm the issue/problem. This will create the avenue to generate ideas through conceptual development and market analysis for the launching of the new ideas.

2.5.2 Brainstorming

Brainstorming sessions are instrumental in generating new ideas that will create base for the development of new products in the market. Google is the best example for giving the employees twenty percent of their working time for thought provoking and it believes that this liberty generates eighty percent of the output from the employees. The most promising ideas will be taken into consideration and platform will be created to bring them into practice. These may include

- Customer need Management.
- Emerging trends in marketplace for products or services.
- Initiation for the substitute product.
- Research and development in New Product Development.
- Understanding and analysing the success and failure stories of entrepreneurs.
- Inculcating the habit of visiting trade fairs and exhibitions for understanding the recent happening in the markets.

- Associating with the government agencies and the experts for brainstorming.
- Government policies and the subsidies in small and medium enterprise.
- Knowledge about the competitor products, and Monitoring the competitors' strategies.

An Entrepreneur can generate the ideas through the need recognition of the customers. The feasibility studies can be conducted to draw the conclusions for the start-ups to understand the demand. The changing lifestyle, attitudes and interests of the customers will awake the thought process to the customers. Based on the expectation of the customers, products or services need to be provided to the customer. The trend is identifying what the customer is looking for by having the tie up with the search engines as majority of the customers do browse for the information on the various social networking sites and the companies will have the track on what customers are looking for in order to provide them the product or services according to their need, want or the desire of the customers.

Idea generation must be creative and viable in the changing environments. Build upon piggyback, extending the thought process to the critics so that their suggestions will further enhance the concept development. The second principle is the quality of the discussion. All the participants should listen to the other's thoughts to stimulate and give spark to the new ideas by providing the opportunity of thought expression. Generally the discussion happens for an hour where the moderator should feel that participants came to the centric point of the thought process and reached to common understanding. Thirdly, there should not be criticism for any idea. The participants should not be afraid of being ridiculed allowing them to speak up their mind without any apprehensions.

For example, an MNC has taken its employees to a resort for an out-bound activity. They have scheduled various programmes, out of which the brainstorming session is one among them where various discussions happened on launching of their new product, how to segment their customers, which markets they need to target, reasons for segmenting and targeting, how to position their product and expected business from the market, competitive advantages, differentiation from the competitors etc.

2.5.3 Problem Inventory Analysis

Problem Inventory Analysis is almost a similar method that provides consumers a list of specific problems in a general product category. It also identifies and discusses the products in the category that suffer from the specific problems. This method is found relatively more effective for the reason that a set of suggested problems generate new ideas. However, problem inventory analysis method is the better method for generating ideas, concept screening, testing the concept and evaluation of the thought process. For example a mineral water company thought of coming up with a square shape design of the bottle as many of the customers reuse the water bottle for water storage purpose in the refrigerator side door. Expecting that the sale of the water bottles will increase they have launched the new designed packaged drinking water bottles. But surprisingly the sale of the water bottles reduced. Then Problem inventory analysis method was used to discuss on the modified thought process. In that discussion they came to an understanding on purchasing behavior that most of the customers buy the water bottles when they are travelling. The space that is provided for the placement of these water bottles will be in the circular form. As the design is changed, they could not place the bottle at the provision which is provided. Because of this reason customer felt inconvenience for placing the water bottle and switched over to the other brands. So, they decided to get back to the regular design of the bottle.

Because of the increasing fuel charges, logistics and supply chain management has direct impact and indirect impact on the cost of manufacturing of the products. For example milk which is a daily requirement and necessity gets the major impact of the increasing fuel expenses. But the price of the milk cannot be increased as the middle and the lower income group may not effort. So, as to maintain the cost of production and to reduce the transportation charges, came up with the innovative thought of extra shelf life milk packets to reduce the cost of logistics as the stock will be given based on the turnover of the packets instead of every day supply, keeping in mind the expiry date of the packaging.

2.6 Encouraging and Protecting New Ideas

Having faced the difficulty in going out and purchasing the food at the place of choice and difficulty in going all the way from the place of living, the concept of door delivery services has come down which is the leading concept as on now in the online markets. Because of the increasing awareness on the organic food the concept of horticulture that is cultivation of the miniature plants at one's own residence is the best example for the new generation ideas.

Because of the shift in the lifestyle, instead of going out and purchasing the grocery and other FMCG products from the nearby markets, customers are preferring to order on line and getting them at the door steps. This has created the opportunity for many of the entrepreneurs to come up with the online shopping websites and dealing with the business. One more interesting point over here is the price of the products, at times the price is lesser on the online websites rather than the physical purchase points. As there will be no intermediaries on online markets, they could able to provide the products at the lesser price to the customers. So, online business idea generation is enticing to the entrepreneurs as there is 200 percent growth in the recent times.

However, the entrepreneurial ventures should look at the sustainability of the traditional formats that already exist. It is every one's responsibility that the giants should not kill the small scale businesses. In spite, they should create separate opportunities for both the businesses. Now-a-days many consultants are available with the ideas to share to the budding entrepreneurs. They train them in all the areas from approaching to franchises, selection of the concept, location, starting of the venture, running it successfully etc.

The government is also giving helping hands in the form of subsidy, training to the upcoming entrepreneurs. For the current generation, because of the internet resources lot of opportunities are there where they can directly interact with the entrepreneurs who are successful in their respective areas. Other firms do not have idea banks but instead encourage employees to keep journals of their ideas.

2.7 Encouraging Creativity at the Firm Level and Protecting the Idea

The organization encouragement and appreciation for creativity effects the creative output of its employees. The intellectual property rights of the entrepreneur are protected by creating awareness on the patent rights, trademark, copy right and not disclosing of the trade secret. As a rule, a mere idea or concept does not qualify for intellectual property protection; and protection comes later when the idea is translated into a more concrete form. At the opportunity recognition stage, however, there are three steps that should be taken when a potentially valuable idea is generated. The idea generated should undergo the screening process – accepted by the members participated in the discussion and recorded as the patent and dated.

If an idea is significant and has potential, the signature of the person who has given that idea and the witness should be notarized. Putting the idea into tangible form is important for two reasons. First, if the idea is in concrete form, is original and useful, and is kept secret or is disclosed only in a situation where compensation for its use is contemplated, may be taken as "property right" or "trade secret" and protected under legal statues. Second, in the case of an invention, if two inventors independently come up with essentially the same thought and apply for the patent only the first person who invented the product will have the opportunity. Next it depends on the circumstances. A firm wants new ideas to be discussed, so a certain amount of openness in the early stages of refining a business idea may be appropriate. On the other hand, if an idea has considerable potential and may be eligible for patent protection, access to it may be restricted.

CaseLet: Jagdish Samal

Mr. Jagdish Samal has ardent interest in gourmet food and enjoys food for pleasure. He loves closed place, yet feeling like being out in the open air far away from all the distractions of modern life. So he explores various regions in India to have diverse food from different restaurants, bistros and cafes.

After class XII, he decided to pursue Under Graduation (BBA) in the city of Visakhapatnam and was new to the city. He observed that there were very few restaurants & cafes, also they remained consistent with their offering. There was no place where people could have all the benefits in one, such as enjoy the time while enjoying their food along with the ambience and also experience of something with uniqueness. He noticed the potentiality to open such a café. After this thought, he visited many restaurants and Café in and around Visakhapatnam. He gathered the information about the operational issues to run a café, capital and working capital requirements, sources of raw-material, type of customers visits to the restaurants and their preferences, and interiors/exteriors requirements of the café.

Then he concentrated on a solid business plan. This business plan spells out exactly what business would be, how it would be profitable and who would be the target consumers. He discussed the idea with friends as he wanted to start up with a partnership model. He went in search of a suitable partner for the firm as being a student it would be difficult to handle the café alone. He chose partnership as the workload would be spread between two of the partners, share decisions and also the thought process from two people will be beneficial as different ideas spurge from two different mind sets. He was also looking at the benefits of shared capital and shared risks. It was also a benefit to him because he was new to the place, language and culture. In all matters partnership could be helpful to him to run the business. After discussions with peers and classmates, Mr. Vikas Choudhary showed interest on idea of start-up and gave nod for accepting as partner by investing his ideas and capital for the business.

After all partnership deeds were finalised, both Jagdish and Vikas were looking for the right location for café and they were searching Vizag's nook and crook for the perfect spot as per their dream and vision. They visited many places but were not satisfied. They visited Dutt Island, a place in Siripuram Junction (one of the main and crowded areas of the city) which was like an open field and full of opportunities. The place had its ceiling broken and damaged but other than that the place was good and it had aligned with their thought process and idea. The view from outside the window was a great advantage and felt serene. Finally, they selected the same area i.e., first floor of Dutt Island, Siripuram Junction. Next day, they fixed a meeting with place owner Mr. Balareddy, discussed about their interest and idea. Mr. Balareddy asked for a time of 10 days to finalize the deal. Few days later, Mr. Jagdish got a phone call from Balareddy that place was sold off to a spa franchise at a higher rate and the agreement had also been done between them. After hearing this they were upset and their interest was pulled down. But they did not give up and started searching for new places again. But they did not find the potential one as Dutt Island. Few days later an unexpected call was received from Mr. Balareddy and enquired whether they found a suitable place yet or not. He asked to meet in the next morning at his office, by hearing his words, they were happy and also excited. Next morning when they went to his office, he told them that the spa franchise to whom they sold the area, had some an issue which was not into his knowledge. As the agreement was withdrawn the offer to take over the place was given and they instantly went for agreement to finalise the rent amount.

Then they finalised the design, the thoughts on the layout, theme, food, equipment and décor, in short they were in brainstorming. Almost each and everything in the selected area required renovation to match the theme. Most of the equipment were bought from Vizag itself, such as refrigerators, oven, stove etc. and for the décor, random materials of theme, they went to Delhi (to invest as low as possible). After few weeks, café interior was ready with innovative atmosphere and modern décor.

After finalising the interior, they concentrated on hiring the Chefs, Waiters and workers for the café. They were very careful about the selection of the staff as they play major role in the future of the business. While they were in process, got news that four new restaurants were going to open soon and they too were in process. By listening to that they saw another space to merge with each other, the two – multi theme and café so that they thought something unique and make a multi-theme plus multi-cuisine café. As it was Vizag's first multi-themed café, had a huge benefit for advertising the café.

Their Strategy/motto was to open a multi-themed restaurant. They wanted multi-themed because if it was considered as any other restaurant/café and if a customer comes in search of variety , they will come once, twice and their visits will reduce as they will be familiar with taste and ambiance.

But, if they are able to keep up with changing preferences and tastes of the customers, they will keep on visiting them. That's why their idea was based on the assumption that if there were three themes, when the customer visit first theme they get a new experience. Then next theme when he comes for the second theme, his experience was entirely new again and again. This thought gives a benefit that the customers will not get bored of the same usual spot. Mr. Jagdish also took suggestions from respective parents, mentors, consultancies, restaurant owners and finally his interest.

After that they had finalised the date for opening. Then due to some technical reasons, it had postponed and it happened twice constantly. At last, 15th November 2017 was the final opening date of the café. For the inauguration news to reach potential customers, they were advertising through social media such as Facebook, Instagram, Word of Mouth and fliers being distributed to the citizens of Vizag. At the time of inception of multi themed café Mr. Jagdish and Mr Vikas had to handle both Café work and manage studies at University as students.

After that, they concentrated on their network to maintain a connection to the area and to attract more customers so for promoting café. They were coming up with new ideas such as Singles party (on Valentine's Day). As time passed by, they got new competition in the market and new restaurants and café came up. Customers also got divided and kept on fluctuating, sometimes the sales were unpredictable. To overcome this problem, they slowly started sponsoring events and started putting up stalls at different fests to popularize, gain customers and earn profit. After this, the concept of online food order and delivery started which became famous. To keep up with the trend, they partnered with Swiggy and Zomato.

Review Questions

1. How do you identify and recognise opportunities with examples.
2. What are the reasons to identify the sources for generating ideas and techniques for business development?
3. Explain the sources for protecting new ideas.
4. What are the trends that are influencing business opportunities?

Applied Questions

1. Identity an entrepreneur in your area and gather the information regarding his/her business ideas.

2. Prepare a questionnaire on a start-up initiative and analyse the idea generation and implementation of ideas.

3. Select appropriate tool and conduct market test for any newly established business.

4. Identify an existing product of your choice and generate the ideas for new product development.

References

1. Alan l. Carsrud and Malin E. Brännback (2007) Greenwood Press, Westport, Connecticut, London.

2. Bruce R. Barringer R. Duane Ireland (2008). Entrepreneurship: Successfully Launching New Ventures, 2/e. Prentice Hall.

3. Hills, G. E., Lumpkin, G. T., & Singh, R. P. (1997). Opportunity recognition: Perceptions and behaviors of entrepreneurs. Frontiers of Entrepreneurship Research, 17, 168–182. Retrieved from http://fusionmx.babson.edu/entrep/ fer/papers97/hills/hill1.htm

4. https://1642598126.rsc.cdn77.org/sites/tbbooks/pdf/Solutions-Manual-Entrepreneurship-Successfully-Launching-New-Ventures-3rd-Edition-Barringer.pdf,

5. https://www.studocu.com/en/document/concordiauniversity/entrepreneurship/ summaries/summary-lecture-1-introduction-to-entrepreneurship/236347/view, accessed on 30-10-2018.

6. Schumpeter, J. (1934). The theory of economic development: an inquiry into profits, capital, credit, interest, and the business cycle. Harvard University Press.

3

Feasibility Analysis

Dr. Rajesh Kumar Pandey
(Associate Professor, SSR IMR, Pune)

LEARNING OBJECTIVES

After reading this chapter, the reader should be able to:

1. Establish connect with the fundamentals of Feasibility Analysis.
2. Understand the significance of the feasibility analysis.
3. Conduct the Feasibility analysis.
4. Gain insights from the case study on Retail Marketing and link it further to the Feasibility analysis in order to gather understanding on the domain.

3.1 Introduction: Feasibility Analysis

Feasibility is the virtue of gaining momentum towards viability of a project. A Feasibility Study is a step towards initiating a new venture idea. It is essentially supportive in addressing the massive question for the Entrepreneurs i.e., *whether the Business is feasible to operate?* Feasibility study may be an essential tool to scrutinize the available idea and then select the best possible move. Further, a well-defined feasibility study may serve as an impressive foundation for constructing a business plan. As against a business plan, which is a working document & gets the idea into action, a feasibility study is more of a validating process for a business idea in consideration to the

Product, Market, Organisation, or Financial feasibility. Feasibility study provides a confidence to build the massive structure of the businesses. While the investment pattern in the feasibility study might be dependent on the magnum of the business projected, however it is advisable to invest in the feasibility study in order to gain a full proof avenue to proceed with the desired business. In economic terms *it is the viability check of the proposed project.* A business owner is committed to a large investment in the venture and aims to enhance the businesses with regular intervals. Accordingly, the risk proportion also gets added and enhances with the increase in business. While the ongoing business affair is certainly important, however these efforts can only survive if the feasibility study was done appropriately. The measures adopted during the study, the application of calculations, foresightedness of the business etc. all these & many more aspects matter while one conducts the feasibility study. Above all one aspect is furthermore imperative i.e., When to conduct this Feasibility study.

3.2 When to Conduct the Feasibility Analysis?

Conducting the Feasibility study is not just a strategic move in terms of the planning business but initiating the process is also a strategic advantage. A timely conducted feasibility study backed by the implementation supports the business acumen. Ideally prospecting a business is the first instance of launching the feasibility study. Emphasizing on the apt time for the study is massively to ensure the economic prosperity of the planning phase as a lot of resources are spent on feasibility study. Feasibility study adds value to the preparation for the business venture. It further adds confidence in the venture owner. The businesses are bound to take risk however the calculated risks support growth of the venture. This feasibility study eventually supports the risk mitigation approach. Every business owner must ensure conducive environment supporting the business functions. The concentration on these aspects can only be with a positive start for the business. A feasibility study supports this positiveness. Hence, the study done at the conceptualisation stage of the business, results better for the venture owner.

3.3 Benefits of the Feasibility Study

Feasibility Study supports the momentum of the businesses and act as the guiding principle. The obvious benefit of such practices gets reflected in the functioning of the business. The Feasibility study supports the *Business Merit Assessment*. As it is very well guided to the budding entrepreneurs that before starting a business, consider the merit of the same like the demand, respective supply, customer base etc. If the market turns favorable, then invest. Such support can be very well expected from the feasibility analysis. This eventually leads to understand the *Market assertiveness*. The financial feasibility is very important to gather for a budding entrepreneur. *Viable Financial Project* has potential to do better in the market. Such market is *worth Investment* and the *Suitability of the Investment* gets established.

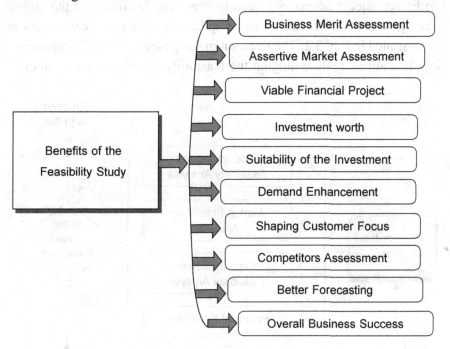

Fig. 3.1: Benefits of Feasibility Study

Source: Author's Study

The feasibility study also supports the *Demand Enhancement* aspect for the businesses. At the start of the business an Entrepreneur may assess that the pace of growth is lesser however the feasibility study has the potential to gauge the future of market. Hence the demand factor has potential to increase in future, such projects are viable projects. The Feasibility study supports in *Shaping Customer Focus* by demonstrating to the entrepreneur the real prospects of the customer base and potential strategy to meet the need. Another massive contribution of Feasibility study is the *Competitors Assessment.* Every business certainly requires complete understanding of the competitiveness in the market. The products must meet the competition to survive. If the entrepreneur is aware of the level of competition in the market, this would help in implementing the business plan and have a *Better Forecasting* done for the business. The feasibility study has the potential to gauge & support the *Overall Business Success.*

3.4 Feasibility Check Chart

The Entrepreneurs necessarily need to check the feasibility of the project before proceeding with the same. A quick check may be enunciated as demonstrated in Fig. 3.2. The decision making factor for the Entrepreneurs plays leading role while judging the feasibility aspects for the business.

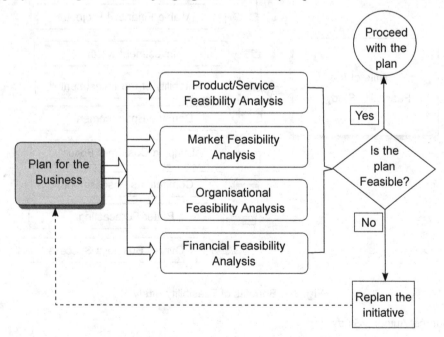

Fig. 3.2: Feasibility Check by the Entrepreneurs

Source: Author's Study

The major sections that need proper considerations while feasibility check are: *Product/Service Feasibility Analysis, Market Feasibility Analysis, Organisational Feasibility Analysis and Financial Feasibility analysis.* While planning for the business if an entrepreneur finds viability in all these sections then moving with the business is advisable. Else it is always better to rethink about the venture. The Entrepreneur shall face external dependency and hence taking an appropriate call will be tough however that's the charm of Entrepreneurship where one defines the odds of the business and reaps the benefits. A potential product for the market may have its market but the entrepreneurs financial feasibility may not support the venture. The organisation may be ready with all the plans for the assets to procure, structure to follow, a defined culture; in short the organisational feasibility might be viable but the marketing viability like desired demand, craze for the product, usage factor etc may not support. Hence, a proper balance shall help in enunciating a business.

3.5 Product/Service Feasibility Analysis

Feasibility as discussed is the viability of the venture. As part of the venture an entrepreneur shall look into gaining confidence from every facet of venture. Products or say Service is an important constituent of venture planning. Selecting the best product as the venture opportunity is very essential. Hence, the feasibility of a product being beneficial for the organisation is essentially needed to be established. The product feasibility shall need to undergo numerous checks & assessments in order to choose the right product for the respective market. The product has to primarily solve need of the consumers. The product design, shelf life, product demand etc. altogether leads into finalisation of the product for the venture.

The Product feasibility analysis shall require answers to questions like *Is it of consumer's interest? Does it solve consumer need? Is it the appropriate time to launch? Etc.* The Product Feasibility study shall attract a good survey to be done pertaining to the product viability in the market. The best aspect to be considered to start a venture is to think about the delivery. Goods or services, either of these ventures must aim at solving the consumers Interest. The feasibility study aims at defining this phase of business planning. If the product / Service have the potential to solve the problem, it has larger potential to be a success in the market. While resolving the problem, it must also ensure the timeliness of the solutions. A successful product feasibility study prepares a base for the venture as rest of the feasibility studies ensure the further functioning of the venture like the market feasibility, operational feasibility, financial feasibility etc.

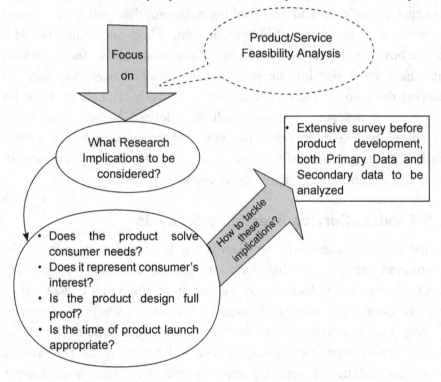

Fig. 3.3: Product / Service Feasibility Analysis

Source: Author's Study

3.6 Industry/Target Market Feasibility Analysis

A business or for that matter the product hunts for its market. The market may be categorised as homogenous & heterogeneous. Also the further classification from business area perspective is the urban market & the rural market. Within the market the product finds its target customer. Segmentation & Targeting supports the market feasibility study and helps in reaching to a juncture where the business owner understands the potential of the business in the selected Market. A few essential aspects considered while Market Feasibility study are as following:

1. **Assessment of Market:** Understanding the potential of business is an essential aspect for a business. Feasibility study of the Market potential helps the business shape its future. The expected size of the market, the expected reach of the product, potential demand creation etc. are all part of assessment of the Market.

2. **Industry attractiveness:** Porter's Five forces Model has been very useful for the business aspirants. The Threat for the new entrant, substitution of the product, Competitiveness in the market & bargaining power (buyers and sellers) helps the budding entrepreneur to be decisive. This enhances the confidence of the business planner and the launch of the product in the market is a very informed decision for the owner.

3. **Target Market Attractiveness:** The target market must be attractive. The Market must be such that the proceeds aren't a matter of concern. Feasibility study enables with such expert steps to avoid any unforeseen situation. The Market attractiveness assessment builds the notion for the owner to place its product and reap the benefits. An attractive market for the product is the initial success upon which the owner builds the momentum of the business.

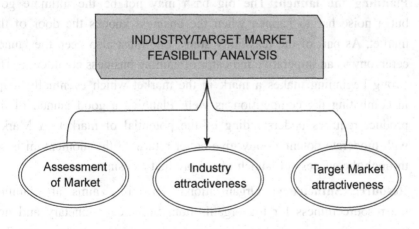

Fig. 3.4: Industry/Target Market Feasibility Analysis

Source: Author's Study

3.7 Organizational Feasibility Analysis

The business aspirant as part of the feasibility analysis needs to understand its state of affairs from managing the organisational set up. The Resources planning, the structural set up & adjustments, the overall business management aspects, all these and many more will be part of organisational feasibility assessment. The key factors to be considered for the organisational feasibility are stated below:

1. **Sufficient Management Expertise:** The brains involved in the business planning must be sufficiently experienced either practically or atleast conceptually. A prior experience in the similar business gain helps the momentum. However, a budding entrepreneur possibly can aim to follow the guidelines of better business plan, where by the Management feasibility necessarily aims at resource management.

2. **Focus on Non-financial resource:** The easiest way to think of business prosperity is to aim for profits. However, the larger businesses largely aim at ensuring a better non financial resource than just financial capital. The human capital, machinery, infrastructure maintenance etc. lead to a better business momentum. The feasibility of attaining such proficiency has to be the aim for a budding entrepreneur.

3. **Planning the launch:** The big bash may not be the ultimate goal but a noise has to happen when the business knocks the door of the market. As part of the feasibility study, one must also keep the launch ceremony as an imperative indicator of gaining business confidence. The strong beginning makes a mark in the market which eventually helps in combating the competition as well. Planning a good launch of the product requires understanding of the potential of market. A Market with moderate potential may give better returns if the momentum is set through the successful launch of the product / business.

4. **Resource Sufficiency:** Organisational feasibility aims at planning the resourcefulness for the organisation. Sufficient monetary and non monetary resources need to be aimed while executing the business. The tangible & non tangible resources for the businesses are pretty essential and the sufficiency of such resources for the business becomes imperative to be studied before starting the business.

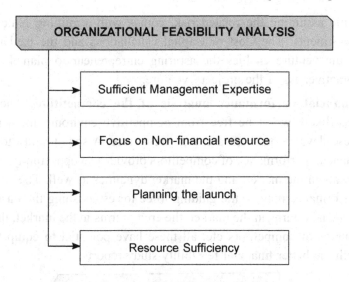

Fig. 3.5: Organizational Feasibility Analysis

Source: Author's Study

3.8 Financial Feasibility Analysis

In common parlance the financial viability of a project is the essential & premium talk before starting a business. An aspirant usually looks for finances first and then decides to launch the product. Ideally, it should go the other way round. The product feasibility has to be the primary concern and accordingly the financial feasibility has to be assessed. The reason being the sources of finances may be varied however the product has to satisfy limited scope of market. If the product feasibility signals a positive path, then the financial feasibility may be ascertained with the following approach:

1. **Financial Assessment:** The business aspirant has to assess the overall financial sources available for the business. These sources could be own funds, it could be borrowed funds. The borrowed funds can further be ascertained through financial institutions, Banks, other lending mechanism in the society like venture capitalists, angel investors etc. Being ready with required funds in hands helps the business aspirant to meet not just regular businesses but the contingencies as well.

2. **Financial Attractiveness:** The investments in business must undergo attractiveness study as well. The Returns on Investment once calculated

while assuming the related risk, comes with a guiding philosophy for investments. The Cost of Capital calculations and the payback period of the venture enables the aspiring entrepreneur to plan the financial attractiveness of the project / venture.

3. **Financial performance analysis of the competition:** The business very likely won't be free from competitive environment. A monopoly these days in business arena is pretty rare. A sound study towards the financial performance of competitors provides an opportunity to learn the threats in the market and the market dynamics as well. The competitors' performance may be the guiding force for establishing the business. The financial returns in the market, the credit terms in the market, the funding sources of competitors etc. all these have potential to equip the owner with the better financial feasibility study reports.

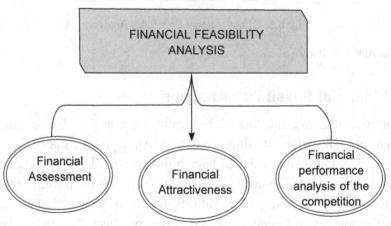

Fig. 3.6: Financial Feasibility Analysis

Source: Author's Study

An overall feasibility study must necessarily be done at the start of the business. However, it should also continue on regular intervals. The feasibility study controls the business planning process, whereby, the venture owner generates the sense of confidence towards realising the project. The Product feasibility study, Organisational feasibility study, Financial feasibility study & Market feasibility study discussed in the chapter provides strength to the business planner in constructing the path of operations. A business venture certainly requires a mammoth planning which includes the feasibility study. The business forecasting, continual operations, effective management and much more are the projected benefits that the Feasibility study provides to the business. Although, it is the start of the business that attracts the feasibility study but a business must keep the study functional on regular intervals. It enables the owner to be on track and necessitate the required diversions in the business plan. Feasibility study is a guiding force for the businesses and must be conducted with utmost seriousness.

CASE STUDY

RETAIL MARKETING: A FEASIBILITY CHECK FOR ORGANISED RETAIL IN RURAL MARKET

Retail Sector is one among the massive growing sector in India. The Nation with a huge population caters a big market for retail business. Indian Retail Industry has immense potential majorly due to the rapid urbanization and penetration of Internet marketing. *India Brand Equity Foundation (IBEF)* projects the developments of businesses and in this context earlier it had projected that by end of the year 2018 Indian retail industry shall achieve CAGR of 13 per cent to reach US$ 950 billion, which eventually was a reality *(www.ibef.org)*. India was ranked first in the Global Retail Development Index 2017, backed by rising middle class and rapidly growing consumer spending. This primarily rationalises the massive talk on development of retail sector and significantly the sector is growing to contribute further in overall GDP. India's retail market is expected to keep increasing and it was projected that it shall increase by 60% to reach US$ 1.1 trillion by the end of year 2020 (It was predictant when COVID-19 did not exist), and the credit goes to the factors like rising incomes and lifestyle changes by middle class and increased digital connectivity (www.ibef.org). While the overall retail market is expected to grow at 12% per annum, modern trade would expand twice as fast at 20 per cent per annum and traditional trade at 10%. Indian retail market is divided into Organised Retail Market contributing 93% of the total sector and Unorganised Retail Market contributing the rest 7% of the sector (www.ibef.org). E-Commerce / online platform for shopping has created a strong revolution in the retail sector and certainly the trend would continue further. The likes of Big Bazaar and Reliance fresh were already creating trends in the business, but with the advent of D-Mart in Indian Market, the business domain has completely taken a joy ride.

The D-Mart inclusion in the business was taken up by surprise by the existing retail sector players. So was the case with Big Basket as well. The brand promoted by Shahrukh Khan, took the market to a next level in urban boundaries. While knowing the fact that the Organised Retail Sector will constitute roughly 10% still the volume is more when considered per unit sales. The Online Retailers or the e-Retailers are a further section of business owners who have entered the market with a new dimension of threats in terms of Pricing and Quality. No longer are the days that the quality of online supplies were compromised, instead they have improved to that extent that it has become the USP for the online sellers. The big idea surrounding the success of the Retail sector or for that matter any sector revolves around the feasibility check of the businesses. The rural section of the society today is still deprived of the full fledge modern retail avenues. A market compound or a designated place for market operations is not new for the rural market but getting the product at door step requires a brainstorming exercise. Professional businesses doesn't run in isolation instead the supply chain require support.

A retail sector survives with the support of product providers, distribution channel and analytics. Hence, a feasibility check for rural sector development for the retail market shall encompass the need to understand the overall supply chain and the related stuff. Rural market shall pose challenges on the distribution channel. The rural market shall pose further challenge on creating demand on new arrivals. The rural market very likely will have challenges on shelf life of products. Retail sector has several facets & product avenues. Not all these facets will have a welcome sign for rural market. The untapped rural market, new & varied customer base, reach and potential to create the demand are a few positives that surround the feasibility of success that organised retail sector may experience in rural market. A budding retail entrepreneur or an existing retail player potential shall run a feasibility check on entering the rural market with the business as the massive dilemma will be the immediate success with competition at urban market or an untapped rural market with potential to grow in future. Sustainability of businesses has always been the priority but rarely that one finds sustainable business if the feasibility analysis was weak for such business.

Questions for Discussion

1. Discuss the essentials of the Retail sector in Indian Context.
2. Explain the significance of exploring Retail business in rural market while highlighting the importance of feasibility check as part of planning the business.
3. "A Feasibility check becomes further imperative when the market is new and demand needs to be created." Discuss the statement in light of Feasibility check for businesses in new markets.

Key Terms

Feasibility: Feasibility means the viability element for any task or operations. The possibility of conducting a task or operations is termed as Feasibility for the operations.

Feasibility Study: Feasibility Study is a process of investigation, review and evaluation undertaken as the project. It is the preliminary evaluation of the Idea where by the Entrepreneur decides the viability of the business idea.

Product Feasibility: A state of assessing the viability of the product to hit the market & survive. Product feasibility generates confidence in the Owner of the product pertaining to the market availability & scalability of the product.

Market Feasibility: A process of understanding the market viability & potential for the product. Market Feasibility encompasses aspects like reach of the product, frequency of purchase, potential of consumers etc.

Operational Feasibility: A state of affair that ensures operational viability of the venture. The Operational feasibility accounts to the likelihood of managing operations i.e., plant & site, trading opportunities etc. The Operational Feasibility assesses the internal environment of the business.

Financial Feasibility: The Financial Feasibility is the state of assuring that the availability of the Finance for the business is not the bottleneck in the path of venturing. The Financial feasibility ensures that the fund required for the venture is available or can be made available through sources.

Product: A product is a matter or offering that can be presented to a market for acquisition, use or consumption. Products provide the business with the opportunity of acquaintance with the buyers. This is the essential matter of thought for the business owner.

Planning: Planning is the first function of Management that initiates the process of managing the ventures. It is initial function of Management which eventually becomes the integral part of all the functions of Management.

Retailing: Retailing is a transactional & trading action corresponding to the sale of goods or services to the ultimate consumer for usage. Retailing as a marketing function enables the producer to reach to the market and sell the products to the customers.

Review Questions

1. What is the implication of the Feasibility Study for businesses?
2. What is the essence of Organisational feasibility study for businesses?
3. Define the way of conducting the feasibility analysis.
4. Write Short notes on:
   (a) Financial Feasibility
   (b) Marketing Feasibility
   (c) Retailing
   (d) Operational Feasibility
   (e) Feasibility Analysis

Applied Questions

1. "The Feasibility analysis is the base of every business." Enumerate the statement while highlighting the benefits of the Feasibility analysis.
2. "Assessing the business feasibility requires a defined process which ensures risk free environment for business." Discuss.

3. "Product/Service Feasibility Analysis is the first step towards the Feasibility study of the business." Explain the statement while highlight essence of product selection for businesses.

4. "Feasibility study is like primary education that builds the foundation of the business." Discuss the statement in light of how & why to perform Feasibility analysis.

5. "An Entrepreneur assumes the risk of developing a venture based on its viability." Discuss the statement while highlighting the significance of Feasibility analysis.

References

1. Taneja, Satish & Gupta, S. L. (2003). Entrepreneur Development: New venture Creation, published by Galgotia Publishing Company, 2nd Revised Edition.

2. Baporikar, Neeta (2007). Entrepreneurship Development and Project Management, published by Himalaya Publishing House, 1st Edition.

3. Ogbari, M. (2016). Entrepreneurship and Business Ethics: Implications on Corporate Performance, IJEFI, Vol. 6.

4. http://ediindia.ac.in/e-policy/Doc/Draft-National-Entrepreneurship-Policy.pdf, accessed on 05/08/2018.

5. https://www.entrepreneur.com/article/38882, accessed on 15/09/2019.

6. www.ibef.org, accessed on 15/09/2019.

❑❑❑

4

Business Plan

Dr. Manisha Gupta
(Associate Professor, School of Business Studies,
Sharda University, Greater Noida)

LEARNING OBJECTIVES

After reading this chapter, the reader should be able to:

1. Understand the components to business plan.
2. Appreciate the benefits of writing business plan.
3. Prepare business plan for starting new venture.

4.1 Introduction

Today new business models have transformed the way business is done. Innovative technologies have played a major role in changing the ways of operating the businesses. Anyone who wants to start a business starts with a question that is *'What's the key to Success?'* The answer to this question is to have a good idea and a smart strategy to carry it out. To achieve success in any new venture one needs to have a business plan.

A documentary representation of the description related to the business products, services, how the business is going to earn its profits, the leadership style to be practised, staffing patterns financing and operations models that has to implemented. A new venture is required to create a business plan while the existing business creates the business plan if there are changes in strategies of operating business.

An effective plan can be created if one has clarity about the idea and its feasibility. The most common business plans originate from the factors such as change in the external environment of the business, unsolved problems of the operations in the internal organization and the problem related to unsupplied demand of the market.

The business plans are created when any entrepreneur seeks funds or investment from external sources such as financial institutions and investors. It is suggested to all start-ups to have a sound business plan as it gives a roadmap to the new enterprise. This can also be of great help to an entrepreneur to uncover the weakness about misperception the market.

The business plan should be able to summarize all that is required to know about the business, in other words it is stated as the *"whole information package"* that includes feasibility study, nature of business, the market analysis and required resources for the business. Basically, the business plan gives a comprehensive overview about the business proposal.

The business plan tries to highlight following aspects of the proposed business:

- What market the business will serve?
- What would be the nature of business?
- What type of product and services the business is going to offer?
- What type of consumers it would be serving?
- What would be the tentative location of the business?
- Describes the Financial situation of the business.
- What would be the legal form of the business enterprise?
- Who would be the operational heads of the business enterprise?

4.2 Benefits of A Business Plan

1. One of the benefits of any business plan is that it gives an opportunity to test business idea i.e., how real the ideas is and what probability does it have to be successful.

2. Since business operates in a dynamic environment and during its life cycle goes through growth and difficulties, a clear statement of business mission would help the enterprise steer through the turbulent business environment.

3. Business model plan is a description on how business is going to spend its funds and excel in the business

4. A business plan gives an overview of the potential customer and their tentative buying behaviour pattern.

5. The business plan gives a review on the major competitors and their strategies plan.

6. Business plan gives clear-eyed analysis for the industry in which business has to operate it gives the overview on the opportunity and threats along with the company's strength and weakness.

7. Business plan chalks out all the benchmarks and standardization of the operations so that proper corrective action can be taken.

8. Business plan gives a brief explanation of the business enterprise's marketing strategies.

9. An analysis of the function and cash flow of the new busy was helps to anticipate the funding needs until the business reaches its breakeven point.

10. A business plan gives the correct assessment of risk associated and the change causing elements of the dynamic business environment.

11. A business plan acts as a resume, which can be used to introduce self to its employees, supplier's vendors, lenders and others.

4.3 Business Plan Elements

4.3.1 Executive Summary

An executive summary of a business plan is the blueprint of the detailed business plan. It gives a summarized point about the key elements of the business plan. Therefore, the executive summary is stated as the most important part of the business plan. The major purpose of executive summary is to capture the attention of the reader at the first instance.

4.3.2 Contents of Executive Summary

A typical executive summary outline for any business includes following sub heads:

- **Mission Statement:** A mission statement literal meaning is "A formal summary of the aims and values of a company, organization, or individual." In few sentences, it describes what are the core competencies of the business, who it will serve and what differentiates it from the competitors.

  Few examples are:

  Google: as *"To organize the world's information and make universally accessible and useful"*

  Wal-Mart: *"We save people money so they can live better"*

- **Company Information:** This section describes the company's founder members ideology, their product, services, key employees etc

- **Business Highlights:** This section deals with the description as to how the business evolved, the major statistics of the growth of the business including pattern of its market share, etc.

- **Financial Summary:** The briefing on the financial status of business in any business plan gives the details of whether the business needs financial expansion or not.

- **Future Goals:** Future goals enables the entrepreneur to assess the future requirement of the finances also.

NOTE: There is a difference between the contents of executive summary of established business and a start up, as for a start up the main motive is to convince the investors who would be providing finances to the project. Therefore, the contents of start up enterprise executive summary can be listed as follows:

  (*i*) The business opportunity

  (*ii*) Taking advantage of the opportunity

(*iii*) The target market

(*iv*) Business model

 (*v*) Marketing and sales strategy

(*vi*) The competition

(*vii*) Financial analysis

(*viii*) Owners/Staff

 (*ix*) Implementation plan.

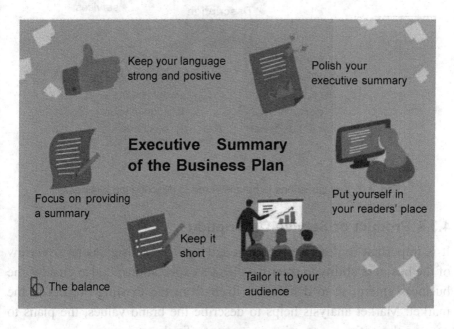

Fig. 4.1: Tips for writing good business plan.

Source: *https://www.thebalancesmb.com/executive-summary-of-the-business-plan-2948012*

4.3.3 Business Description

This section deals with the description of all the aspects of the company. It may include the mission and vision statement of the company. The ideology and the value system of the leaders of the company. It also describes the unique selling propositions (USP) of the company and what is the business plan to seize.

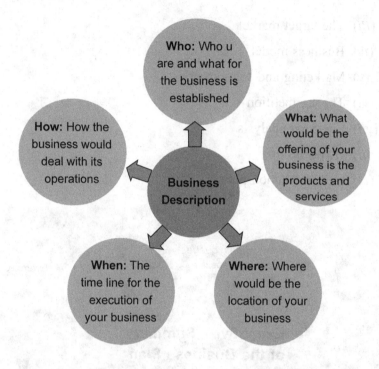

Fig. 4.2: Key Questions to be answered to describe the business.

4.3.4 Product or Service Description

It is important to describe products and services as it gives an overview of the business ability to cater the client's expectations. It also enables the business enterprise to distinguish itself from the existing players in the market. Market analysis helps to describe the brand values, the plans to convert the entire prospective customer to final consumer.

The product and service description section include following inputs:

   (i) Description of offered product and services

  (ii) The pricing details of product and services

 (iii) A comparison between the products and services offered by the competitors

 (iv) Information regarding the sales efforts of marketing department

  (v) Methods how the order will be processed or fulfilled

 (vi) Intellectual property or legal issues need to be addressed if any

(vii) Future prospects of offering (product and services)

4.4 Mission Statement

A mission statement states the purpose of the business. In the mission, statement the business goals and the philosophies are stated in the form of few succinct sentences. This outlines the future course of action for the business. The mission statement portraits the business outlook towards its customers, employees, suppliers and community.

Example: Mission statement of TCS *"To help customers achieve their business objectives by providing innovative, best in class consulting, IT solution and services. Make it a joy for all stakeholder to work with us"*

A mission statement is meant to answer the following questions:

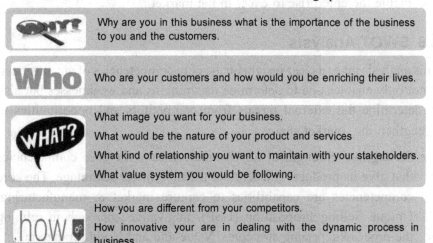

Fig. 4.3: Questions that should be answered in Mission Statement

4.5 Market Analysis

Market analysis helps to describe the brand value, the plan to convert all prospective customers to final consumers. This helps to enhance sales and develop a loyal clientele. The market analysis section of a business plan in general includes following information:

- **Description of the operating Industry:** A detailed statistics of the industry that includes the forces which govern the sector such as bargaining power of the suppliers, bargaining power of the buyers, threats of the substitutes, threats of the new entrants and the Rivalry within the Industry. These forces can be well explained using Porter's Five Force model.

- **The target Market:** A well define demographic profile of the population is expected to be known to the marketer, because it gives a better understanding of the segment to be targeted for the positioning of the product and services.

- **Initial investigation:** Well-structured test marketing would enable the marketer to successfully commercialize their product and services.

- **Competitive Analysis:** In the era of globalization there are n number of substitutes available in the market, hence, it is required to have a healthy competition in the market. To be well informed about the competitor's strategy and the type of product and services would enable the enterprise to excel in the market.

4.6 SWOT Analysis

This analysis gives a clear insight on the core competencies of any business. It not only enables one to determine its strengths and weaknesses but also to determine the external threats from competitors and opportunities to strengthen the market share

- **Strengths:** Strength of any business means the core competencies that give its products and services the first mover advantage. The core competencies are capabilities to capture market & manufacturing, Unique Selling Proposition (USP), innovative approach in refining the processes, pricing strategies, Value-add and brand reputation.

- **Weaknesses:** Studying weakness would enable the business to analyse the areas where the business needs to improve. Hence, weakness is the negative factors that diminishes strength. The factors under weakness that must be answered are.

  (*i*) What are the processes that need to be improved?

  (*ii*) Which are the areas that need to be worked upon in order to have competitive edge?

  (*iii*) Are there any gaps in your operational team?

- **Opportunities:** These are determination of the new avenues to be invaded, where business can identify for growth and greater profitability. (Example new market, export potential, joint venture proposal).

The scanning of opportunity of a business can be understood by study of following market aspects

(*i*) Market summary: It emphasises to determine the market segments, the requirement of the potential customer.

(*ii*) Market trends: It represents the substitute products and competitors offering in the market.

(*iii*) Market growth: It determines the anticipation of the overall growth in the demand of product and services in the market.

(*iv*) Market needs: It focuses on the trending changes required by the customers in the existing products.

- **Threats:** Threats in business are determining the aspects of external environment, which are dynamic, and changing which adversely affect any business operations in future. (Example: imported products, new entrants, political and economic changes)

It is very important for a successful business to have an operating plan which includes business threats. These threats determine the factors (external in nature) can affect the performance of business and other strategic decisions. For example, in tobacco industry, the major threats could be government policies, the changing perception of population regarding being more health conscious, excise duty etc.

4.7 Marketing Plan

The marketing plan section of a business plan explains how an entrepreneur is going to get its customer to buy to product/services

The section include in Marketing Plan can be stated below:

- The Unique Selling Proposition (USP) of the offerings(product/ services)
- The Pricing Strategy adopted for the achievement of sales target.
- The intermediaries chosen that is the Channels of Distribution Plan
- The Promotional Mix plan (design of Advertising and Promotions)

A thorough market research is to be taken on the above sections. The marketing research enables the entrepreneur to get an insight on the entire marketing mix to be implemented for the successful launch of the product/service in potential market. The market plan cannot be devoid of competitor's analysis. The marketing plan can be summarized by answering following questions:

4.7.1 Unique Selling Proposition

- Answer to the features of the product and services that fulfils the needs of the consumers.
- Elaborate on the physical attributes of the products and services and the difference it has in comparison to the competitors.
- Answer the benefits that the customers will get by the usage of the product.
- Answer the extra benefits that the consumer would get besides fulfilment of basic needs. For example- a floor cleaner would clean the floor but also benefit with better health.

4.7.2 Pricing Strategy

The pricing strategy must be competitive and still enable the entrepreneur to gain reasonable profit. In a marketing plan, it is important that the pricing strategy should be defined as to how the enterprise is going to be gained. The word "reasonable" here implies that the price of product and service should be marked in such a manner that the consumer is willing to pay.

The price should be calculated by the cost individual in manufacturing; the benefits estimated and compare the products and services with the similar available products and services in the market.

For an effective pricing strategy, it is important to answer following questions:

- Whether all fixed and variable cost have been included while calculating the cost of the product; it should also include freight costs, administrative costs, and/or selling costs, for example.
- The price that is quoted is competitive in nature. That is, if the price is high why is it so, whether the consumer is willing to pay and if the price is low how are you in the industry able to do so.
- The kind of return on investment that is expected from your product/ services in a specified period.

4.7.3 Sales and Distribution Plan

The sales and distribution plan would enable to know how the customers are going to get the product and services. What mode of distribution network to be used would be decided if the business plan answers following questions:

- What would be the mode of distribution of goods/services. Would it be through E- retailing or physical form of retail or through personnel selling, or through the mail?

- What level of distribution channel must be adopted whether zero, one two or three level? In zero level there is no intermediary it is from manufacturer to consumer. In one level of distribution channel there is one intermediary between manufacturer and consumer it can be retailer or wholesaler, and so on.

- What would be the waiting line for the raw material and finished product?

- How is the product packed and labelled for the shipping?

- What is the minimum inventory level to be maintained to ensure that there is no delay in fulfilling the gap between demand and supply?

- What is the payment facilities, return policies and after sales support if required.

4.7.4 Advertising and Promotion Plan

A well-designed advertising and promotion plan enables the entrepreneur to design a message that can be sent to the target audience with effectiveness. In addition, design a promotion mix that can successfully portray the USP (Unique Selling Proposition) of the product and the services offered.

There are literally thousands of avenues of promotional mix available, few can be named as:

- Advertisement.
- Sales promotion.
- Publicity.
- Trade shows.

4.8 Financial Projections

Financial projection is a very crucial and difficult part of the business plan especially when one is just at the stage of raising seed money. Well designed financial projection whether short term and medium term is essential because it draws the serious attention of the investors.

A detailed financial projection in a business plan includes sales volume forecast, expenses budget (like advertisement budget, training cost), cash flow statement, annual balance sheet and profit and loss statement. A general accepted accounting principle should be used to report the financial projection.

4.8.1 Sales Forecast

Sales forecast gives a clear insight of how a company would manage its work force, cash statements, and other resources. Sales forecast is easy for a pre-established firm because predictions can be done on the base of trends past and anticipate the future accordingly. But in case of a newly established firm the only raw data available is the competitor's sales volume and their trends and the prospective consumer demand. Sales forecasting can be appropriately done through a proper understanding of the market trends the industry environment. This will give the investor the confidence that the forecasting is not merely guesswork.

The sales forecast should be narrowed down by stating the monthly sale, quarterly sales and annual sales so that the business plan should give a clear picture of your proposal to the investors.

4.8.2 Cash Flow Statement

Cash flow in simple language can be defined as the incoming and outgoing of the cash. Incoming can be determined through sales forecast and outgoing is revealed by the expense statement of the firm. The lags of revenue payments should be calculated in the cash flow statement as there can be clients who deal in credits rather than paying in advance.

Table 4.1: Cash Flow Projection Spreadsheet

	Year						
	Previous	Current	Next 1	Next 2	Next 3	Next 4	Next 5
1. Income							
(a) Financial Commitments							
(b) Gifts and/or Funds from Endowments							
(c) Fund raising							
(d) Rental Income							
(e) Plate Collections							
(f) Non-committed contributors							
(g) District or UUA Grants							
(h) Others:							
(i) Others:							
(j) Others:							
(k) Others:							
Total Income	0	0	0	0	0	0	0
2. Expenses							
(a) Personnel							
(b) Administration							
(c) Programming							
(d) Contributions							
(e) Debit Service							
(f) Others:							
(g) Others:							
(h) Others:							
(i) Others:							
(j) Others:							
Total Income	0	0	0	0	0	0	0

4.8.3 Profit and Loss Statement

The profit and loss statement also termed as "Income Statement". The P & L statement of any business shows the revenues earned and expenses of any business in a given period of time that is (in a month, a quarter or a year).

Following information are required in order to state the P&L statement of firm:

• The transaction list that is all the purchases made by the firm.

- Any petty cash transaction or cash transaction for which you have a receipt.
- List of all sources of income.
- Information on reduction of sales, discounts and returns.

Table 4.2: Profit and Loss statement Template

INCOME STATEMENT	
For the year ending December, 31, 2017	
Revenues:	
Sales Revenue	$500,000
Other Revenue	$0
(Less Sales Returns & Allowances	0
Total Revenues	$500,000
Cost of Goods Sold	150,000
Gross Profit	**$350,000**
Expenses:	
Accounting	$2,500
Advertising	25,000
Amortization	0
Bad Debt	1,000
Depreciation	50,000
Employee Payroll Tax	15,000
Employee Wages	100,000
Entertainment	0
Insurance	2,000
Interest Expenses	12,000
Miscellaneous	5,000
Rent	24,000
Software	0
Telephone	2,500
Utilities	7,000
Web Hosting	500
Vehicle Expense	12,000
–	0
–	0
Total Expenses	**$258,000**
Net Income Before Taxes	**$91,000**

4.8.4 Balance Sheet

The balance sheet is the balance between the two sides namely assets and liabilities. Many components of both the sides are more than periodical sales and expenses. For example, any property, equipment, or unsold inventory owned is an asset with a value that can be assigned to it. The same goes for outstanding invoices that have not been paid.

The balance is the trade off between what one has and what one borrows.

The three important sections of any balance sheet are:
- Assets – Anything that has value and owned by a company
- Liabilities – This provides a list of debts a company owes to others
- Capital or Equity – This is the amount invested by the Shareholders

Below is shown the template of T shaped Balance sheet

Table 4.3: Horizontal form of balance sheet template

Liabilities	Amount	Assets	Amount
Capital	xx	Fixed Assets-Land, Bldg.	xx
Loan Taken	xx	Current Assets	
Current Liabilities		• Cash/Bank B/s	xx
• Outstanding Expenses	xx	• Accounts Receivable (Debtors)	xx
• Bank Overdraft	xx	• Bills Receivable	xx
• Accounts Payable (Creditors)	xx	• Inventories	xx
	xyz		xyz

The company's Act 2013 had proposed a vertical form of balance sheet for the disclosure of maximum information as the horizontal form of balance sheet had restricted information.

Table 4.4: Vertical form of balance sheet.

Particulars	Note No	Figures as at the end of current reporting period	Figures as at the end of previous reporting period

I. EQUITY AND LIABILITIES
1. Shareholders' Funds
   (a) Share Capital
   (b) Reserves and Surplus
   (c) Money Received against Share Warrants			

Contd...

Table 4.4: Vertical form of balance sheet

Particulars	Note No	Figures as at the end of current reporting period	Figures as at the end of previous reporting period
2. Share Application Money Pending Allotment			
3. Non-Current Liabilities			
(a) Long-term borrowings			
(b) Deferred Tax Liabilities (Net)			
(c) Other Long-term Liabilities			
(d) Long-term Provisions			
4. Current Liabilities			
(a) Short-term Borrowings			
(b) Trade Payables			
(c) Other Current Liabilities			
(d) Short-term Provisions			
Total			
II. ASSETS			
1. Non-Current Assets			
(a) Fixed Assets			
(i) Tangible Assets			
(ii) Intangible Assets			
(iii) Capital work-in-progress			
(iv) Intangible Assets Under Development			
(b) Non-current Investments			
(c) Deferred Tax Assets (Net)			
(d) Long-term Loans Advances			
(e) Other Non-current Assets			
2. Current Assets			
(a) Current Investments			
(b) Inventories			
(c) Trade Receivables			
(d) Cash and Cash Equivalents			
(e) Short-term Loans and Advances			
(f) Other Current Assets			
Total			

4.8.5 Break-Even Projection

The Break-Even Projection enables to determine the revenue that has to be collected by sales, so as to cover costs of operating a business. This is an important point because as the business reaches the breakeven point it starts its growth phase and starts giving profits to the firm. The breakeven point depends on three Key assumptions:

1. Average per unit sales price (per-unit revenue)
2. Average per unit cost
3. Monthly fixed cost.

4.9 Conclusions

A business plan is a very important strategic tool for entrepreneurs. A good business plan not only helps entrepreneurs to focus on the specific steps necessary for there to make business ideas succeed, but it also helps them to achieve both their short-term and long-term objectives. Many venture capitalists agree on the fact that for a successful start up not just a great idea is essential but a perfect black and white version in the form of business plan is required. In fact, an excellent business idea might fail if the entrepreneur cannot formulate, execute and implement the strategic decisions taken which is only possible through a well structures business plan. Hence, it can be concluded that a business plan is necessary for any start-up venture-

(a) To raise money for business.

(b) To make strategic decision about type of product and service, designing the segment, target market and positioning strategies.

(c) To help to identify the strength, weakness, opportunities and threats of the business.

(d) To communicate the idea to the stakeholders and get required funds and helps to launch the business successfully.

4.10 CASE STUDY

Starting a Business Repairing Bicycle*

Sheila works as a departmental manager responsible for all non-food products in a store close to where she lives. She has a team of eight people working for her and they appear highly motivated and consider Sheila a good manager. Although Sheila loves her job, her ambition has always been to start her own business and she feels that the time is now right to plan a future in self-employment.

Over the past few years Sheila has saved regularly, putting a small amount of money aside each month into a bank savings account. This has built up and will provide Sheila with some investment capital. She is, however, fully aware that she will have to raise additional funding if she is to realise her dream and create a viable business that will support herself. Sheila is very keen on cycling and is seen as something of a local 'hero', having won a couple of high-profile professional races two years ago. Sadly, last year she was involved in an accident and damaged her left knee. Following this accident, she had to retire from racing, but luckily, she was insured and has recently been awarded a small payout. Sheila plans to invest all pay-out in the new business.

Although she can no longer ride professionally, Sheila is still very keen on cycling and believes there is a great opportunity in the local town to open a bicycle shop, selling new and second-hand bicycles and providing a high-quality repair facility. Her vision is to open a bicycle shop close to the town centre, with enough showroom space to display a range of high-quality new and second-hand bicycles and with sufficient room, either behind the showroom or next door, to repair bicycles. Sheila's unique selling point (USP) is to offer a 24-hour turnaround service for customers, together with a pick-up and delivery service. These premises and the associated services will not be cheap. Sheila has some funds from her savings and from the insurance payout, but she will need to raise some additional investment capital to secure the appropriate premises, fixtures, fittings, equipment, and a van. She will also have to select, train and employ staff, and fund the numerous other business costs during the critical start-up and development stages. Although Sheila is at the very early planning stage, she knows that she must research and evaluate the financial, operational, marketing, legal and control aspects of this proposition in detail. She must also secure the various consents and adhere to the numerous laws and regulations, if she is to have any chance of securing additional finance for this venture. Now she needs to start putting together her business plan.

Q: As a management professional, develop a Business Plan for Sheila.

(*Source*: © The Association of Business Executives 2017 J/504/4410 Business Plan for Enterprise Start-up QCF Case Study Tuesday 5 December 2017)

Key Terms Discussed

(a) Business Plan

(b) Breakeven analysis plan

(c) Mission statement

(d) Market analysis

(e) Financial projection

Review Questions

1. Define business plan, also discuss the key elements of business plan.

2. Why is it important to do monthly cash flow analysis in business plan?

3. Why is location selection the most important aspect of any business plan?

4. Before starting any business, what are the important elements to be investigated.

Applied Questions

1. 'Business plans that look good on paper, may fail in practice' Comment about this statement.

2. You have been requested to assist ABC company to write out its business plan covering the next three years. Briefly explain how you would go about assisting them and explain the major sections this plan should cover taking care to use relevant examples where appropriate.

3. Assume that you are starting a business unit for service-based Application what primary study would be done and how you will prepare the business plan to present in front of investors.

References

1. Harvard Business School Press 2007, 4; Barrow & Barrow & Brown 2008, 7-8.).

2. Harvard Business School Press, Pocket Mentor 2007, Creating a Business Plan, Harvard Business School Publishing Corporation.

3. Barringer, 2015, 103-105; Harvard Business School Press, 2007, 24-26.

4. Ward,S (2018,October) Executive Summary of the Business Plan. Retrieved from http:// www.thebalancesmb.com.

5. Gray,R.B(2016,December) How to write a company description for a Business Plan. Retrieved from http:// www.smallbusiness.patriotsoftware.com.

6. Duermyer, R (2018,March) Business plan–Product or Service Selection Retrieved from http://www.thebalancesmb.com.

7. Abrams, R (2003) The Successful Business Plan: Secrets and strategies, Fourth edition, Palo Alto, CA.

8. Gregory, A (2018, October). What to include in the Market Analysis section of a Business Plan. Retrieved from http://www.the balanceamb.com.

9. Hayden, J (2015, April). How to Write Great Business Plan: Market Opportunity. Retrieved from http://www.inc.com.

10. https://cleartax.in/s/financial-reports.

11. Daniel, R (2018, July). Financial Projection. Retrieved from https://www.the balancesmb.com.

5

Industry and Competitor Analysis

Dr. Nandita Mishra
(Dean & Professor, MITCON Institute of Management, Pune)

LEARNING OBJECTIVES

After reading this chapter, the reader should be able to:

1. Understand the business and environment trends
2. Understand the concept of competitive strategy for a firm
3. Find the Competitive Intelligence Framework for the Entrepreneur

---

5.1 Studying Industry Trends

Entrepreneurs in the next decade will differ in age, gender and origin than their predecessors. The shifts in small business ownership will create new opportunities for many and will change the global scenario. Today's entrepreneurs are younger than the previous generation's entrepreneurs and now lot more women entrepreneurs are seen. The glass ceiling that once had limited women's corporate career paths has instead encouraged more women to the small business sectors. The rise in entrepreneurship has originated from many economic, social and technological changes. Layoffs and downsizing also drive people to become entrepreneurs. There has also been an emergence of entrepreneurial education. Different types of entrepreneurial education will expand over the next decade and improve the success rate of businesses launched.

77

Entrepreneurship is the unique capacity and willingness to develop, organize and manage a business venture. Entrepreneurship across the country is evolving, but there are lot of challenges at every level. At this juncture, economy needs entrepreneurs who can create work, either by new businesses or by expanding the existing businesses or by collaborating with other players. The society needs entrepreneurs that help people grow and develop and thus add economic value by developing knowledge. The Indian start-up ecosystem is just taking off. It is projected that by 2020 there will be 11,500 firms from just 3500 firms in 2016. Between 2010 and 2014, the infusion of venture capital and private equity increased from US $13 mn to US $1818 mn. Angel investment has also multiplied eight times. India comes across as an under- penetrated consumer driven market and the demographic dividend has a scope for exponential growth. This is despite the multitude of operational regulatory and taxation issues. According to a report of Grant Thornton (2016), India is ranked third amongst the top five countries in the world in terms of start-ups, with 10,000+ start-ups. US Ranks number one on the venture list with 83,000 + start-ups. Total technology driven start-ups are expected to increase to 11,500 in 2020 from 4300 in 2015. To understand the IP protection issues it's pertinent to analyse the composition of the Indian start up industry.

Table 5.1: Composition of Indian Start-up Industry

Technology	Non Technology
Start ups – 4300	Start ups – 5700
% Share – 43%	% Share – 57%
	Engineering – 17%
	Construction – 13%
E-Com – 33%	Agri Products – 11%
B2B – 24 %	Textile – 8 %
Consumer Products – 12%	Printing & packaging – 8%
Mobile App – 10%	Transport & Logistics – 6%
SaaS – 8%	Outsourcing & Support – 5%
Others – 13%	Others – 32%

Source: Grant Thornton, Start-ups India an Overview 2016

Technology based start-ups comprise mostly 43% of the start-up Industry in India. Innovation in various sectors like healthcare, education, financial services, logistics, travel and tourism, the list could be endless, is driving start-ups in India. The country has evolved as the third largest start-up ecosystem in the world and there is a rise of interest from industry giants, aspiring entrepreneurs and international investors. By leveraging emerging technologies like IoT, Big Data and analytics, artificial intelligence, block-chain and machine learning, these start-ups are completely restructuring and revisiting the way business is done in the country. Seed capital, VC Funding and Impact Investments is the current trend in entrepreneurship. E-commerce and Fintech were the frontrunner in 2017.

Industry analysis focuses on the potential of an industry. A new venture needs a more-in-depth analysis to understand market and industry trend. Determining the market conditions for feasibility analysis is very important for new firms. An entrepreneur must answer some pertinent questions before anything else. (i) Will the new venture survive in the industry it's planning to enter? Or is it again a me-too concept? (ii) Does the industry support innovation or is underserved? This can work both as an advantage and as an disadvantage, depending on how the entrepreneur spans every activity. (iii) Can the new venture avoid some negative side effects or hazards of the industry?

Firm level performance and Industry level performance affects the performance of a new entrant. The firm level performances are set by the firm's assets, products, culture, teamwork, employee culture, internal resources and ethics. The industry level factors include threat of new entrants, rivalry and competition, bargaining power of supplier and bargaining powers of buyers. The firm's profitability is attributed more to the industry in which the firm competes. In order to assess the industry attractiveness, the new firms should;

(a) Study the Business and Environmental Trends

(b) Assess the Five Competitive Forces Model

Business and Environmental Trends

On a broader scale, business owners are also thinking about major in-dustry trends and new technologies that will significantly impact the way they operate in the year ahead. The current industry trends in the Indian Entrepreneurship scene unfold the following:

(*i*) **Health Tech:** In India quality health care is confined mainly to the urban areas. However, with the current government's vision of health care and health insurance for all, a growing number of health tech start-ups have taken the initiative to bridge the gap. The current start-ups or enterprises in the health care start-ups are not only focussing on diagnostic and medicine delivery but also on addressing problems arising due to consumer lifestyle, mental stress, genetic disorders, palliative care and many others. To name a few health care start-ups it like Practo, Health Kart, Zoctor, 1 mg, Portea, Lybrate, JustDoc, Pharmeasy, Netmeds and Mera Medicare have revolutionised the health tech entrepreneurship. The main influencer in health care start-ups is the digitisation wave that has increased the pace of innovation in artificial intelligence. People's awareness on health-related issues and disorders have also paved the way for health tech.

(*ii*) **Fintech:** Bill Gates, Co-Founder and former CEO of Microsoft commented that, digital technology provides a low-cost way for people in developing countries for all their financial transactions if financial regulation environment is supportive. As a year of financial services, 2017 saw the emergence of promising start-ups in finance domain. The focus in fintech has been the cashless economy, thus giving rise to digital wallets, internet banking, digital mobile apps etc. Demonetisation has redefined the fintech sector and has paved the path for digital payment firms.

(*iii*) **Travel Tech:** In terms of contribution, the Travel and Tourism industry is ranked 7th globally. According to Google India- BCG report, the India's travel market is expected to become $48 bn industry. Indian online travel industry has a penetration of only around 19%. Indian start-ups in the online travel business like, MakeMy Trip, Cleartrip, ibobo, Yatra, ixigo and Expedia has made travel business look attractive and lucrative.

(*iv*) **Logistics Start-up:** The fine line between disorder and order lies in logistics. Technological intervention introduced by start-ups in the space of logistics has paved the way for dramatic improvements in productivity transparency, end-to end visibility, fuel cost efficiency, real-time tracking and accountability. The likes of Blackbuck,

Grey Orange, Ringo, and Delhivery are potential unicorns. Zomota biggest acquisition in the logistic space is Runnr, to strengthen the food delivery capacity.

(v) **Consumer Services:** E-Commerce, hyperlocal food and grocery delivery saw a drop in funding in 2016. However, Morgan Stanley report says online food and grocery segment would become the fastest growing segment, expanding at a CAGR of 141% and contributing $15 Bn to the economy. Swiggy, Food Apnada, Satvacart, Grofers, Godrej Nature's basket, Big Basket and Daily Ninja have opened huge opportunities in consumer services space.

(vi) **Deep Tech:** Artificial Intelligence has emerged as promising technology that can help to deliver services to different segments efficiently and effectively. Big Data is the foundation of AI. There has been an increased application of AI in health tech, fintech, edtech and consumer tech and across all sectors.

(vii) **Recurring Revenue Techs:** Instead of offering a product or service at a larger, onetime fee, many business owners are seeing the benefits of switching to smaller, monthly fee models. The success of Netflix compels one to consider recurring revenue model.

(viii) **Edtech:** The growth perceived in the educational start-ups is of course boundless as the industry is on everyone's radar, but it cannot be denied that edtech start-ups face huge number of competitors. So, the challenge remains, how these entrepreneurs can stand out tall in such a congested space. In the EdTech sector there are far too many start-ups and there is high possibility of crowding out. Even though education across the country is evolving, there's a variety of resistance to transformation at each level, change in any business cannot come so smooth, edupreneurship is also no exception. Innovation in public education can be clogged or slackened on the hands of a couple of stakeholders from teachers to taxpayers to school boards and local government officials. Edtech start-ups also have challenges of pricing strategies that probable clients can afford to pay. This is of course a complicated calculation, balancing the need and capability of the stakeholders and also making profit or even reaching break-even at the beginning, may impose a serious challenge. In the edtech world, all that matters is deliverables, action items, getting things completed, showing results and iteration. Whereas in the traditional academic domain, it slants to all about discussing, philosophizing and debating, so the edtech start-ups face the problem of a clash in the way they are expected to operate, and they do operate. In order to merge the two categories of thoughts, the thought-orientated academic players with the action-oriented edupreneurs, it necessitates that there is a clear communication of value points from edupreneurs to academic decision-makers.

5.2 Finding a Competitive Strategy and Developing New Strategy using Michael Porter's Five Forces

5.2.1 Threats of New Entry

Every entrepreneur needs to ask certain questions before starting any business. How easy it's for others to enter the market, with little or no variation in their goods? Is his business technology protected? Has he created barriers to entry? When and how can he make the business scalable? And most importantly, is the market regulated? If competitors can enter the market with little money and effort, one needs to adapt the strategy to handle potential competitions.

5.2.2 Threat of Substitution

The Five Forces model of Porter prompts the entrepreneur to explore the chance of his/her product getting replaced with an alternative that solves the same need. Answers to these questions can help understand the strategy. So an entrepreneur needs to ask what differentiates his product from his competitions? How many such alternatives are available in the market? What is the switching cost for the customer?

This is exactly what iPod did to the CD market. The CD for years had been giving customers a portable way to listen to music, iPod did the same using new technology. Price isn't always the reason that customers switch to a substitute product. After all, the iPod was much more expensive than a CD player, but people were willing to pay a higher price for a device that held thousands of songs. The same goes to explain how Kodak lost its position in the photography segment.

5.2.3 Bargaining Power of Suppliers

Supplier also thinks the same way as any business does. Any change in their prices thus affects the profitability of the entrepreneur. The entrepreneur must always evaluate how many suppliers does the firm have, how unique is the product or the service of the supplier, can it be replaced by alternate suppliers and how does the price compare amongst all the suppliers? The entrepreneur therefore develops his own strategy to protect the business.

5.2.4 Bargaining Power of Buyers

The situation differs from firm to firm. In case of B2B the bargaining powers of buyers is more compared to that of B2C. One needs to determine whether buyers have the power to drive the prices down. The questions every entrepreneur should answer therefore are, the control the buyers have on his business, what is the order size of the buyers, could the buyer switch to other supplier and what is the ROI of the product or service of the buyer. These questions help determine to leverage how clients can dictate cost in a service industry specially. The more customers one has, the more power one enjoys.

5.2.5 Competitive Rivalries

The four forces discussed above, i.e. (1) Threats of new entry, (2) Threats of Substitution, (3) Bargaining powers of suppliers and (4) Bargaining powers of buyers largely affect this last one. The number and strength of the existing competitors is extremely important in determining the market competition. Questions like, quality of the entrepreneur's product or service, number of competitors in the market and the power of the biggest competitor determines the entrepreneur's success. What will the customers gain or lose to switch to a competition product or service? The distinct feature of the entrepreneur's product or service decides his market success.

Paytm the Indian e-commerce payment system and digital wallet was founded in 2010 by Vijay Shekhar Sharma. It initially started off as prepaid mobile and DTH recharge platform. In 2014, Paytm wallet added payment links to Indian Railways and Uber as an added option.

Using the Five Forces model discussed above, one can correlate the reasons of Paytm success. With a user base of 150 million and 7 million merchants across India, Paytm has facilitated many small merchants and traders to sign up without a bank account. This is the uniqueness of the product. The Paytm wallet balance can further be used for shopping or making any other payments. The ease of making payments has made it more acceptable than its competitors. Users didn't have to link their accounts with debit or credit cards, thus allowing financially excluded section into its fold. This is where Paytm's rival lost the market to Paytm. In fact Paytm put the cart before the horse, which at times works in business due to the first mover advantage. Paytm used the Feet on street Approach, the salespersons visited all possible retail hotspots, street vendors, schools, colleges, mobile shops, merchants and micro-merchants. The ease of technology made even the Uber and Ola drivers use Paytm for their personal transactions.

5.3 Gaining Competitive Intelligence

Competitive intelligence (CI) means gathering information on risks and opportunities and analysing this data to develop insights and strategies. It helps a firm to assess their competitors' strengths and weaknesses, markets. For an entrepreneur it's imperative to gain competitive intelligence from social media, newspaper articles, trade fair, exhibitions, meets and most importantly the market.

In the early phases of strategy development, the PEST framework can be used to understand the landscape in which the firm operates. The environmental and legal aspects of the PESTEL analysis are not included in the discussion below as it overlaps with the political, economic and social environment.

Exhibit-I: Pest Framework

Political	Economic	Social	Technological
Environmental Regulation	Economic Growth	Income Distribution	Government support
Tax Policies	Interest Rates	Demography	Industry focus

Contd...

Exhibit-I: Pest Framework

Political	Economic	Social	Technological
Trade Regulations	Government spending	Life style changes	Inventions and innovation
Contractual/Labour Laws	Employment Laws	Entrepreneurial Spirit	Rate of Technology Transfer
Government Policies	Taxation	Education	Life Cycle of Technology
Competition Regulation	Exchange Rates	Fashion Trends	Energy Consumption & Cost
Political Stability	Inflation rate	Social Welfare	IT & Internet Usage
Consumer Protection	Stage of Business Cycle	Living Standards	Mobile & Digital Technology

An entrepreneur needs to select the product line and business strategy in line with the PEST Framework indicated above in Exhibit-I

Competitive Intelligence can further be divided into Communication Intelligence, Financial Intelligence, Technical Intelligence and Human Intelligence.

Exhibit-II: Competitive Intelligence

Communication Intelligence	Financial Intelligence	Technical Intelligence	Human Intelligence
Organization History	Financial History	Technical Literature	HR Policies
Web Contents	Financial News/ Deals	Patents & Patents Application	Employees
Social Media	Investors Presentation	Product Specs	Consultants
Marketing Communications	Annual Reports	Factories & Service Centre	Sales/Field Officers
Advertisements	Financial Documents	Manufacturing/ Production Centre	Customer Services

An entrepreneur should never miss the FOUR Data Points of Competitive Intelligence:

1. **Sales Information:** With reference to sales channel, sales target, specific conversion offers, announcements of specific offers. This helps the entrepreneur to know the rivals in the product lines, launch of new products in the market and any promotion offers made. Such information allows one to be competitive in the market.

2. **Product Releases:** How the products have evolved over time? Entrepreneur must stay alert on identifying new markets, trends, opportunities and new products. In a rapidly developing digital society, companies gain significant advantages by learning what their competition/ rivals are doing to secure business.

3. **Promotion:** Entrepreneurs pay special attention to promotion in advance of any special events. Website comparison and knowledge of various other competitors helps the entrepreneur to modify the pricing and optimize marketing initiatives. A very common for example is the offers given by tours and travels or OYO rooms, Airbnb and many others before the beginning of any vacation. Similarly, the great Indian festival offers of Flipkart and Amazons of the world also determines their sales optimizations.

4. **Corporate News:** An entrepreneur should always focus on the corporate news of its competition to design its own strategy. News on special events coverage, blogs, CSR activities and a host of other social initiatives creates lots of buzz for the entrepreneur.

Website, newsletters, social media, regulatory bodies, customer reviews and a plethora of other activities can help the entrepreneur find CI. It depends on the industry and the specific company goals.

Competitive Intelligence will allow an entrepreneur to

1. Identify market gaps
2. Develop unique value proposition
3. Identify methods to attract customers
4. Detect areas of strength and weaknesses
5. Appreciate customers' need and perspective

5.4 Understanding the Competitive Analysis Grid

Once the entrepreneur decides to enter an industry or a domain, it's pertinent that the entrepreneur develops Porter's Five Forces Model. The entrepreneur should thereafter prepare the Pest Analysis and Competitive Intelligence Grid of the firms operating in the industry. An in-depth investigation and analysis of the competition allows one to assess the competitor's strengths and weaknesses in the marketplace and helps the entrepreneur to choose and implement effective strategies.

What should the entrepreneur know before getting started?

1. Who should be considered as competitor? Firms offering similar, dissimilar or substitute products in relation to the products or services of the entrepreneur are considered as competition. A very common example is the manufacturer of plastic containers. There are many manufacturers in direct competition and also indirect competition who will satisfy the customers' need to some extent, although it's not what the customer wanted but ended up buying because of product usage, salesmanship, price or product features.

2. Should the entrepreneur analyse all the competitors? There are several markets where it's relatively easy to name every competitor. There are still markets where the number of players is large. In order to study the market in depth, the 80/20 rule should be followed. It is most probable that 80% of the market will be accounted for by 20 % of the player. The entrepreneur should focus on the 20 % of the players. When using this approach it's also important to keep abreast with the upcoming players, for they might use a new strategy to bring in the differentiating factor.

3. How should the entrepreneur limit the competition? There can be a broad range of strategies a businessman can employ. Price change, new packaging, customer service and new product development are some ways through which one can limit corruption.

4. Conducting and Preparing the Competitive Analysis Grid- Conducting research to gather competitive information, analyse the competitive information determining the level of competition and then determining its own competitive position is required for preparing the competitive grid.

The entrepreneurs should keep in mind the following questions while analysing the competitive grid.

1. Who are the top three or four competitors?

2. What are the range of products and services they offer?

3. What is the marketing strategy or tool of the competitors?

4. How do they fair in customer service?

5. How does the price of the competitors compare?

6. Most importantly, what is the differentiating factor of the entrepreneur?

Given below is the Competition Analysis Grid to be designed by any entrepreneur.

Exhibit-III: Competitive Analysis Grid

Name	Competitor 1	Competitor 2	Competitor 3	Contnd...
Product Features	Advantage for you	Even	Disadvantage for you	Advantage for you
User Engagement/ Marketing Tools	Enter your thoughts about the competitors engagement with the user	Enter your thoughts about the competitors engagement with the user	Enter your thoughts about the competitors engagement with the user	Enter your thoughts about the competitors engagement with the user
Differentiator	How the product is different	How the product is different	How the product is different	How the product is different
Price	State the price	State the price		State the price
Customer Service	What customer service is provided by the competitor	What customer service is provided by the competitor	What customer service is provided by the competitor	What customer service is provided by the competitor
Level of Competition	High	Low	Moderate	Not in comparison

Once all the above information is fed into the grid, the entrepreneur should be able to locate its strategy. The competitive analysis grid should be a regular feature and not a one-time analysis. Competition can change very rapidly, new players can emerge, or the economy might undergo an upswing or downswing. It's only when the entrepreneur clearly understand the competitive advantage, the market position can improve.

It's not only the business strategy, fund requirement or regulatory environment that challenges entrepreneurs; they also face legal issues and more so the intellectual property protection, In many instances, structuring the correct set up for the IPR prevents future complications and mitigate the regulatory issues.

The main features that define entrepreneurship are:

1. It could be an entrepreneurial venture or a new business.
2. It's financed by an individual or small group of individuals.
3. It's built on technology and innovation.
4. It has been in existence during the last 3-5 years.

Every entrepreneur goes through the various stages

PRE-Start

1. **Discovery Stage:** Where a scalable product/ service is identified, that has a huge potential for the target market.
2. **Validation:** The product identified hits the market looking for the initial client or customer

Growth

1. **Efficiency:** The entrepreneur looks for increasing the client or customer base
2. **Scale:** The entrepreneur looks for increasing capacity to grow in a sustainable manner

Post Maturity

1. **Maintenance:** This stage is focused on maintaining the markets and get maximum benefit
2. **Sale or Renewal:** There is a huge decision to sell the company or let it get acquired by a giant

A good business plan comprises of potential demand for its products and services, the nature of the competition, entry barriers, the unique selling proposition, technology and strategy partners, raising fund, projected start up costs, marketing strategies and the like. New and innovative ideas are the key to successful business for start ups, safeguarding creative expression and original knowledge is equivalent to retaining competitive advantage.

5.5 Case in Point- EdTech Entrepreneurship

Glossaread is taken as a case study for K12 and STEM startups in the early –growth stage. It is about bootstrapped entrepreneurship looking for either seed funding or Series A round of funding. The EdTech Startups in the discussion are driven by technology and make learning easy and fun. They are more relevant in the study of K12 Model as we explore their strategy to decide education entrepreneurship in this domain and identify patterns to predict successful business models. **Glossaread** was founded by Chandrabhanu Pattajoshi, a product focussed person with cross media experience across TV/Radio/ Data/Internet and a wide experience of running businesses across different geographies.   The concept of Glossaread came to him, when a bunch of engineering college students mentioned that the present generation doesn't subscribe to the idea of buying the full book for a few chapters or only some short relevant portion of a chapter. On the other extreme were the professors training the students for engineering entrance exams and giving capsule modules for solution but had no protection of their intellectual property He says that the entire education market today stands at 150 bn $ USD and higher education alone at 75 bn $ USD. However, higher education in developing countries like India can at times be unaffordable. Students from the economically weaker sections can't afford Course Books or Reference Books. Glossaread saw an opportunity in this! Glossaread breaks up the chapters of the course books/ reference books and makes the book more affordable through e-learning/digital learning/ satellite/ and online tutorials. Since all chapters from a book are not necessary, relevant chapters from different books are compiled and made available to students. Glossaread is already into engineering and would soon be targeting the management education domain. He further emphasizes that the biggest challenge India faces is the abysmal low internet speed of 5.6 mbps.

Differentiating factor: The cause of Glossaread was in the common interest of publishers, private tutors and coaching centres. Digital piracy is a challenge in today's world but by making chapters of books available at a cost cheaper than photocopy, the current generation users will go for more convenient and genuine options than unauthenticated and fake content.

The key pain points the entrepreneur faces are (1) go to market strategy, (2) customer acquisition (3) cost of sales (4) operational challenges (5) product replication and (6) long sales cycles. Given that the gestation period is longer in new ventures, entrepreneurs will have to overcome such hurdles to prove their efficacy. In case of K 12 Edtech startups there is also the challenge of red-tapism and bureaucracy in working with schools, convincing them to even pilot a project. Most schools and colleges must be wary of the number of pitches received daily. It is therefore a long sales process. This also means there are lots of similar products in the market and entrepreneurs might be severely underestimating the breadth of competition.

Source: Mishra, N. & Chakraborty, T. (2018) [EdTech Entrepreneurship: Sustainability Challenges and the Way Forward]

Case Questions

1. Discuss the challenges for Glossaread in the new venture, using Michael Porter's Five Forces Model and PEST Framework.

2. How should Glossaread develop its Competition Analysis Grid?

Key Terms Discussed

Industry Trends, Competitive Analysis, Business Environment, PEST Framework, PESTEL Analysis, Bargaining Power, Threat of Substitution, Competitive Intelligence, Competitive Analysis, Grid,

Review Questions

1. Compare and contrast the PEST Framework and the Competitive Intelligence Framework

2. Define entrepreneurship and the stages in the life of an entrepreneur.

3. Take an entrepreneurship business you would like to venture into and chart out the prelaunch research you should be doing.

Applied Questions

1. Analyse the current business and environment trends in context to the Indian start up composition?

2. Taking Michael Porter's Five Forces Model discuss the Health Start-Ups in India.

3. Chart out the Competitive Grid for an entrepreneur entering into the baby –food business in India.

Suggested Additional Reading

1. Fleisher, C, S., & Bensousson, B, E (2015, February 12) "Business & Competitive Analysis: Effective Application of New and Classic Methods", Pearson FT Press; 2 edition

2. Oster, S, M (1999, March 25) "Modern Competitive Analysis", Oxford University Press, 3 edition

3. Krishnamurthy, A, G "Dhirubhai Ambani Against all Odds" MCGraw Hill Education: Leadership Essential Series.

4. Article-How to Start a Startup in India- Idea to Execution, www.digest.myhq.in

5. Article- 50 Best Small Business Ideas to Start with $10k in 2020, www.profitableventure.com

References

1. Aronsson, M. (2004), "Education Matters- But does Entrepreneurship Education? An Interview with David Birch". Academy of Management Learning & Education.

2. Build to Scale (2017) Edtech Report.

3. Dutta, D.K., Li,J., Merenda. M. (2011). "Fostering Entrepreneurship Impact of Specialization & Diversity in Education". International Entrepreneurship Management Journal, 7(2), 163-179.

4. Jaarboek, K.S. (2013) Innovation and Sustainable Development through Entrepreneurship.

5. Klofsten, M., & Jones-Evans, D. (2000) – "Comparing Academic Entrepreneurship in Europe – The case of Sweden & Ireland". Small Business Economics, 14(4), 299-309.

6. Sawyer, K. (2012) Explaining Creativity: The Science of Human Innovation. Oxford: Oxford University Press.

7. Clark C., & Gonnelle, C. (2016) Three lessons for Impact Investment Education Programs.

7. Winne, P.H. (2010) Bootstrapping learner's self-regulated learning, Psychological Test and Assessment Modeling, vol. 52, no.4, pp. 472-490.

9. Lynch M., (2017, December 4). "Why Educators Make Some of The Best Edtech Entrepreneurs". The Tech Advocate. Retrieved from https://www. thetechedvocate.org/educators-make-best-edtech-entrepreneurs/

10. Marissa L. (2018, March 6). 5 Ways Education Technology Startups Can Get the Funding They Deserve. Bright Magazine. Retrieved from https:// brightthemag.com/edtech-startup-funding-research-education-technology-automation-bc47e789e2c6

11. D'Cunha S. (2016, October 13). Why Mark Zuckerberg Thinks An Indian EdTech Startup Is Worth Millions. Forbes Contributors. Retrieved from https://www.forbes.com/sites/suparnadutt/2016/10/13/why-mark-zuckerberg-thinks-an-indian-edtech-startup-is-worth-millions/#6e376f57c04d

12. Sinha P. (2016, March 18). Why do edtech startups fail? Tech Asia. from https://www.techinasia.com /talk/edtech-startups-fail

13. Shumski D (2013, Nov 20). 5 failed education startups you should study. Education Dive. from https://www.educationdive.com/news/5-failed-education-startups-you-should-study/196134/

14. Indian Tech Startup Funding Report (2017). Retrieved From https:// pages.inc42.com/annual-indian-tech-startup-funding-   report2017/?utm_ source=website&utm_medium=annual-report-article&utm_ campaign=top-3-angels

15. Mishra, N.& Chakraborty, T. (2018) "EdTech Entrepreneurship: Sustainability Challenges and the Way Forward", Sustainable Development: A Value Chain Perspective, Tiger Print, pg 211-230.

❑❑❑

6

Initial Ethical and Legal Issues Facing A New Firm

Dr. Rajesh Kumar Pandey
(Associate Professor, SSR IMR, Pune)

LEARNING OBJECTIVES

After reading this chapter, the reader should be able to:

1. Explain how to develop an ethical culture in an entrepreneurial organization.

2. Explain the criteria important to selecting an attorney for a new firm.

3. Argue the importance of a founders' agreement.

4. Provide an overview of the business licenses and business permits that a start-up must obtain before it starts conducting business.

5. Discuss the differences among sole proprietorships, partnerships, corporations, and limited liability companies.

6.1 Introduction

Establishing a new enterprise isn't that exciting as it gets detailed & discussed. It requires utmost focus on the ethical and legal quotient. Firms are prone to issues that may surround the establishment of the new venture. Along with all the entrepreneurial traits, the knowledge corresponding to the legal agenda of the entrepreneurial venture must be known thoroughly to the entrepreneur. While we consider Entrepreneurship as an art & skills of transformation and change, however it operationally requires strong legal base to support the establishment. Entrepreneurs are considered as the leaders of the economy. They are the self-motivated individuals who find opportunities for success in the industrial domain and society at large. Entrepreneurs are stated to be the Change Agent in the society. Entrepreneurship in this context becomes an essential aspect of societal growth. Hence, being ethical is imperative in this regard. Ethical business decisions support the business growth and sustainability of the business has more certainty.

Strong organisational culture has the potential to promote the ethical and legal atmosphere at the organisation. The entrepreneur must ensure legal appropriateness in the context of framing the Founder's agreement, seeking business permits & licenses, appointment of attorney etc. All these matters require expertise and concrete investment of time & energy leading to a satisfactory existence of the business. Entrepreneurs build base for the Industrial society to flourish and hence being safe on legal front promotes the entrepreneurial instinct. Initial ethical & legal issues are one among the primary concerns for the Entrepreneurs. Rather planning the mitigation of legal risk, it is better to be well prepared for ethical sound and legally strong venture.

6.2 Ethical & Legal Aspects of Entrepreneurship

Ethics in Business is the behaviour which corporation must adhere in its regular operations within the environment where it operates and in the community. Business ethics pose challenges for entrepreneurial ventures as the environment is dynamic and businesses are result oriented. In the world of business, norms are set to determine appropriate behaviour and decision-making. Business ethics is a larger umbrella, covering every aspect right from corporate governance to CSR. Business ethics while explaining sounds pretty subjective in nature. Ethics & legality go hand in hand for businesses. Being legally appropriate, leads to being ethically strong. Maintaining ethicality & legality in businesses ensures smooth functioning of operations and adds to the effort towards sustainability business.

Fig. 6.1: Maintaining Ethicality & Legality in Business

Source: Author's Study

6.2.1 Integrity

Organisational operations necessarily need to be free of any distort whether product wise or any other functions. Integrity has a strong relevance to ethicality of the business. The value system of the organisation must be adhered and it must be the integral part of the organisational operations. Integrity in functioning is observed through its basic intent of meeting the reliability quotient of the business. Customers have belief on the service providers; this set of belief suffers if the organisation compromises on the integrity. Utmost quality of the product, distribution channel's effectiveness, harmony in employee relations, product's capability to serve more than expected, delivering the promise, all such and many more accounts to integrity of the organisation.

6.2.2 Organisational Spirit

An organisation is as strong as its people. Gaining Organisational spirit requires conscious effort towards people development. Spirit towards team bonding, spirit towards maintaining integrity, spirit towards delivering results, spirit to adhere to compliances, spirit towards progressiveness etc. helps organisations to gain momentum. Organisations are pool of people; every Entrepreneur must be a people's manager. Howsoever, entrepreneurs gain expertise on machinery; the human value can't be discounted.

This spirit of belongingness & ownership need to be inculcated in employees and the same may only happen if the entrepreneur is well versed with the same.

6.2.3 Transparency

Openness is an important virtue for an Entrepreneur. Here Transparency refers to the openness and clarity in business operations. Right from the business values shared with external entities till the relations with internal stakeholders that include Employees. Transparency in operations reflects in organisation's approach towards setting expectations with employees, managing deals with the suppliers & dealers and ensuring fairness with the stakeholders.

6.2.4 Accountability

An Entrepreneur although being the owner of the business yet must not solely take the onus of progressing ahead instead must adopt the Gandhian philosophy of Trusteeship. Developing the sense of belongingness & ownership towards the business must be the motto. The sense of accountability is towards the delivery of services to society, welfare of employees, overall product processing etc. Accountability ensures execution of responsibility to utmost care and endurance.

Entrepreneurial Story – 1: VERGHESE KURIEN

Dr. Verghese Kurien, the gem of India is referred as the Father of White Revolution (Milkman of India). Dr. Kurien was co-founder of 'AMUL' and Founder - NDDB (National Dairy Development Board). He was not money driven in his cause but massively worked on bringing change for the common man. He introduced the prospects of modern technology and marketing to the dairy farmers. Kurien's cooperative venture was built on the logic of mass consumption and mass production must go hand in hand. This was his simple but compelling logic, which eventually the world adopted. The revolution is attributed to have empowered millions of Indian milk producers, who are an economic resource. "Without their involvement, we cannot succeed. With their involvement, we cannot fail..." remains his simple but fail-safe inspiration. His venture had its own challenges in the form of competition in market from MNCs especially Nestle, challenge of maintaining the cooperative business with balanced commercial intent with societies interest. Awarded with the civilian awards in the Nation, Kurien's life is big learning for budding entrepreneurs in terms of their intent towards supporting the mankind. Key factors as take away from Kurien's innings in Entrepreneurship would be the societal care, innovations with people involvement and leadership.

6.3   Creating Strong Ethical Culture

Shared assumptions, Shared Values and Organisational beliefs culminate into Organizational culture which governs the way people perform in organizations. An organization assists its employees to learn and grow in their jobs and careers with a positive culture. The outlook, attitudes, values, goals, and practices shared by a group, organization, or society is referred as Culture. Morality gets interpreted by Cultural norms, and varied cultures may have varied beliefs on right and wrong choices. Cultural and business ethics focuses on three main areas – *employees, environment, and consumers* –these three items are common to any business regardless of geographical region.

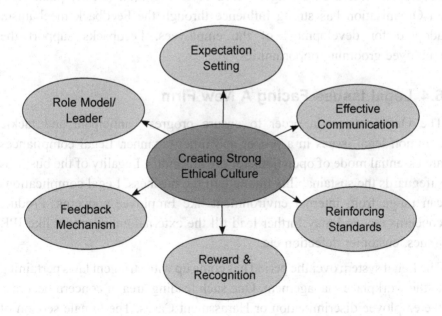

Fig. 6.2: Creating Strong Ethical Culture

Source: Author's Study

Developing a strong Ethical culture in the Organisation certainly has a huge dependency on the leadership profile of the Organisation. "Walk the Talk" prevails while expecting an ethical environment. The employees follow their leaders, they consider them as role model and hence it becomes very imperative that leaders are ethical in their approach. This certainly helps in expectation setting as well. Every Entrepreneur must ensure that they set the right expectation with the employees. This helps the Organisation to develop a progressive culture and desiring attitude. Expectation setting is well supported by the effective communication by the Entrepreneur. Entire Organisation must adhere to prompt communication principle in order to fetch desired results.

Organisational approach must adhere to the set standards for the operations and its functions. Reinforcing the standards on regular intervals supports the growth of the progressive culture at the Organisations. These standards may be in the form product quality, norms &policies, standards of delivery function, standards of talent acquisition & management etc. The Talent retained must be appreciated for the efforts. A strong culture may get developed with a deserving Reward & Recognition (R&R) plan. Also an Organisation has strong influence through the Feedback mechanism adopted for development of the employees. Feedbacks support the employee grooming opportunities.

6.4 Legal Issues Facing A New Firm

The Organisations in order to ensure progress, anticipate and tackle common legal issues in a proper and timely manner. Legal compliances are essential mode of operations for organisations. Legality of the business safeguards the sustainability quotient of the business. Legal complications can range from internal environment like Employee concerns, Product concerns etc. and may further lead till the external environment like IPR issues, customer defection etc.

The Legal system over the period has come up with stringent laws pertaining to the workplace management. One such leading area of concern becomes the employee discrimination or Harassment Cases. The female section of the organisational population has been equipped with the support from the Legal system towards any untoward experience leading to their loss of dignity. Also whether it is gender or physical status or any discrimination in job, the same is strictly prohibited. Budding Entrepreneurs must take a note of this aspect. Legal compliances won't be possible without proper documentations. Business records essentially need to be maintained to avoid any legal complications. Similar is the consideration towards the Intellectual Property Rights (IPR). The entrepreneur must either ensure that there isn't any violation of IPR or must seek IPR protection of its creation.

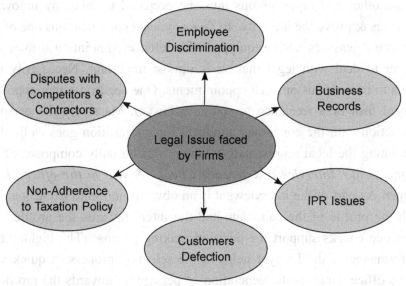

Fig. 6.3: Legal Issues faced by the firms

Source: Author's Study

Non Compliances lead to negative publicity and that eventually leads to dissatisfaction among customers. In the case of B2B environment, maintaining legality of the business ensures the longer tenure of the deals. Else defection of the clients is obvious. Another prominent area for entrepreneurs to make a note is the adherence to the Taxation policy. Taxation is the major source for earnings for Government which intern gets invested in public welfare & facilities. Tax evasion is a legal offence. Further to all these legal matters, entrepreneurs must also ensure that there isn't an opportunity towards legal disputes with competitors and contractors. The issues can be pertaining to the advertisement war, Product IPR, brand ambassador, labour issues (Contractual) etc.. Tactfully an entrepreneur must tackle these legal issues that may hinder the existence of the organisation.

6.5 Selection of the Attorney/Lawyer

Legal system is a good support to industrial establishments. While at one end the organisations must be legally sound to avoid any complications, on the other end organisations must be prepared to face any untoward instances & prove the integrity. To face any legal complications one of the important measures is to be equipped with defence. Appointing an attorney/ lawyer to deal with legal matters is utmost important. Necessarily one needs to be cautious on such appointments. One needs to either approach a legal firm or a freelance to source a lawyer. Massively the personal interaction with the concerned applicant for the position goes well while appointing the legal representative. The process usually comprises of the segments like *Interviews, Reference Checks & visit to the office of the lawyer.* As part of the interviews it is an obvious notion to get acquainted with the profile of the candidate and the intent towards the profile. The reference checks support the decision making purpose. The highlighting performance of the Lawyer helps in the selection process. A quick visit to the office supports the generation of perception towards the profile of the candidate. An organisation need to be cautious on such associations as they represent the organisation on external front. A thoughtful decision in appointment of the attorney supports the will power of the Entrepreneur and protects the interest of the organisations.

6.6 Founder's Agreement

A Founder Agreement is an imperative document which governs the rights and obligations of founders, their responsibilities, their shareholding, their exit clauses, etc. The company's founder undergoes to govern its business affairs, which requires framing a document that is termed as Founder's agreement. The Agreement establishes the liabilities, obligations rights & responsibilities of each founder. On common parlance, matters that are not covered by the company's operating agreement, this agreement may regulate the same.

Contents of a Founder's Agreement

A founder's agreement may contain the following clauses:

- Details of the parties to the agreement and the business relation between the parties.

- The duties of each founder and its execution.

> Appointment of Attorney: PROCESS
> - Interviews
> - Referencing
> - Background check
> - Visit to Office

- Representations and warranties of each Party.
- Regarding intellectual property associated with the business
- Equity holding details, guidelines on transfer of shares
- Remuneration payable for duties performed.
- Remedies for breach of the agreement.
- Dispute resolution.
- Governing law of the agreement and governing law of the dispute resolution clause.
- Other provisions such as survival of clauses, severability, etc.

Entrepreneurial Story – 2: TULSI TANTI

Suzlon – One of the world's leading wind power players is the result of Tanti's personal vision and leadership. Tulsi Tanti, an entrepreneur, explored the possibilities of non-conventional energy. He brought glory to the indigenous and smart spirit of contemporary India. Tulsi has the burning desire to operate on the global stage. He aims Suzlon to emerge as leader among the wind energy companies in the world. He has the determination to fulfil the aim and reach to desired destination. The Government of Maharashtra had made an announcement to support the creation of wind power, Tanti and team took the opportunity & developed wind power plan. Tanti, strategically worked on the desired change in the Industry & developed the idea of offering a complete package of wind energy services. Despite his serious conduct and modest appearance, Tanti is known for his shrewd and aggressive takeover tactics.

6.7 Obtaining Business Licences and Permits

Entrepreneurship must be encouraged as one of the career options and its promotion through curriculum at Schools & Colleges must continue to gain progressive results. Building entrepreneurial culture in the education system right from secondary to higher education shall have a definite value addition to the National Income. The knowledge on Business Licensing & Permits supports the momentum of the budding Entrepreneurs.

The government agencies issue the Business licenses which permits the organization or Business entity to operate business within the government's specified jurisdiction. Licenses issued by the local government have been permitted for starting the business activities. Usually a business requires the following types of licenses – Fire Department Permit, Air and Water Pollution Control Permit, State Licenses (Law of the land), Taxation enrolment, Health Department Permits etc. The process of gaining license differs from one type of business to another, based on various determining factors like the number of employees, sector, the type of business, the place of business etc.

6.7.1 Company or LLP Registration

Proprietorships or partnership firms are the preferred choice for entrepreneurs knowing the fact that registration from the Central Government isn't compulsory. The Registration of a company and LLP is regulated by the Ministry of Corporate Affairs. The Entrepreneurs who have plans for initiating a business with an annual turnover of more than ₹ 20 Lakhs are advised to obtain an LLP or Company registration to receive the benefits of the Government. The registered Company or LLP has a separate legal identity and the promoters enjoy limited liability. Registrations help the businesses to get easily transferable status and the entity will have perpetual existence. Hence, before commencing a business, it's better to consult an expert and register a company or LLP. The law although doesn't mandate the registration of MSMEs yet the registrations do help the companies to get the governmental support.

6.7.2 GST Registration

The entities and individuals who have an overall annual turnover of more than ₹ 20 lakhs in most States and ₹ 10 lakhs in Special Category States are essentially required to attain GST Registration. Also, any person supplying goods (intra-state supply) is required to attain GST Registration, irrespective of turnover. In addition to these parameter, various other criteria have been mentioned under the GST Act for GST registrations. It is imperative for all Entrepreneurs to get conversant with the GST norms and obtain GST registration within a stipulated time frame of starting a business.

6.7.3 Udyog Aadhar Registration

Udyog Aadhar Registration is available for entrepreneurs who wish to incorporate a small business – Micro, Small and medium enterprises (MSME). Based on the investment in Plant & Machinery made by a manufacturing concern or investment in equipment made by a service provider, the Udyog Aadhaar Registration eligibility is decided. Once, the Udyog Aadhaar registration is ascertained by the business, it enjoys several subsidies and schemes specially granted by the Government for supporting small businesses in India.

6.7.4 FSSAI License or Registration

FSSAI – "Food safety and standard authority of India" is the body / authority responsible to verify the safety and standardization of food products across the nation. Retail stores, Restaurants, food & beverages etc. must mention the registration of FSSAI on the packets & display the registration certificate in the premises. The license or registration under FSSAI is divided into three categories:

• FSSAI State License

• FSSAI State Registration

• FSSAI Central License

6.7.5 Import Export Code

Import Export Code is obtained from the DGFT department by all companies involved in Import or Export of goods/services from India. It is essential for the business to have a PAN and a Current Account in a bank.

6.7.6 Shop and Establishment Act License

To regulate the conduct of business essentials like the working hours, child labour, payment of wages, safety and general health of the employees, "The Shop and Establishments Act", was enacted. The State Governments issue the license or registration under Shop and Establishment Act. The norms vary from state to state. The respective State Government authorities need to be approached for obtaining Shop and Establishment Act License.

A few documents that a budding entrepreneur must maintain include PAN Card, Address Proof, NOC from the land lord (if on lease), Application letter to Municipal Corporation / Panchayat, Memorandum and Article of association, Certificate of incorporation of the company, Director's details, Insurance papers & other financial documents proving the capital arrangement, Telecom Authority letter etc. Further, a business may also have to essentially obtain permits from the fire department, or the pollution control board, or maybe the local healthcare system. It all depends on the type of business you are willing to operate. Hence, before incorporating the business, entrepreneurs must make sure that they understand the legal and regulatory requirements.

Exhibit-2: A Restaurant In India: Licenses Required

- FSSAI Food Safety and Standards Authority License
- Health / Trade License
- Eating House License
- Fire Department
- Lift Clearance
- Liquor License
- Signage License
- Music License
- Certificate of Environmental Clearance
- Shop and Establishment Act
- GST Registration

Source: www.posist.com

Entrepreneurial Story – 3: SUBHASH CHANDRA GOYAL

Subhash Chandra Goyal, the man behind the advent of satellite television channels, is a well acclaimed personality. It was Subhash Chandra's vision that brought satellite TV industry in India the desired success. It inspired others to follow the venture. Zee TV the Chandra's brainchild is the first service provider in India to launch Direct to Home services. Zee group of companies positioning strategy supported it to tap the huge opportunity offered by digital communication services in the Nation. Subhash Chandra understood the significance of creating a high-quality media conglomerate. He is credited to introduction of employee stock options in the television industry. He is the chairman of the Indian conglomerate - Essel Group. In May 2014, to mark the completion of 90 years of his Essel Group, a sum of 5000 crores was donated towards his Foundation depicting social inclination. The Chandra group consists of Zee Media Corporation Limited, Siti Cable Limited, Dish TV India Ltd., Zee Learn Ltd., Essel Finance and many others. Dr. Chandra through his trademark show Subhash Chandra Show, has engaged with youth from across India and interacted on different topics. A Man representing masses at Parliament has a perfect blend of professionalism, socialism and business acumen.

6.8 Forms of Businesses

Businesses are known through varied forms. This in a sense provides varied opportunities for the budding entrepreneurs to look upon. The career seeking individuals opt for their choice

> **Forms of Businesses based on Service:**
> * Manufacturing Business
> * Service Business
> * Trading / Retailing Business

in professional career and varied businesses present opportunities to them. Massively on the grounds of core activities, three major kinds of businesses have been identified:

6.8.1 Manufacturing Business

The manufacturing business procures products with the purpose of using them as raw materials in making a new product. Hence there is a transformation of the products purchased. The raw materials, labour, and factory overhead gets combined in its production process by a manufacturing business entity. The manufactured goods will then be brought to market for sales to customers.

6.8.2 Service Business

Service businesses provide intangible products (products with no physical form). These firms offer professional skills, expertise, advice, and other similar products. Examples of service businesses are: Banks & Insurance, salons, repair shops, Educational Institution, accounting firms, and law firms.

6.8.3 Merchandising Business / Trading / Retailing

Such businesses buy products at wholesale price and sells the same at retail price. These sorts of businesses are also known as "buy and sell" businesses. They fundamental is to earn profits by selling the products at prices higher than its purchase costs. A merchandising business necessarily sells the product without changing its original form. The examples of such businesses are like grocery stores, convenience stores, distributors, and other resellers.

The forms of businesses may also get segregated based on ownership. Presented below are the basic forms of business ownership:

6.8.4 Sole Proprietorship

Sole proprietorship is a form of business that is owned by only one person. It is certainly easy to set-up and it is the least costly among all sorts of ownership. The owner faces unlimited liability which means that the creditors of the business may go after the personal assets of the owner if the business cannot pay them. Such kind of sole proprietorship businesses is usually adopted by small business entities.

6.8.5 Partnership

The partnership businesses are such businesses which are owned by two or more persons who contribute resources into the entity. The partners adopt the

Forms of Businesses based on Ownership:
- Sole Proprietorship
- Partnership
- Corporation
- Cooperative

practice of dividing the proceeds from the business among themselves. In general partnerships, all partners have unlimited liability. In limited partnerships, creditors cannot go after the personal assets of the limited partners.

6.8.6 Corporation

Corporation is a business set up or organization which has a separate legal personality from its owners. The Ownership gets represented by shareholding. The owners (shareholders) enjoy limited liability but have unlimited involvement in the company's operations. The board of directors, an elected group controls the activities of the corporation.

6.8.7 Cooperative

Cooperative is the business organization that is owned by a group of individuals and is operated for their mutual benefit. The persons forming the group are referred as members. Cooperatives may be incorporated or unincorporated. The examples of cooperative set ups are like water and electricity (utility) cooperatives, cooperative banking, credit unions, and housing cooperatives.

6.8.8 Entrepreneurial Story – 4: SHIV NADAR

Shiv Nadar's business strategy acumen, management style and ambition to be leader in the business were the major motivation to lead the venture. The corporate restructuring exercise over the years resulted in several companies. He has reached pinnacle of success by his hard work, vision and entrepreneurial spirit. Shiv Nadar is the founder and chairman of HCL. Also, the social instincts led to creation of the Shiv Nadar Foundation. HCL was incorporated by Nadar in the mid-1970s and by constantly reinventing his company's focus, he transformed the IT hardware company into an IT enterprise over the next three decades. He was awarded with Padma Bhushan in 2008 for his efforts in the IT industry. With 100 offices worldwide, the high-tech entrepreneur nurtured HCL to become a billion-dollar group. This led to creation of wealth for himself, his associates and investors. Nadar's visionary approach kept him moving across these years.

CASE STUDY

BEVERAGE OF CHOICE

An Organizational Journey of Silvassa Bottling Company

The Beverage Industry is one of the very innovative Industries where the taste of people varies a lot & hence the companies must be on their toes in learning the preferences of the Customers. The beverage industry being huge setup, may get segmented in various ways to cater the right person with right product. The several ways that the Industry may get segmented broadly can be classified as *Alcoholic, Non-alcoholic and sports beverages, Natural and synthetic beverages and Energy Drinks.* Beverages have been part of human life since ages however the advent of the Carbonated & Non-Carbonated beverages has taken the Market to a greater height. To understand the business scenario of beverage Industry one has to deep dive in the potential of the Industry. Franchiseindia.com stated that Beverage Market (Carbonated & Non-Carbonated beverages) in India is ranging to ₹ 14,000/- crore and has the potential of growing by 30% per annum. In a similar study indiaretailing.com, states that Beverages market shall grow 3.5 times of its present size by 2020. The key players like Pepsi & Coca Cola have a greater influence on the market with total 60% of the stake. Parle Agro is another giant in the market.

Amidst this huge competition, Silvassa Bottling Company (SBC), a relatively local product in the eyes of the giants, has encroached a significant share of the market. Established at the end of the 90s (1999), it never competed with the giants however gradually the key players started noticing the growth of SBC and a healthy competition erupted. The joint efforts of (Partners) Mr. Rahim Roy and Mr. Nizar Thanawala have taken the company to greater heights. The company started its operations with 300 ml glass bottle of Royal Club Soda and gradually today 8 products of the company are served in 300 ml glass, 600 ml plastic, and 1.5 L plastic bottles. The company intensified its network through allocating agencies for distribution. The company major focus was on reaching the rural areas. With more than 30 key distributors it has today covered areas of Western Maharashtra i.e, Dahanu, Palghar etc., South Gujarat region Vapi, Valsad & Surat, and Union Territory of Dadra and Nagar Haveli. The company today has to its credit the following products: Royal Club Soda, KC Cola, Gina Orange, Gina Lemon, T2, Jajira, Gina Lemon Juice & Lichi Juice. The company's financials aren't in a safe position. The revenues are at the lowest position in the last six years. Approximately ₹ 22 Cr revenue in the year 2016-17 is even lesser than what it realized in 2011-12 (₹ 23 Cr). The peak position in terms of revenues was in the year 2014-15 with ₹ 34 Cr. Even the delicious fish has to ponder when the Shark takes the turn. Coca Cola & Pepsi's dealers came up with their competitive strategies and backed by the innovative products of these companies, SBC had to face the heat. The reality is on records i.e., a decreasing trend over the years. One specific turn in the economy also had its impact on the results of 2016-17. A few months of the 3rd & 4th quarter of 2016-17 had the pinch of demonetization as well.

SBC considers its quality, access to manpower and distribution as its strength and marketing efforts as its area of improvement. While the huge competitive market and the Market Research function is a big threat to SBC, however the region being industrial belt and more of educational institutions mushrooming in the region of its operations has given hint of opportunities. SBC has its own share of challenges. Broadly, the company is exposed to challenges in the form of competition in the market, perception of people towards brands and innovations. SBC has been strategic in its approach. One of the primary strategies adopted by the SBC was Growth strategy under the umbrella of Grand strategies. While the revenues may indicate a downfall during the recent past years yet the organization over the period has grown with respect to its reach and product profile. They extend support to new vendors to settle down and then commercialize their business. Also one of the strategies SBC follows is cash / account transfer model. This supports them in cash flow management. Especially the local drive is all on cash / account transfer. Silvassa Bottling Co. has its respective dilemma sounding very similar to any beverage company however it has its own uniqueness. Taste Vs. Health being one of the leading troubles, quality shall tackle the same. As an aspiring company SBC would like to concentrate on their market share that again brings into account further investment in scale of production. Amidst all the challenges & dilemma, SBC is strategizing further to survive and excel.

Questions for Discussion

1. Discuss the nature of Entrepreneurship exhibited by the Owner in the case.

2. Analyse the state of Silvassa Bottling Company while highlighting prospects of the company amidst prevailing competition.

3. Suggest the future course of action for SBC while critically evaluating the dilemma surrounding the company / Entrepreneur.

Key Terms

Entrepreneurship: Entrepreneurship is creation of value by people working together to implement an Idea through the application of drive and a willingness to take risk

Legal Compliances: Legal compliances are essential mode of operations for Organisations. Legality of the business safeguards the sustainability quotient of the business. Legal complications can range from internal environment like Employee concerns, Product concerns etc.

Attorney: Lawyer to deal with legal matters

Founder's Agreement: It is a document that governs the rights and obligations of founders, their responsibilities, their shareholding, their exit clauses, etc.

Business Licenses: The Business license or registration is issued by government agencies which permits the organizations or Business entity to conduct business operations within the government's specified jurisdiction.

LLP Registration: Limited Liability Protection (LLP) Registration ensures that the entity would be a separate legal identity and the promoters would enjoy limited liability protection.

FSSAI License: "Food safety and standard authority of India" (FSSAI), is responsible to verify the safety and standardization of food products nationwide.

Organisational Culture: Shared assumptions, Shared Values and Organisational beliefs culminate into Organizational culture that governs how people perform in organizations.

Sole Proprietorship: These are the businesses owned by only one person.

Partnership: A partnership is a sort of business venture owned by two or more persons who contribute resources into the entity.

Business Ethics: Ethics in Business is the behaviour which corporations must adhere in its regular operations within the environment where it operates and in the community.

Review Questions

1. Define Ethical Entrepreneurship.
2. What is Strong ethical culture for Organizations?
3. What are the Legal issues faced by the Organisations?
4. What is Sole Proprietorship & Franchisee?
5. Write Short Notes on:

   (*i*) Founder's Agreement

   (*ii*) Selection of Attorney

   (*iii*) FSSAI License

   (*iv*) IPR Issues

   (*v*) Ethical Entrepreneurship

Applied Questions

1. "Ethical and Legal aspect of the Entrepreneurship is essential matter to be considered towards venture management". Discuss.
2. "Organisational Culture essential defines the fate of the Organisation. Creating that strong culture at Organisations not only require a departments involvement instead it is a top to bottom approach ensuring completeness in strategizing the action plan". Discuss.
3. "Initiating a Business not necessarily require only enthusiasm, it necessarily undergoes a process of ensuring authoritative approvals." Explain the statement while highlighting various considerations for obtaining the Business Licences and Permits in Indian context.
4. "Budding Entrepreneurs have multiple opportunities & ways to enter their dream venture." Enumerate the statement while citing relevant examples.

References

1. Taneja, Satish & Gupta, S. L. (2003). Entrepreneur Development: New venture Creation, published by Galgotia Publishing Company, 2nd Revised Edition.

2. Baporikar, Neeta (2007). Entrepreneurship Development and Project Management, published by Himalaya Publishing House, 1st Edition.

3. Ogbari, M. (2016). Entrepreneurship and Business Ethics: Implications on Corporate Performance, IJEFI, Vol. 6.

4. http://ediindia.ac.in/e-policy/Doc/Draft-National-Entrepreneurship-Policy.pdf, accessed on 05/08/2018.

5. https://www.accountingverse.com/accounting-basics/types-of-businesses.html, accessed on 25/08/2018.

6. https://www.posist.com/restaurant-times/resources/licenses-required-to-open-a-restaurant.html, accessed on 30/08/2018.

7. https://www.entrepreneur.com/article/38882, accessed on 25/09/2018.

8. https://www.indiafilings.com/learn/licenses-required-business, accessed on 25/09/2018.

9. https://www.thebalancecareers.com/how-to-choose-a-lawyer-2164685, accessed on 05/10/2018.

7

Financial Viability of New Ventures

Dr. Bhavesh P. Joshi

(Professor, Manav Rachna International Institute of Research and Studies, Faridabad, India)

LEARNING OBJECTIVES

After reading this chapter, the reader should be able to:

1. Understand the concepts and tools required for evaluating the financial performance of an entrepreneurial firm.

2. Comprehend the concepts and tools for funds management, funds sourcing, valuation and financial management of entrepreneurial firms with the help of ratio analysis.

3. Understand guidelines required for successfully starting and growing an entrepreneurial venture for financial success.

4. Appraise the concepts of financial management for efficient utilization of resources, funding from venture capitals and exit strategies.

7.1 Introduction

Internet bubble 1999-2000 had impacted the way new ventures used to exist and survive in the business world. An entrepreneur is a risk taker and when he decides to explore the opportunity and comes with a unique idea. He is willing to have and practice in broader sense the knowledge of business and allied areas impacting his future plans. So in business perspective he should be dealing with finance and accounting, marketing, management, operations and so on, to succeed. And if it's a technology driven idea then acquisition of specialized knowledge in the allied areas needs to be added to it.

The background work what he had already completed helps in it like recognition of the opportunities and generating of ideas. Political, Economic, Social, Technological, Environmental and Legal (PESTEL) analysis helps him in achieving this. These generated ideas should have feasibility and viability so need proper analysis of resources, opportunities and threats. With this he needs to access the new venture's financial strength and viability for getting financed internally or externally with funding from institutions. So decision for getting funds from a Venture Capital or from other financial institutions also plays a pivotal role.

Developing an effective business model requires proper planning in the form of a business plan, this helps in strategizing venture's growth and prepare after evaluating the challenges of growth.

This chapter specifically deals with the financial viability of the new venture. Viability in financial perspective needs decision on the financial performance of today and predicting the future based on the present cash flows. This statement in itself had two parts; 1) generation of sufficient funds as return as profit to meet the present obligations to the customers, employees, creditors, government etc. and 2) during the phases when the venture is not able to generate profit, sustaining during the tough times with saving for future or an exit plan for sustenance of another venture.

To make it simpler the chapter is divided into following broader points for discussion:

1. Financial Statements and Financial Analysis for Financial Planning
2. Working Capital Management and Venture Capital

7.2 Financial Statements and Financial Analysis

7.2.1 Financial Statements

As an entrepreneur the individual is supposed to wear different hats of expertise. Finance being the life blood of an organization, needs utmost care to be taken while taking decisions. Today's decision is going to impact tomorrow's survival and sustenance. So the financial plan must be prepared while keeping future in mind.

Sources of funds are not, free they bear cost with them. Cost like interest to be paid if debt financing is done and dividend in case the funding is raised through equity. Even in the case of funds deployed by the entrepreneur from his own resources it had an opportunity cost, the return which he could have foregone because of investing in his own venture. Raising funds for a new venture are comparatively tougher due to new concept or idea which may not be funded by the ordinary financial institutions. Because of these reasons the financial resources consumed today had a cost that might be paid in the same financial year when the tax is being paid or would be paid in future.

So, projections of such financial resources need judicious decisions about the need of funds in near future and how to finance them. Generally the short term financing is costly then the long term financing. Due to the time factor involvement and risk association with the project the due diligence is to be made before raising capital. Even these judicious planning may fail due to their being based on the historically available information which may change as per the change in the business environment and the unexpected downturn in the demand of the products or increase in the cost of raw material. Next part of the discussion will carry this point further where entrepreneur would be planning for short term and long term financial plans of the venture.

With a modest starting, a new venture plans to grow exponentially and get funding from the open markets in the form of debt or equity, as per the financial needs of the venture. This venture being a separate legal entity (a concept in accounting which differentiates between the promoter of the venture and its promoter/owner) needs to file returns so a better understanding of the financial statements make him ready to handle the statutory requirements imposed on such legal entities.

Generally in the business daily the public limited entities share the financial information with the stakeholders who are interested in the financial performance of the company. This annual information is prepared as per the statutory norms set by Institute of Chartered Accountants of India (ICAI) in India. The final draft is audited and made available for the information to the regulatory bodies, stock exchanges, and other stakeholders. These stakeholders can be the financial institutions like banks, raw material suppliers, employees of the company, or prospective employees who are interested in knowing more about the company, government who is interested in the profit and taxes to be collected in future due to excellent performance of the institution and owners who can be the promoter or even the shareholders of the company. They all are looking for this valuable information because it ensures their interest at present and in future too. This sharing of quarterly and annual information helps these stakeholders judge that their interests will be served in future or not in the ongoing financial year.

Accounting Standard Board (ASB) an committee under the ICAI issues and supervises the accounting standards. These are the set accounting concepts and conventions that helps in synchronization and ensures standardized reporting through the company's financial statements.

As promulgated by ICAI the accountants had Indian Generally Accepted Accounting Principles (Indian GAAP) and or Indian Accounting Standards (Ind-AS) following the International Financial Reporting Standards (IFRS) to prepare and report through the financial statements.

As an overview of the accounting information that takes place between the entries which are made and finally the financial statements are created can be understood by the following eight steps taken by an accountant as accounting cycle:

(*i*) Recording of business transactions in journals

(*ii*) Posting of entries from journals to ledger accounts

(*iii*) At the end of the fiscal year making of adjustments and posting to the ledger accounts.

(*iv*) Preparation of summary of accounts balances

(*v*) Preparation of income statement from revenue and expense account balances

(*vi*) Closing of revenue and expense accounts to retained earnings.

(*vii*) Preparation of post-closing summary of account balances

(*viii*) Finalization of balance sheet and statement of cash flows.

As per the Schedule III of the Companies Act, the general instructions are there needed for the preparation of financial statements.

The primary financial statements having the financial information about the company are:

I. Balance Sheet

A venture starts modestly with amount invested by the owner or stockholder. With the growth and passage of time, it also grows. So for an entrepreneur it is important to check how much this venture had created for its own existence and for the owner or stockholder as the residual claim on it. Residual claim because in case of liquidation of a venture, the owner and stockholders get at the end after the payment of dues to all those who owes. In other words the claims of the owners are at the end of the life of the venture.

As the name suggests it's the balance statement of assets and liabilities generated/created in a particular financial year. This is created at the end of the financial year. In India we follow 12 months period as a financial year that starts from the 1st April of that year and ends on the 31st March of the very next year. For example it starts on 1st April of 20X0 year and ends on the 31st March of 20X1.

Assets for the organization can be created by increasing liabilities from the owner (capital) or from other financial institutions. So, keeping a check on the balance helps in knowing whether the venture is profitable in comparison to the amount invested or last year's performance.

This asset and liability statement of the company shows the direction in which the venture is going. In case of growth in the value of the venture, it can go to bank or any financial institution and borrow funds to meet current obligation or needed investment for future growth.

For the preparation of the balance sheet the following accounting equation is followed:

$$\text{Assets} = \text{Liabilities plus Capital}$$

This equation shows the financial position of the venture on a particular day with the assets, liabilities and valuation. As in accounting we follow double entry system, and for every transaction there are two entries to be made. So this equation remains balanced.

Entrepreneurship in India   120

So it is a statement that consists majorly of three broader aspects:

(a) Assets

(b) Liabilities

(c) Capital

All of these determine the capital of the business entity and is presented in the financial reports as Balance Sheet.

(a) Assets: Things that the business *owns or is owed*.

So in a balance sheet one of the portions is known as assets; it is the resource (with economic value) tangible (property, plant, equipment etc) or intangible (goodwill, patent, copyrights etc) on which the venture had the ownership rights. As these are being owned by the company, so it can utilize them for generating profits of future.

Tangible asset based on the time factor and convertibility into cash or cash equivalent are classified as current assets and fixed assets are the one which take long to very long time to get converted into cash. Because of wear and tear the value of the fixed asset decreases with the passage of time, hence the decreased values must be reported in the books of accounts to reveal the current and correct position of the venture. This decrease in value is known as depreciation; in this the depreciated value is deducted from the latest value of the fixed asset to reach the current value of such asset. While the decrease in the intangible assets value is known as amortization.

(b) Liabilities: debts the business *owes*.

If a liability is to be paid within 12 months or during the same financial year it is known as current liability like venture owing from banks as overdrafts, trade creditors (creditors from whom the raw material is purchased but not paid), tax liabilities for the current year, etc. and long term liabilities are the financial obligations to be met or to be repaid after 12 months.

Its examples are accounts payable, taxes payable, accrued expenses, notes payable, bonds payable etc.

(c) Capital: also known as owner's equity or stockholder's equity (depending on the business entity)

This is the cash put in the business by the owners and the stockholders; hence this is the other kind of liability for the venture or any legal business entity.

As per the accounting equation this is the remaining amount after the deduction of the liabilities from the capital;

$$\text{Assets} - \text{Liabilities} = \text{Capital}$$

This increases with the accumulation of claims on the assets of the owner/stockholders, which is due with the growth of the company. It increases with the increase in the retained earnings (the amount of profit which is left after payment of interest, taxes and dividends).

II. Income and Expense Statement or Profit of Loss Statement or Statement of Revenue

As these names suggests that this it tries to measure the profit or loss made in a accounting period; which is generally a financial year consisting of twelve months. The operating results are shown by this statement as it is on accrual basis. This statement captures how the business entity had consumed the resources in monetary terms i.e the expenses and been able to generate the resources i.e., profit, for the promoter and other stakeholders (including the shareholders). This is the report card of the operating activities for the period that can be for particular month, quarter or for the whole fiscal years.

The net income generated or loss incurred in the financial year is the result of inclusion of all the profit and loss transactions, including the exceptional entries that had occurred due to the previous periods as adjustments. In case of extraordinary items for the financial year it should also be reported and separate treatment is to be made within the income statement.

Comparative analysis of P&L statements of previous years or with the peer group business entities helps in analyzing the financial capability of the organization. With this it could yield better results either by reducing the cost or expenses or by increasing the profit. Decisions need to be taken with regard to the generated profits, as the same amount can be distributed to the equity shareholders as dividends, else it can be kept as retained earnings for future projects or opportunities.

These leads to the profit made by the business in a financial year and are presented as Profit and Loss Account Statement for the period ending. In India financial year is between 1st April to 31st March subsequent next year.

III. Cash Flow Statement

Cash is among the most important factor for the smooth functioning of the venture. Information discovers the inflow and outflow of the venture within the reporting period, as was being done for the P&L statement. This cash analysis helps in taking decisions on actual basis of cash movement. Based on this actual cash flow movement the decision maker (user of this accounting information) can take a call whether the venture will be needing to raise funds from market in the form of debt, equity or both, it capability for dividend distribution to the stockholder or as retained earnings for future decisions. Even in case of dividend distribution it can be observed whether it is generating funds for this from the operating activities or not, otherwise it may not be sustainable in long run. If the cash cycle is reduced with the improvement in the accounts receivable from its debtors in the short run it can impact on the working capital of the venture. It is always better for the venture to have a proper control over the inventory, as this reduces the cash related burden due to blockage of funds on inventory.

Cash flow at a business entity level takes place from three different modes, operating, investing and financing activities.

The *operating activities* involve movement of cash i.e, inflow or outflow. Inflow of cash can be through the sales transactions, collection of interest, income or dividends, notes receivable etc. the outflow of cash from the venture can be due to payment of interest, inventory purchase, suppliers, salaries, taxes etc.

For the venture the *investment activities* can have cash inflows from sale of intangible and tangible assets that venture owns, loan principals payment received, sale of foreign securities, equity shares etc. while the cash inflow in the investment activities can be due to funding to other entities, buying of assets tangible as well as intangible assets.

Financing activities for the venture includes cash inflow from the sale of its own equity shares, bonds or other forms of debt to the investors, etc. while the outflow can be dividend payment to the equity shareholders, debt repayments, repurchase of own equity shares etc.

These financial statements balance sheet, profit and loss account and cash flow statements are prepared as per schedule III of the Companies Act. Still there is space of creative accounting and accounts freeness to avail free degree of scope in reporting of earnings and the valuation of assets. in studies of depreciation accounting it had been found that this freeness is creatively utilized by the accountants by using the depreciation method and life span of the assets being depreciated for getting written off from the balance sheet.

Even though standardization, reporting formats, concepts and conventions exist still due to scope and broad nature of accounting, nature of business and reporting provides space for creative accounting. At this juncture proper financial analysis helps in taking futuristic decisions based on financial data of the venture.

7.2.2 Financial Analysis

For evaluation of a financial health of a venture financial data available (on the financial statement) helps in taking decisions at present for reaping benefits in future. The intention behind such financial analysis is to judge the financial performance, position and liquidity aspect of the venture. This can be done through following the three steps as part of the Financial Analysis Framework:

   (*i*) Trend analysis-Comparison of ventures past financial performances over a period of time

   (*ii*) Competitor analysis- Comparison of its financial performance with that of the other peer group competitors

   (*iii*) Industry analysis- Comparison of the financial performance with that of the industry average performance for the considered period for analysis.

With the help of these the analyst or the user of this financial information can understand and appreciate the link between the financial statements and the data contained in it.

Different businesses have different capital requirements, debt-equity composition, management vision, competitors and risk which makes the ratio of one venture different from the others. Hence ratios needs same grounds for comparison so the ratios too can be created between the different financial years for the same business entity, same entity with the industry averages, its peer companies, relevant industries to name a few. But they should be comparable.

The ratios that can take values from the financial statement are broadly divisible into:

(A) Liquidity Ratios

As the name suggests it tells about the business entity's financial capability to meet its short term financial obligations:

(*a*) **Current Ratio:** It tells about the venture paying capacity of its short term liabilities with respect to the current assets that it has.

Formula is Total current assets/ Total current liabilities

(*b*) **Quick ratio or the acid test ratio:** This ratio tells about the ventures capability to utilize its current assets for the payment of current liabilities for the year.

Formula is Total current assets-inventory/ Total current liabilities

(*c*) **Cash Ratio:** In this ratio the liquid assets like cash, marketable securities like equity shares etc with respect to the current liabilities of the venture. This ratio tells about the ventures ability to meet its short term liabilities with respect to the liquid assets

Formula is Cash + Marketable Securities/Total Current Liabilities

(B) Profitability Ratios

Reduction of cost factors and expenses leads to more profitability for the venture. This ratio analysis leads to understanding of the profitability attained by the venture in the ongoing financial year versus its performance with itself, peer competitors and industry average to see the direction in which it's moving in positive direction or declining performances. This utilization of ventures resources is possible with the effective control over the expenses and cost reduction in production of goods and services.

(a) Net profit margin

Net profit to the net sales ratio provides is the measure of usage of each rupee after deduction of the expenses. Improvement in the net profit margin with the passage of time is a good indicator of profitability and its sustenance in future.

Formula is Net profits / Net Sales

(b) Return of equity (ROE)

With every rupee invested the venture wish to generate maximum returns, this rate of return on such equity investment is measured through this ratio. As net profit margin growth in this ration over period of time is a good sign of growth, or vice versa.

Formula is Net profits / Shareholders equity

(c) Return on investment (ROI)

This ratio is an indicator of the overall effectiveness of the venture to generate profits with the total investments made in the assets. So this convertibility of the assets to the net profits is something which strategically all ventures plan, its visibility and sustenance is showcased with the growth of this ratio during the trend analysis.

Formula is Net profits/ Total Assets

(d) Gross profit martin

Profitability for a venture after the deduction of cost of goods sold is a good measure of real profitability that the venture had made during the financial year. Its comparison with the past performances, peer competitors, industry average can help in deciding the point of concerns like focusing more on increasing of sale and reduction of cost of goods being manufactured and sold as this will make the resulting profit more and available for future expansion, modernisation, and diversification as per strategic goal of the venture.

Formula is (Sales − Cost of Goods Sold)/Sales

(C) Efficiency Ratios

These ratios are the Asset Management, they are the measure of conversion and efficiency with which a venture can convert its resources for selling and conversion into cash is something which decides the effectiveness of that venture. In cash conversion from raw material to final goods and later sales (including credit and cash sales)

(a) Inventory Turnover Ratio

Funds are utilized by the venture in buying of current assets like raw material, which is processed and later converted into finished products. The COGS to inventory ratio is an indicator of speed with which the inventory gets converted into sales.

Formula is Cost of Goods Sold/ Inventory

(b) Fixed Asset Turnover Ratio

This ratio is the measure of ventures capability to utilize its tangible assets like property, plant and equipments into sales, it is feasible only when the company is getting demand from the markets and producing to meet those demands on time; to get sales

Formula is Sales/Fixed assets

(c) Total Asset Turnover Ratio

Beyond the fixed assets venture do have other assets, so in a financial year how effectively it was able to utilize the total assets for making sales is evaluated with this ratio.

Formula is Sales/Total assets

(d) Average Collection Period

As stated earlier too that the sales is not always a cash sales it is most of the time a credit sale. The efficiency with which the venture can get its receivable back by collecting and converting credit a sale into cash is measured by this ratio. It depends on the business policy, credit policy, market conditions, and other factors which impacts the ventures credit conversion cycle.

Formula is Accounts receivable/Average daily credit sales

(D) Leverage Ratio

These ratios are the Debt Management Ratio that captures the degree with which the venture is able to utilize the finances, specifically the debt raised or borrowed funds.

(a) Debt ratio

The portion of total assets that's being funded by the raising of capital in the form of debt is measured by this ratio. A debt driven venture would be having a higher ratio in comparative to the equity funded one.

Formula is Total Debt/ Total Assets

(b) Debt to equity ratio

Total debt to the portion of funds raised through the shareholders equity is a measure of funding by debt or by equity.

Formula is Total Debt/Total Shareholder's Equity

(c) Times interest earned

Payments with regard to the debt aspects associated to its being part of the capital structure of the venture; firstly its the cheapest source of funding and secondly it saves taxes as its interest payment reduces the taxable amount. Its beneficial in to have it in the capital structure if the venture is capable enough to generate and meet the interest obligations without effecting on the financial efficiency of the venture.

Formula is Earnings Before Interest and Taxes/Total Interest Charges

(d) Fixed charge coverage

If the long term assets are a major part of the capital structure then the fixed cost that the venture had to bear every financial year would be more, this impacts of the profitability of the venture which it might give as dividend to its shareholders or can retain for future use.

Formula is Profit before taxes, interest and lease payments/ Total interest charges + lease obligations

In case of Profit and Loss statement (P&L Statement) the first point of information is the Sales of the venture. It a comparative analysis is done it shows the trend. If it's growing than the reasons for it could be like increase in sales due to

(*i*) Volume

(*ii*) Price

(*iii*) Combined effect of volume and price

(*iv*) Sales mix etc.

These can be a reflective of the better capacity utilization of resources (man, machine and material) or vice versa if sales is showing a downward trend.

In other words it's the relationship between the sales for the year and the profitability that shows the operational efficiency of a venture. The relationship between these factors can be understood from the following equations:

(i) Listed price of the product or services – Discounts or rebates = Net Price

To make its products or services effective either the venture can make the listed price competitive, otherwise needs to offer discounts or rebates as per the nature of the business

(ii) Net price* Volume = Net Sales

Volume plays a pivotal role in the decision making, some organizations get benefitted due to the volumes which they can attain with the effective prices so that the net sales is beneficial for them.

(iii) Net Sales-Distribution Cost – Production Cost of Goods Sold = Gross Profit

Reduction in the distribution cost through effective distribution channels and usage of operating leases venture can reduce its cost even if when the sale is normal. If different modes of cost reduction (depending on the nature of business) like business outsourcing, contract manufacturing, etc. are adopted by the venture than too it can increase its gross profit.

(iv) Gross Profit-Marketing & Sales Expenses – Administrative Expenses = Operating Earnings Before Interest Taxes and Amortization (Opr. EBITA)

Operational efficiency of a venture is visible with the trends when the earnings are sustainably more and constant before the payments interest to shareholders, payments to the tax authorities, loss of intangible assets.

Other point of cost reduction can be the reduction in the marketing and sales expenses by adopting different modes of channels to reach to the customer.

Administrative expenses are there as support to the operational activities of the venture, if they can be made effective it helps in generating better operational efficiency for a venture in a particular financial year or continuing it with efficient utilization of administrative resources in the offices.

(*v*) Net Sales/Opr. EBITA = Operating Earnings Before Interest Taxes and Amortization Margin (Opr. EBITA Margin)

This margin is a indicator that how effective are the operational activities of the venture and how successful it had been to generate earnings before the payments of the interest, taxes and amortization.

With a sustained Operational EBITA Margin, the venture showcase not only the sales being growing but also its able to reduce its operational costs effectively and efficiently.

At this juncture the decision maker finds the Income Statement margins of utmost importance and specifically those which are expressed as percentage of sales. Some of them are as following:

(a) Gross Margin Percentage = (Sales − Cost of sales or Cost of Goods Sold)/sales * 100

This margin can be increased by two ways

Firstly by increasing the sales; dependent on the external factors like market competitions, acceptability of the product or services, etc.

Secondly by reducing the cost of goods sold (COGS) it is internal in nature as its the internal efficiency of the venture to reduce or eliminate cost of product or services by reducing the cost of manufacturing or servicing to the customers, reducing the defects, efficient utilization of available resources etc..

(b) Operating Margin (EBITA Margin) = (Profit before Interest & Tax/Sales) * 100

If the venture is able to save a major portion of inflow of funds in the form of sales of goods and services, it would be effectively be able to pay for the Interest to be paid to long term liabilities and taxes on the amount generated during a financial year.

(c) Cash Operating Margin (EBITDA Margin) = (Profit before Depreciation/Amortization, Interest and Tax/Sales) * 100

Depreciation is considered as an internal source of funding while as it impacts on the value of the tangible asset without the cash flow (involvement in inflow and outflow). This margin shows the ability of venture to pay for obligations from the sales of the financial year.

(d) Profit before tax margin percentage = PBT/Sales * 100

This margin shows the portion of the tax that is to be paid to the tax authorities as a stakeholder interested in the growth of the venture. Remaining amount will be available for the shareholders who are also interested in the financial growth of the venture to get benefitted in the form of dividends or retained earnings resulting into the profit maximization or wealth maximization of the stockholders.

Operational efficiency of a venture is visible in the cash flow being generated by the Cash Flow from Operations (CFO). For financial analysis of Cash Flow Statement the important ratios can be evaluated to see the financial viability of the venture:

(a) Cash flow adequacy

This ratio shows the capability of the venture to meet its primary obligation; it's a ratio of Cash Flow from Operations to the funds engaged in the long-term debt raised, assets purchased and payment of dividends for the financial year.

CFO / (Long-term debt + purchases of assets + dividends paid)

Increase in this ratio during trend analysis, indicates that the venture is generating sufficient funds through its operational activities and is sound enough to raise debt obligations and make their payments; for future operations adding of assets by its operational efficiency to keep this efficiency improving with the market conditions; payment of dividends to its existing shareholders and keep them getting benefits of such investments in the past and become a lucrative option to the prospective shareholders.

(b) Long-term debt repayment

Debt is raised by the venture to purchase assets for the future expansions and improvement of the current operational efficiency with the changing technology and up-gradation to meet future demands. So within a financial year if the venture is able to generate sufficient cash flows to meet such payments of long-term debts it also shows the operational efficiency of the venture for which it exists in the market. This ratio is long-term debt payments made to the Cash Flow from Operations for the financial year.

Long-term debt payments/CFO

(c) Dividend pay-out

Same as debt the venture also raises equity from the open market through issuing of equity shares and preference shares. A venture with a good dividend payout attracts the interested investors who wish to get benefitted with the growth of the venture in the form of dividends (as part of profit) and capital appreciation as part of wealth maximization in the long run. It is a win-win for both as venture gets funds and investors get return on such investments with the associated risk of price movement of the shares. A sound venture can pay such dividends with cash generated is a good sign of its operational efficiency; that could be due to adoption of cost reduction measures, profit maximization planning etc. It is a ratio of dividends to equity and preference share holders to the Cash Flow from Operations for the financial year

Dividends/ CFO

(d) Reinvestment

With the passage of time the assets value and utility both depreciate. Even due to improvement in technology and market conditions the venture may need to upgrade its existing asset base. This needs cash to purchase of assets. This ratio of assets purchased to the Cash Flow from Operations is the measure of ventures being able to generate sufficient cash for reinvestment and maintenance of asset structure.

Assets purchased/ CFO

(e) Debt coverage

Ratio of total debt to the Cash Flow from Operations is the estimation of the number of years required for the repayment of the total debt raised with the cash flows available with the venture during the financial year.

Total debt/ CFO

(f) Impact depreciation write-offs

Cash for the venture is also generated from the non operating activities like depreciation (of tangible assets) and amortization (intangible assets), being the adjustments and writing off of the amounts from the book value of assets. Investors might be interested in evaluating the pace with which the assets are depreciation and contributing towards the cash flow from such activities.

$$Depreciation + amortization/ CFO$$

All of the above stated ratios (a) to (f) are part of sufficiency ratios. They all help decision maker in estimating the self sufficiency of the venture to meet its primary obligations.

The other category of such ratios is Efficiency ratios:

They help in estimating the efficiency attained by the venture in the respective financial years.

(g) Cash flow to sales ratio

Cash during the operating activities is generated from operations, investment and financing activities. Sale is not always in cash it can be a credit sale too. So its necessary to evaluate how much of cash is coming from the sale being the part of operating activities. Such realization helps in supporting the venture by not raising funds from the market for its business activities.

This is the ratio of Cash Flow from operations to the sale for the year

$$CFO/Sales$$

(h) Operating index

Operating activities leads to income from continued business activities, so this ratio of Cash Flow from Operations to Income from continuing operations is a measure of efficient utilization of resources and business capability to prove the existence of the business.

$$CFO/Income\ from\ continuing\ operations$$

(i) Cash flow return on assets

Moto of any business entity is to utilize its assets efficiently so that it could be able to generate more cash in the form of sales. This is the measure who capture the same with Cash Flow from Operations to the assets utilized

$$CFO\ /Total\ assets$$

7.3 Working Capital Management and Venture Capital

Management of cash is of utmost importance for a new venture, specifically in the case when it is lacking information. Preparing an optimal mix of debenture and equity is the need of the hour for a new venture, because with this information it can decide about the duration for which it needs funds so it needs funds at cheaper rate for long duration or it requires to have funds at higher rates for a shorter duration. Presence of such accurate information helps a lot to such ventures.

For the existing venture who is aware of the demand and supply of the goods and services can decide about expansion, diversification and modernization of its existing capacities and venturing into new business domains. For the long term fund requirement it should look for cheaper rate of interest to be paid, which is generally with the debt funding. But if the requirement is seasonal or demand based like inventory purchases then it could search for funding options which may be costly, reason being they are unplanned, but to meet the demand they will be needed to retain its position in the market.

The management of short-term assets and liabilities is known as working capital. The net working capital for a venture is the difference between the current assets and current liabilities, its always good to have a positive new working capital, that means having more current assets to pay for the current liabilities.

But this doesn't stand true every time, due to the dynamism associated with the business operations and market factors.

For the financial viability of the venture the decisions that impact its financial capabilities are

(A) Decisions Regarding the Management of Inventory

For smooth business operation and to meet the demand of the product and services the venture needs to maintain raw material. Some of this raw material will get into the work-in-progress (WIP) and later the finished goods. But with this these investments are the blockage of funds which otherwise might have been utilized to generate returns. The other side of the same coin is that if it is not maintained that it may further lead to costly raw material purchases during the production period. So the entrepreneur or the financial decision maker should have to take a call between the holdings of large inventory and the cost blocked with them.

(B) Accounts Receivable Management

The other aspect of working capital management that impacts the short term capital requirement is the presence of credit sales. These credit sales lead to debtors or accounts receivable. These are the short term assets of the venture. These unpaid bills remain part of such assets as receivables. Depending of the credit policy of the venture it could have credit limit for days, weeks or months. It is always beneficial for venture to have a shorter cash conversion cycle, as it supports with the short term availability of funds to meet short term capital requirements.

(C) Cash Management

To meet its short term obligations the venture needs cash. But keep cash in idle form is not good for the venture. So for cash management it needs to decide about the cash to keep in hand for such requirements and cash to be kept in other liquid assets like investments in the interest yielding short term securities. The other decision of cash management is to ensure the efficient handling of the cash equivalents like checks, which if in bank will be yielding returns in the form of interest.

The presence of call money market; which is an option to get returns from such short term investments and also acts as a source of short term finance for ventures needing funds with ease. Cash that is available and idle can be invested for months and even for days to get returns.

Venture Capital (VC)

Venture capital is a type of private equity and is different from the other private equity investing like Mezzanine, Buyout and Distress.

Distress type of private equity is having more of the characteristics of the Hedge fund than that of the private equity. The difference is due to the investment in securities; Venture Capital invests in private securities while the Hedge Fund invests in public securities. They make profits by buying of distressed ventures with a pure intention to make profit by reselling of these securities. With the dynamism in the business environment the differences are blurring with the passage of time and increasing completion too.

Mezzanine as term was coined in mid 1980s as a form of debt with equity participation. It is a type of private equity where the investments are made in the late stage of the venture. This is a form financing with subordinated debt (next to bank loans and financing) existing with the additional equity participation like that of warrants to buy the common stocks. Now it had took a different structure where it had emerged as a next level of debt financing for highly leveraged buyouts (LBO)

Buyout investing is bigger and the largest category of private equity. Its different from the Venture Capital and mezzanine in the sense that in this the investors take the majority stake and have the major control over the portfolio companies. They can go for such large buyouts where they invest buy buying the equity stakes, buying from the other shareholders including the junk bonds and even the mezzanine investors. Due to this characteristics they are called as leveraged buyouts (LBO). Such LBOs do participate in regular trade in the market for the mid segment companies.

While Venture Capital is a financial intermediary that channelizes the funds of the depositors towards the business entities and individuals. This makes them different from the *angel investors* who used to invest their own funds instead of the investors' capital.

A financial intermediary will be a Venture Capital with the presence of the following characteristics:

1. Channelizes investors' capital and for returns invest the capital raised directly in portfolio companies.
2. Investments in the private companies and take active participation and monitor the portfolio of companies
3. These VCs investments make it tough for the ventures to trade and rise on a public exchange.
4. VC's make returns by selling of the investment or making on Initial Public Offering (IPO) on a stock exchange.
5. A VC's funds are invested to raise the internal growth of venture.

These VCs are always in search of good prospects for investment so they keep an eye on new opportunities. They screen through various options and funnel down to the most prospective venture for investment. For screening it goes through *term sheets, valuation, structure and due diligence* it includes valuation of asset, type of security, timing of investments and controlling rights in the venture.

This is win-win situation for the venture capitalists and venture. as it acts as a source of funding for the promoter and the VC gets the return yielding business entity.

CASE LET

With a modest starting as Oravel in the year 2011 Mr. Ritesh Agarwal (an 18 year old young Indian) had started this venture. Though it was formally launched in Gurgaon in the year 2013, this branded budget hotel chain across India had shown how a brand is built. This venture had grown up and now is known as OYO Hotels & Homes (when it was launched in 2013 it was known as OYO only), considerably a long chain of leased and franchised hotels, homes and living spaces. This is one of the World's fastest growing hotel chains with its operations in more than 800 cities, 80 countries, 43000 Exclusive hotels and 1.2 million exclusive rooms all over India, UK, UAE, Dubai, China, Singapore and Indonesia. It became a unicorn in September 2018.

Milestones set by the OYO Hotels & Homes

2013: Mr. Ritesh Agarwal (then 18 years of age) was selected for the Thiel Fellowship and a funding of $100, 000. With this and the idea a concept of branded budget hotel was born as OYO in Gurgaon.

2014: OYO got its first Series A funding

2015: OYO got a funding of $25 million, in the same year its app was launched and so was the expansion that was there. Later it received Series C round of funding from Softbank

2016: was the year when this hotel chain had achieved the 1 million check-ins mark and launched internationally in Malaysia

2017: Its business was established in Nepal

2018: It got its operations expanded in other foreign countries like UK, UAE, Dubai, China, Singapore and Indonesia. Other achievement was it became the Unicorn of Indian origin.

2019: Raised $2-2.2 billion debt from the consortium of Nomura Holdings and Mizuho.

2020: It is amongst the World's fastest growing hotel chain with presence in 80 Countries. Was able to raise $807 million of Series F for the announced $1.5 billion in the year 2019.

According to the various sources Softbank had infused $506.75 million and holds 50.6 percent stake in the hospitality unicorn OYO Hotels & Homes through SVF India Holdings, while its promoter Mr. Ritesh Agarwal holds 25.87 percent through the RA Holdings.

On observing the history of OYO Hotels & Homes it had been a journey from a modest idea to becoming a unicorn with international presence. Financial management and financial decision making had kept this brand build and survive even during the tough times when the other brands were not able to bear the financial burden and they are now out of the business.

Key Terms Discussed

PESTEL Analysis: Political, Economic, Social, Technological, Environmental and Legal Analysis.

Format of Financial Statement: Available and updated through the Schedule III of the Companies Act, the general instructions are there needed for the preparation of financial statements.

Balance Sheet Equation or Accounting Equation: Assets = Liabilities plus Capital.

Assets: Things that the business *owns or is owed.*

Liabilities: Debts the business *owes.*

Capital: Amount invested by the promoter of the venture.

Balance Sheet: Statement of assets and liabilities generated/created in a particular financial year.

Profit and Loss Statement: Also known as income statement shows the revenue and expenditure made during the financial year.

Cash Flow Statement: Is a statement of cash movements' inflow and outflow due to the operating activities, investment activities and financing activities of the business entity.

Review Questions

1. How the organizing and financing of a new venture is different than the existing business entity?

2. How the financial performance of a venture be measured with the available information in the financial statements?

3. Why the working capital management is important for a entrepreneur?

4. How the short term and long term financial planning does is done by an entrepreneur?

5. What are the different types and costs of Financial Capital for a new venture?

Application based Questions

1. Decisions for a new venture are always tough even the trade-off regarding the inventory management? Comment. Is it similar case in the cash management too?

2. To have capacity building and rapid growth Venture capitalists (VCs) primarily invest in young, fresh and high-technology driven companies, how a new venture can make itself a lucrative option for such VCs to get funding?

3. Credit policy of the venture is impacted by the profit margins, interest rates and the probability associated with the repeat orders? Elucidate with relevant examples.

4. Ratio analysis helps in taking decisions based on the financial health of the venture? Do you agree? If yes, then please mention the application of important Cash Flow Statement ratios.

5. With the succession strategy the businesses should be ready with the exit strategy too? Selling of the ownership by the entrepreneurs' is also a strategic plan and for this venture capital provides support? Comment.

References

1. Andrew Atherton, (2012), "Cases of start-up financing", International Journal of Entrepreneurial Behavior & Research, Vol. 18 Iss 1 pp. 28-47.

2. Barry Christopher B. (1994): "New Directions in Research on Venture Capital Finance" Financial Management, Vol. 23, No. 3, pp. 3-15.

3. Narayansamy C., Hashemoghli A. and Rashid R. M (2012): "Venture capital pre-investment decision making process: an exploratory study in Malaysia" Global Journal of Business Research, Vol. 6, No. 5, pp. 49-63.

4. Hall J. And Hofer C.W (1993): "Venture capitalist decision criteria in new venture evaluation", Journal of Business Venturing, Vol. 8, pp. 25-42.

5. Jeng L.A and Wells P.C. (2000): "The determinants of venture capital funding: evidence across countries" Journal of Corporate finance Vol. 6, pp 241-289.

6. Venture Funding Support: https://www.startupindia.gov.in/content/sih/en/compendium_of_good_practices/angel_and_venture_funding.html.

❑❑❑

8

Building a New-Venture: Financing and Funding

Dr. Nandita Mishra
(Dean & Professor, MITCON Institute of Management Pune)
Amruta Desai
(Freelancer, Marketing & Creative Ventures)

LEARNING OBJECTIVES

After reading this chapter, the reader should be able to:

1. Understand how to build teams for a new venture
2. Identify various sources of Financing
3. Understand how Strategic Partnerships helps new-ventures

8.1 Building a New Venture: Over View

The entrepreneurial bug seems to have really caught on with today's generation. Every college graduate, high school drop-out, house wife or even corporate employees seem to want to start their own venture. Is it an easy task, many may wonder? Most start up ideas do not get past the idea generation phase with the fear of how they would manage to generate funds.

Building a new-venture can be a great opportunity for someone who is self-motivated, driven and meticulous with finances. There are many lessons that one can learn from being a start-up owner or by working as an employee for a start-up. The most popular reasons to start working on a new venture would include having a unique business idea, working towards one's financial independence, investing in one's own abilities and having the flexibility to grow at one's own pace.

Paramount to the success of a new-venture is having a strong team to rely on. Getting one's team ready is crucial to the growth and ease of operations of the new start-up.

8.2   Hiring Key Employees

Hiring for any venture can be hard, but hiring for start-ups may be even harder. The most essential aspect in the success with hiring would be having a clear picture of the various job roles and the skills required for the personnel who fill be filling those roles. One can use these guidelines to pick out the best talent for the new-venture:

1. Have an Exciting Vision and Mission for the New-venture

During the initial days of any venture, one may not be able to afford fat pay-checks to the employees and this could be a set-back in hiring good talent. But if one wants the best talent to come and work, one should be able to impress them with an exciting and unique vision and mission. Most people today would want to work for something that they are passionate about and gives them a purpose in life. If an entrepreneur can decipher these underlying unmet expectations and desires of the venture's future talent, they will come out as a winner!

2 Hire Committed People and they will Never Fail

All new-ventures may already have some fans. These are those people who are passionate about the company's products and services; they are already convinced about the goodness of the brand and always spread a good word about it. Positive word of mouth can never hurt and it can bring the new-venture more fans and more new talent. Most new pop culture apparel start-ups like www.souledstore.com and www.bewakoof. com hire their fans. They ask their fans to send them a short write up about why they love their brand and accordingly call them for interviews to hire them for the various vacancies.

3 Remote employees may be the new way forward!

The new-venture may be situated in a city where there is a dearth of talent, but that shouldn't stop an entrepreneur from hiring the best. When an entrepreneur decides to hire remote employees, they end up with the whole world as their option to create a global talent pool. One can have a pick from the best of best from around the globe. If remote working is not a viable option, then one could hire employees who could work for a few days a week from the venture's office and a few days from home. Offering such flexibility will surely attract new talent.

4   Create a fun work culture and build a strong brand presence from the first day itself

A company with a good work culture has a greater chance of attracting good quality talent. If one is able to keep their employees happy, these employees will want to bring in their friends to work for the venture. Great people will want to work for any company if it has a great work culture and they will work hard and the attrition rates will also be low.

Building a brand right from day one may help an entrepreneur to stay in the minds of both his customers and future employees. Doesn't everyone want to work for a popular brand? Most people want to advance their careers by working for brands that are renowned and offer them many opportunities to grow. So as an entrepreneur, one should look at being active on social media, conferences and meet up communities.

5 Challenging Projects Invite the Best Talent

The best talent in the market does not want to work on mundane or boring projects. If they are given something that challenges them, they will be more inclined and interested to work with the company. Stimulating and ambitious projects will keep the workforce engaged and they will thank the entrepreneur for it.

6 Keep the Conversation Going Online

Most smart phone and internet users spend a lot of their time online. Maintaining a blog with relevant content and contributing content to other websites are a great way of keeping the conversation going about the start-up. One can even inspire someone to join their team by simply posting interesting and relevant content on the company's website.

7 Networking and speaking at events are a good way to send out a message about the new-venture

Speaking at events may be a good opportunity to send the message about the vision of the company to future prospects and also to future employees.

An entrepreneur can expand their talent pool, by just networking or speaking at relevant events.

8.3 Recruiting and Selecting New Employees

8.3.1 The Challenges Faced when Start-ups hire new Employees

Hiring for a new-venture with limited cash reserves can be a daunting task. Hiring the wrong fit for a job can be potentially harmful to the new-venture. There are many challenges that a start-up could face as a new company on the start-up block:

1. The pressure of getting the operations moving

To start any business, there is going to be a huge outflow of cash to fund the new processes, to buy material, to establish a distribution channel, to market or advertise the new product\service. In the rush to recover these initial expenses, managers may conduct the hiring process in a hasty manner which could be detrimental to the success of the new start-up.

2. No prior hiring experience

Most new-ventures do not have the finances to maintain a separate HR department. In such a case, the finance or operations department takes on this added responsibility of hiring new personnel. Since there are no fixed hiring procedures, the quality of the talent being hired may suffer. In most cases, aptitude tests and skill tests are not conducted and the personnel being hired are not the right fit for the job.

3. Poor Negotiation skills

Due to the lack of experience in the field of HR, salary negotiation with employees may become a perplexing task. An experienced employee who is skilled at negotiation may end up getting a salary that is higher than the market rate and someone may end up not being compensated at par with their skill level. Due to such issues, good candidates may get driven away and the entrepreneur may end up attracting the less deserving ones.

4. Poor clarity about the organization's culture

Ideally, a good organization should be clear about their organization's culture in all forms of its communication, especially when communicating about recruitment and selection. But at the initial stage, the entrepreneur may not have a clear picture of the work culture. If the entrepreneur hires someone who does not into fit into the work culture, the integration of him\her into the work force will not be easy. And if the start-up owner ends up hiring someone who does not match the company's culture, the employee's tenure in the start up may be rather short and frustrating.

5. Lack of efficiency of assessment tools

If a start-up lacks clarity about its yearly, monthly and weekly targets, it cannot set up clear target for its employees and it would be hard to measure their performance. This asymmetry affects the promotion and appraisal mechanism and causes confusion and may lead to inaccurate results. Due to these poor evaluation methods, the employees may feel dissatisfied and may not be very interested in contributing to the growth of the new-venture.

8.4 Understanding the roles of the Board of Directors, Board of Advisors, Lenders and other Professionals

8.4.1 Roles of the Board of Directors

Strong internal governance is the foundation of any new-venture. This solid foundation has its roots in establishing a concrete Board of Directors. Most start-up owners get so caught up in product development and getting their product to go-live, that they fail to pay attention to creating a reliable and concrete board of directors. After the first financing round, when the investor demands a seat on the board, the founder members realize that they need to build\establish the board of directors.

Organizational continuity can be ensured only when there is a strong foundation in place for start-ups. Initially, it is essential to list up to three (3) members of the board, which comprises usually of the founder member and his co-founders. Developing the board of directors is quite a major task in itself.

The board needs to accomplish the following main duties:

1. Setting salaries
2. Planning financial ratios
3. Hiring of the senior management
4. Providing guidance for transparency and company compliance
5. Approving budgets
6. Issuing debt, stock and options
7. Have a say in declaring dividends

The popular social media website 'Digg' was founded in 2004, it quickly shot to fame and Google tried to buy them out for Two hundred million dollars in 2008, but due to the persuasion and urging of the then board of directors, the CEO 'Kevin Rose' turned down the deal. Sadly, the website ended up being sold for Five Hundred thousand dollars in 2012.

This is an example of how things can go awry if the board of directors do not operate diligently and the board is unable to provide the entrepreneur with the best advice.

IPO's, Exit strategies, mergers and acquisitions are also overseen by the board. Strategic Partners are required all along the supply chain and introductions with such partners are handled by the board members. As a founder, it is easy to become blind-sided and lose long-term stake in one's own venture. If it can happen to Steve Jobs, it can happen to anyone. So, it is of prime importance to plan one's long-term stake in one's own start-up before inviting other investors to the board of directors. Founder members should have an ongoing dialogue about the strategic objectives and it should be written down so as to finalize it. Legal help may be sought to understand what type of structure will be conducive to the new-ventures long term growth strategy and goals. If the new-venture goes up for many rounds of funding, there would be a variety of investors and it could lead to a complex organizational structure. At the initial stage, it is good to have roughly 3 to 5 members on board and at a later stage it is advisable to have 5 to 7 members. Before bringing anyone on board, it is essential to set the roles and responsibilities in the bylaws of the company. Most venture capitalists and angel investors would want to join the board and would have their own set of terms, so it is wise to be well prepared to negotiate with them to meet a middle ground on terms.

It would be wise to get an independent director first before offering a seat on the board to a VC who has invested money in the new company. Conventionally, the initial investors are offered a seat on the board. But off late this school of thought has slightly changed and an independent director with an expertise in the area of service of the start-up is given preference as the first member of the board. A reliable independent director can act as a tie-breaker on the board and can make or break the governance of the start-up.

8.4.2 Recruitment of the Board Members

Directors internal to the venture that are not the founders' could be initial investors who do not comprise the founder member's family and friends. Independent directors can be colleagues having a strong base in the start-up's industry or possessing a rich background in administration and governance. Founders need to come up with a structure for the interview process to be used for selecting members on to the board, inclusive of angel investors and venture capitalists who would like a seat on the board.

8.4.3 Adding a Member to the Board

While adding new members to the board, one can ask the following questions to ensure that the new members are adding value to the start-up:

1. In which way will this new board member add quantifiable value to building the start-up?

2. How is the board member interested in the company? Does he\she have a mentoring or profit or structure perspective?

   If the only motive is profit, there stands a chance of a fiduciary breach.

3. What kind of a compensation structure can be offered to the board members?

   Most board members are given a percentage of equity and the ones that do not are usually board observers. Angel investors and venture capitalists are not to be offered extra cash compensation as a member of the board, as they already have a sizable stake in equity.

5. An annual evaluation of board members is usually advised and are the members willing for the same? Are they willing to be rotated?

8.5 Role of the Board of Advisors in A Startup

A group of individuals selected by the founder member to provide advice and help the new-venture grow and meet its goals is an advisory board. Entrepreneurs will usually select advisors based on the skills required or based on the existing voids to be filled in the start-up. For example, a lawyer could be hired for additional legal advice, for Marketing and branding purposes: a PR specialist can be hired or an investor could be brought in for fundraising advice.

When an entrepreneur hires an advisory board, it speaks a lot about his\ her persona. It shows that the entrepreneur is smart enough to identify the areas of void and is not hesitant in asking for help in filling the gaps. No start-up entrepreneur can become successful all by himself, he certainly needs a board of advisors to guide and help him. An advisory board can be of great help provided the entrepreneur listens to them. Mark Zuckerberg (Facebook, CEO) failed to pay heed to the warning given by the safety advisory board, that the user data on Facebook could be seriously compromised. Because of this negligence, the information of about eighty seven million users of Facebook may have been compromised and given to 'Cambridge Analytica' which was a major political consulting group during the US Presidential elections of 2016. There needs to be respect for the advisory board as they are there to guide and assist the start-up to reach their goals and accomplish their mission.

When does a start-up need an advisory board?

Now in this case, there are two schools of thoughts:

The first states that the business should be built first and only then help\ advice should be sought. The second school of thought states that it is good to have an advisory board right from day 0. This route makes sense to a lot of entrepreneurs in many ways as there are a plethora of questions that need to be answered before starting a business: Will there be a market for this product\service, how will market testing be performed?, How should the business ideally be structured? It always helps the entrepreneur to have a board to bounce his ideas off and make sense of the above mentioned and other important questions.

The advisory boards are meant to be fluid. As and when the organization grows, the make-up of the board will change along with it.

How to understand that it is time to have an advisory board for the new-venture?

When it is observed, that a, particular goal cannot be accomplished with the current resources of the company, when the management needs the guidance and help of some extra skills or when the team seems to be stuck in a rut, most start-ups realize that they need the help of an advisory board.

As an entrepreneur, it's beneficial to put together a smart, invested board of advisors to help the start-up get through the beginning years and beyond.

Twelve start-up founders from Young Entrepreneur Council (YEC) have mentioned what is most important when choosing an advisory board.

Hand over the equity over a period of time

"It is extremely difficult to find the right advisers for your business. You need to make sure they have a strong work ethic, sufficient spare time to commit to the company and that they can provide solid advice and resources to your business.

Instead of giving advisers all of their shares at once, consider having their equity vest over time so you have a fair solution if these factors do not line up, which is often the case."

—Doug Bend, Bend Law Group

Bring in a large number of advisors

"I would get a large board of advisers at low equity cuts (between a quarter and a tenth of a percent) so that you can really create a huge list of people that can help you with your initial launch. The more advisers you get the easier it will be to get more, and the more you have for your launch the bigger your splash will be. I've seen quite a few companies pull this off (about me being a fantastic example)."

— Liam Martin, Staff.com

Be Selective of whom to pick

"Most people will informally advise you. Have as many of those kinds of advisors as you like. For your actual board of advisors you should be a lot more selective.

They get small portions of equity, so they should really know what they're talking about and really help you with the business. They should have experience in start-ups or your field. They should be somewhat noteworthy, have an experience or strong personal brand. Plan on three to five people. The spots should be coveted."

—Carlo Cisco, Select

Seek only counsel and not advice

"It's important to seek people who can provide counsel instead of people who just give advice. Anyone can give you advice, but counsel is a very specific type of advice that comes from people who have vast knowledge or experience in the area of your business.

You should always try to surround yourself with people who have more experience or are more knowledgeable than you are. You do not have to be an expert in every area of your business, but you should put together a council of people who are the most knowledgeable about every critical area of your venture. It's your job to know what those areas are."

—Arian Radmand, CoachUp

Go after dream advisors

"I would advise an entrepreneur preparing to put his/her board of advisers or board of directors together for the first time that there is potentially no more important task than this in the early phase of starting a company. An advisory board lends credibility, industry expertise and a wide range of introductions and advice that can be crucial to one's early days as an entrepreneur.

A dear friend of mine, venture capitalist Emily Melton, advised me early on that "if you want to build a Fortune 500 company, start with a Fortune 500 board." I took that advice to heart and always went after dream advisers in the wine/ beverage/technology/media industries."

— Alyssa Rapp, BottleNotes

Listen to the advisors that the start-up hires

"Your advisers should be people that you're truly excited to listen to. Don't put people on your list who you wouldn't be excited to chat with for 20 minutes.

That said advisory boards are not as practical as you would think. While you will certainly benefit from your advisers' feedback, a board is also an important way to build and maintain your network. Think about who has helped you in the past, who will be there in the future and who you want to bet on."

— Bhavin Shah, Refresh

Don't rush into any decision

"I know many companies that have given away cash or stock options to advisers too quickly, often before getting to know them well or understanding their commitment to the company. Don't rush into it. Most advisers worth their weight will happily spend time with you and prove their value long before they ask for an official role or any kind of compensation."

—Robert J. Moore, RJMetrics

Look for those who can bring in different perspectives

"Don't fill the room with a bunch of people who will think the same way. It will generate a crippling form of groupthink. Bring different perspectives to the table, because they'll offer a more comprehensive and effective solution. Get a good money guy, operations guy, marketing guy, etc. You'll be able to gain better insights that consider all areas of your business."

—Andy Karuza, Brandbuddee

Look for persons who are filled with passion

"Don't chase a title or a company. Instead, look for board members that are excited about your business and vet them based on their skills, experience and availability. This will help you build a passionate board that is committed to your success."

—John Berkowitz, Yodle

Get more skin in the game!

"Don't rush it, and don't feel like you have to put a board together right away. By making sure your board members want to be engaged and involved, you can avoid wasting resources like time and money.

Furthermore, make sure your board members have some skin in the game and have made an investment in the company. This will prove to you that they believe in the company and the leadership, and that they will be willing to work hard to associate themselves with a winning business."

—George Bousis, Raise Marketplace

Seek a Specific set of features

"When building our advisory team, we drew our dream team of advisers on the whiteboard. We included specific, sometimes famous and out-of-our-reach people.

Once we had a team we were happy with, we identified the important factors that drove us to include each person on the dream team. Were they a subject matter expert in our space? Did they know influential investors?

Once we completed this exercise, we were left with specific features, experiences and connections we were looking for in each seat. The rest was easy. We networked to meet people with those specific sets of features. Once you know specifically who you're after, people will help you find them."

—Brennan White, Watchtower

Ensure to be respectful at all times

"Anyone worthy of being on your board of advisors will be an extremely busy business professional. Be respectful of their time and do your homework in preparing and structuring every interaction."

—Björn Stansvik, MentorMate

8.6 Role of Other Professionals in A Startup

A person working for a start-up usually has to don many hats. Finding the right person who fits perfectly in the start-up can be daunting. The below mentioned roles are the ones that exists in most start-up organizations.

The CEO

The main founder member, who in most cases is the CEO, is the first component of any start-up. He\She has to always be in the selling mode for all of his\her time. The CEO should be spreading a positive word about his\her company at every possible opportunity and he\she should use all his time to network and build new contacts.

Other than raising funds and recruiting for the start-up, his\her main focus should be on maintaining a continuous dialogue with the clients and making sure that the company is building a service\product that the client actually wants and is willing to pay for.

The Front End Engineer

Coding skills are the need of the hour in today's time. If the start-up owner is not skilled at coding, it is advisable to hire an engineer to do the same for the start-up. HTML and CSS should be considered as a mandate for the front end engineer, but it's a lot better if they are also skilled in UX and also possess design skills.

The Back End Engineer

"Full Stack" engineers are available and they specialize in both front and back end programming. It is rather better to have two separate engineers who handle their own specialities. The front-end engineer can focus on the looks of the company website, user acceptance testing etc. The back-end engineer can focus on how the website actually works.

The back-end engineer must be able to pick\choose the programming language which is to be used, he should be able to design the first version of the website, also be able to establish the hosting.

Marketing Manager

Someone who lives and breathes messages and content marketing should be an ideal fit for this role. They should be skilled at drafting emails, writing content for the company's website. The ability to manage social media marketing and the ability to reach out to reporters and maintain consistency across all forms of communication is a necessity.

The Marketing Manager should be able to set the tone, feel and brand for the company by working with outsourced designers and maintaining a keen eye for design. Having a competent content marketer with a strong sense for visuals can save the company from spending huge amounts on branding. The start-up should essentially look out for someone who can don many hats at the office and can assist with printing things, picking things up and dealing with the day's latest catastrophe.

Wild Card

This isn't a one size fits all type of employee. This job role is specific to what the start-up specializes in or needs. This depends on that missing part of the puzzle that the entrepreneur needs to get right for the start-up to get off the ground. The start-up may want to hire a product manager if they are building their product right from the scratch. If they already have the product ready and need someone to do cold calls or visit prospects, then they need to hire a salesperson. If the start-up plans to hire a minimum of 10 people in the coming year, then it may need a recruiter for the same.

Once the team is ready, it is essential that they work together unitedly and they succeed at meeting the goals of the start-up. Laying out clear expectations can be one way of ensuring that the team succeeds. Before the person joins the start-up, ensure that they are informed that they may have to wear multiple hats and work long hours, but the pay-off can be extremely rewarding.

8.7 Understanding the Various Sources of Personal Financing

8.7.1 The Various Sources of Personal Financing

As a start-up owner, the first idea for raising funds that comes to mind is usually whether one can raise the money through personal finances. The start-up founder may think of friends and family who could lend the money to him\her, use up his\her own personal savings or sell something of value to obtain some cash. Let us explore these options of personal financing further in details.

8.7.2 Using up the Founder's Own Savings

When an entrepreneur invests his own cash in his start-up, he raises funds for his new-venture that is cheap (i.e. low cost of capital). Also since the cash is already available to him, he does not have to wait for long periods for cash availability. Often an entrepreneur starts a business when he is prompted by some change in personal circumstances – e.g. loss of his job, desire to start something new\innovative, inheritance etc. When an entrepreneur invests his own money, he\she retains a lot of control over his enterprise. Bankers and potential investors sense a strong sense of commitment from the entrepreneur when he\she has invested his\her own money in the enterprise.

8.7.3 Re-mortgaging

This is one of the most popular ways to raise loan-related capital for any new-venture. This works in a rather simple manner. The entrepreneur mortgages his private property and invests either all of that money or some of it into his new-venture. This form of financing is low-cost although the risks are high. In case there is a failure of this new-venture, then the property will also be lost. But, the falling house prices and credit crunch has made this form of financing harder.

8.7.4 Borrowing from Family and Friends

This is a lot more common source of financing than anyone can imagine. It is easier, quicker and cheaper to raise this form of finance as compared to taking a bank loan where there are stringent interest and repayment terms. Family and friends who are supportive and convinced of the entrepreneur's ability and his\her business idea will provide money to the entrepreneur. Though this may be a convenient source of financing, it may stress the entrepreneur if the business is unable to do well as was expected.

8.7.5 Making use of Credit Cards

A lot of entrepreneurs use their credit cards to fund their new-venture and it has become a popular way to finance new-ventures. It works in a very simple way. The entrepreneur makes payment every month for the various start-up related expenses using his credit card. Then fifteen days later, he receives a credit card statement by post and he makes the payment against the same within the credit-free time available to him. A benefit of using these credit cards is that, he gets an access to a credit-free period of roughly thirty to forty five days.

8.7.6 Going the Hard way by Cutting Costs

The entrepreneur runs a few extra miles to save up cash for his business. Sometimes, he does not pay himself a salary or does not take out any money for himself from the profits he earned. He re-invests all the profits back into the business. The entrepreneur will have to don many hats and perform many job roles at once, by doing this he saves on the salary that he would have had to pay an employee if he would have hired someone. In most new-ventures, entrepreneurs are looking at various ways to save some moolah.

8.8 Preparing to Raise Debt and Equity Financing

8.8.1 Debt Financing

There are a few things that one needs to know before raising debt or equity financing for their new-venture. Primarily there are two options available: leverage the debt in the business or raise funds from investors (equity). Discover the best source of finance for the business and go for it, don't just blindly follow the herd.

Debt means that the entrepreneur is borrowing money from someone or from some institution. In most cases one will be re-paying in monthly instalments, over a time period that is fixed and it will be according to a predetermined rate. Now, this could vary according to whom the entrepreneur is raising the debt from. Is the start-up owner raising the debt money from investors, are they using a credit line or a working capital loan or using convertible notes?

The biggest and most apparent advantage of using debt over equity is the ownership and control. The entrepreneur can make all decisions and retain all the profits; he cannot be kicked out of his own venture. Another plus point is that the liability will be over when the entrepreneur would have finished re-paying the debt. One can borrow only what one needs and repay it accordingly, the entrepreneur will essentially never have to pay more interest amounts than what is needed. It certainly looks like debt is a lot cheaper. Something that is also overlooked is that having debt in the capital structure will help with tax deductions.

There is also a downside to debt financing. The entrepreneur will always have to repay the debt amount on time whether the business is making profits or not. The entrepreneur will have to make mandatory monthly payments and this may be a huge burden on a new-venture. If the entrepreneur does not have a clear distinction between personal and business line of credit, he could face collateral damage to his personal belongings like his home, car, child's college fund etc. Variable interest rates may also come back to haunt him\her with a drastic change in repayment terms. Having too much debt in the capital structure may impact the venture's valuation and profitability and can also cause the terms for raising equity in the future to become inferior.

8.8.2 Equity Financing

In this form of financing, the founder member will have to exchange ownership rights with the investor against the capital that he provides to the business. This can happen in the form of fund raising from angel investors, platforms for crowd funding, VC firms, and close partnerships and also in the form of IPO's.

In this case, no fixed repayments will have to be made. In most cases, the investors may receive a percentage of the profits earned by the business. There are sometimes hybrid agreements that are made that include benefits and royalties to early investors.

Equity fund raising can bring in more cash as compared to what debt financing can. Growth can be far slower without equity fund raising. Flexibility is the biggest benefit of having equity in the capital structure. The entrepreneur is not under the stress of making debt service payments if the start-up is not making profits. The entrepreneur will not have to make rash or hasty decisions so as to make profits to repay the debt in this case and hence he can make wise and informed decisions that will help his business grow. When one brings in an equity partner, one is bringing in someone with vested interests in seeing the start-up succeed. Their experience, influence and connections can help the start-up grow.

The primary issue with giving up equity is the loss of control. Every micro factor of the business may get affected as the entrepreneur gives up a portion of his\her decision making control to the investors. If the ownership percentage that the start-up owner retains in the business is small, he\she will have to split a major share of the profits. If one doesn't have the right connections or the ability to pitch the new-venture, raising equity can become arduous and consume a lot of the entrepreneur's time.

One can raise funds for their company mainly using their own personal savings, debt or equity.

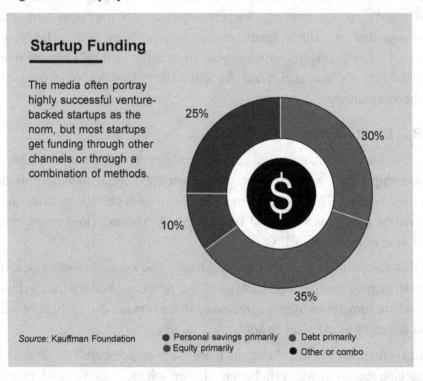

Startup Funding

The media often portray highly successful venture-backed startups as the norm, but most startups get funding through other channels or through a combination of methods.

25%

30%

10%

35%

Source: Kauffman Foundation

● Personal savings primarily   ● Debt primarily
● Equity primarily   ● Other or combo

As shown in the chart above, start-ups prefer debt in their capital structure. As per the Kauffman Foundation's survey that comprised of five thousand new-ventures, more than one-third of entrepreneurs used debt as a primary component to get their company started.

Equity is often associated with glamour, big money and all things fancy but in reality only ten percent of the start-ups funds come from VC's and angel investors. And as start-ups begin to flourish, they continue to raise less of equity and rely more on debt.

8.9 Understanding Angel Investors and How they Help Start-ups

8.9.1 Business Angels

A wealthy individual or a group of such individuals who invest their money or provide equity financing to early stage businesses and new-ventures are called as Angel investors. They provide financing in the form of private equity or 2nd round funding for growing small businesses that need the funding to grow. Once the seed money is established from friends and family or from the founder member's personal savings, the angel investors provide either equity or debt financing to the company for it to survive and grow.

If the venture has a high amount of perceived risk or if the credit market is tight, then it becomes hard to obtain debt financing. In such a case, private equity financing is the next logical step to raise funds.

A few angels form a part of 'angel investing groups' while some angel investors prefer to be on their own. Some investors are very knowledgeable about investing in new-ventures while others just go with their intuition. Some angels take initiative in being involved in the company that they invest in, whereas some others don't care much about being involved. Angel investors have many differences but they have this thing in common and they usually invest in small businesses only that they assume can give them a high ROI – perhaps as much as twenty to forty percent. The failure rate of new-ventures being very high, these angel investors expects a gigantic return on their investment.

Amazon.com, Starbucks and Apple are three of the most renowned companies that got angel investments at their start. It can be an arduous process to source funds from angel investors. These investors look for business plans that are air-tight. Only ten percent of the business plans submitted receive funding from these investors, as these investors are very diligent and they weed out business plans that are not competitive. Small venture owners will have to make multiple presentations to these investors to secure an investment.

It is unlikely that a new start-up owner may secure funds through an angel investor right away, but one may make excellent contacts to source funds from at a later stage. A lot of these angel investors will provide the entrepreneur with sound business advice. Certain types of industries stand a greater chance of getting investment over the others. Mostly hot and high growth industries interest angel investors as they expect a high ROI on their investments.

According to a research done by 'Innovencapital'; the below charts **show the** investments made by angel groups in India from 2012 to 2018.

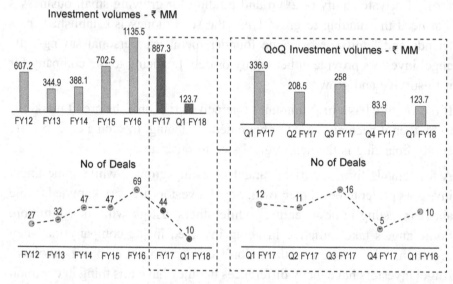

The pie-charts below mention the demographics of the start-ups that have received funding,

Demographics of startup Funded

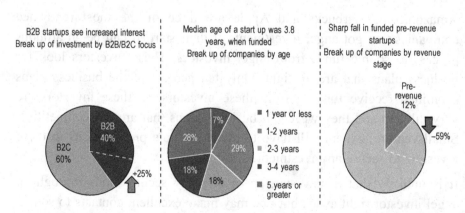

8.10 Understanding Venture Capitalists and How They Help Startups

8.10.1 Venture Capitalist

Start-ups often seek financing from venture capital (VC) firms. Such firms are able to provide strategic assistance, capital, and introductions to new prospects, employees, partners and a lot more.

VC financings are rather hard to procure.

8.10.2 How to Procure VC Financing?

It is essential to understand that most VC companies focus their investments around a certain few criteria as mentioned below:

Specific sectors (digital media, mobile. SaaS, software, biotech)

Stage that the company is currently in (seed rounds, later stage of rounds)

Geographical location of the company (e.g. Mumbai, Bengalore, NCR, Chennai)

Before approaching a VC, it is best to ensure that one's company is in alignment with the area of focus of the VC's company. Most VC's are inundated with emails from start-ups and they tend to ignore them due to the lack of solicitation and because of the sheer bulk of the mails that they receive. If the entrepreneur wants the attention of a particular VC, it is advisable to get an introduction from another entrepreneur, a trusted colleague or a lawyer friendly to that firm.

The venture process can be very lengthy and tiring. Initially one will have to present their idea to a VC, which will be followed up by many conversations and meetings followed by multiple presentations to all the partners of the VC fund; followed by the issue and negotiation of the term sheet. Numerous legal documents are drafted and negotiated by the lawyers of both sides to evidence the investment.

The initial documentation of most VC financings is done by a 'term sheet' which is documented and developed by the VC firm and presented to the start-up owner.

A document of prime importance is the term sheet, as it is a sign that the Venture Capital firm is quite serious about investing in the start-up and wishes to proceed with finalising and preparing legal documents pertaining to the investment. Once the VC firm gets an approval from their committee which handles investments, they proceed to issue the term sheet. The issuance of term sheet does not guarantee that the deal will materialize, but in most cases term sheets that are finalized usually result in completed investments.

The term sheet would ideally cover all of the prime components of financing:

1. The valuation given to the new-venture (Having a higher valuation will mean that the entrepreneur will have to face lesser dilution).

2. Issues pertaining to control like the makeup of the members on the Board of Directors.

3. The sort of veto or approval rights that the investors would enjoy.

4. Post-closing rights related to the investors, such as the participation rights in future rounds of financing and the rights to receive financial information on a periodic basis.

The founder members of a new-venture usually hold common stock in the start-up. VC's and angel investors make investments in the start-up in one of the following ways:

1. Convertible promissory note:

The angel investor\VC will be given a note by the company, which can be converted into the company's stock in the next financing round. This note will mostly have a date of maturity which will often be twelve months from the date of issue, and will likely bear an interest rate of 4-8 %. At this point in time, no valuation has been set for the new-venture. The investors may want to convert the notes into stock issued at the next round of financing at a discounted rate on the actual price paid in the next round of valuation, wherein a twenty percent discount is usually common, sometimes having a 'cap' on the company's valuation for the purpose of conversion rate. Seed rounds usually see such convertible notes.

2. Simple Agreement for future equity (SAFE)

These are an alternative to the above mentioned option of convertible notes. They are certainly not debt instruments. A SAFE does not have a maturity date or an interest component associated with it. An investor in this case makes an investment in the start-up that can be converted to stock in the next round of fund raising. As in the case of notes, the SAFE's can be converted with discounts and\or with caps on valuations. VC's are not keen on investing in SAFE's, though they have proven to be useful for start-ups at the initial stages.

3. Convertible preferred stock investment

This preferred stock gives the investors more preference over the common shareholders when the company is being sold. Preferred stock can also be converted into common stock of the co. Series A financing rounds issue convertible preferred stocks in most cases. A benefit to using convertible preferred stock is that it allows the start-up to issue stock options to its prospective employees and it will be available to them at a reduced price than what the investors pay for it.

A few popular start-ups in India have been funded by the VC's mentioned below:

Helion Venture Partners

They usually invest in consumer service oriented businesses and in tech powered businesses. They are a 605 Million dollar company and they focus on early to middle-stage venture funds that participate in future rounds of fund raising in collaboration with other venture partners.

Investment Structure: Invests between two to ten million dollars in each venture having revenue of less than ten million dollars.

Industries: Mobile, Financial Services, Education, Retail Services, Healthcare and Outsourcing.

Start-ups Funded: Yepme, TAXIF or Sure, MakemyTrip, NetAmbit, PubMatic.

ACCEL Partners

This VC firm was established in 1983 and has a global presence in India, China, London, Palo Alto and New York. They usually make investments in internet tech ventures in multiple stages.

Investment Structure: They have made investments between half a million dollars to fifty million dollars in their portfolio of companies.

Industries: Mobile and Software, Internet and Consumer Services, Cloud -Enabled Services, Infrastructure.

Start-ups Funded: BabyOye, BookMyShow, Probe, CommonFloor, Myntra, Flipkart, Freshdesk

8.11 Understanding How Business Incubators Help Startups

8.11.1 Business Incubators

The primary purpose of a start-up incubator is to help an entrepreneur to grow his business. They help to solve many problems that start-up founders face like providing work space, mentoring, training, providing seed funding etc.

Both public and private entities run such start-up incubators and are usually non-profit in nature. Many universities act as incubators and some business schools like Columbia or McCombs provide their students and alumni the opportunity to participate in entrepreneurship development programmes. Successful entrepreneurs, governments, civic groups also act as incubators.

In today's time wherein tech start-ups are on the rise and the media also focusses on them, incubators aren't just limited to just one industry. An incubator's focus can vary by region. North Carolina houses five major incubator farms. NYC houses several incubators for both fashion and food. There also exist many all-purpose incubators that consider several kinds of start-ups from different industries.

'The Batavia Industrial Center' was the first start-up incubator, that formed in 1959 in response to Batavia, NY's high rate of unemployment and to just start up with something in a vacant industrial building. Given the origins of why start-up incubators came into existence, it is no surprise that these incubators had started to make a strong comeback in the time of recession.

The most common start-up incubator services involve the following:

1. Help with the basics of business
2. Access to angel investors and venture capital
3. Identification of the management team
4. Helps with developing business etiquette
5. Assistance with regulatory compliance
6. Assistance with technology commercialization
7. Higher Education Resources are provided to them
8. Access to mentors and advisory boards
9. Legal counsel and assistance with intellectual property management
10. Opportunities for networking
11. Assistance with marketing
12. Access to high-speed internet

Most companies spend roughly two years with a business incubator during which they share office space, telephone and other resources with other start-ups so as to reduce operation costs and overhead costs of everyone involved. If an incubation programme seems to interest an entrepreneur then he\she needs to be prepared with a detailed business plan. A screening committee will review whether the start-up owner meets the criteria or not and accordingly accept or reject him\her. Incubators have limited space, equipment and finances and hence are selective about which businesses to choose. They would want to choose businesses which have a greater probability of becoming successful.

An entrepreneur should find a business incubator that is in alignment with their sector to improve the chances of being selected. We have mentioned a few business incubators in India for reference:

1. The Indian Angel Network (IAN) Incubator

IAN has set up an incubator with the support and assistance of the "National Science and Technology Entrepreneurship Development Board" and the "Department of Science and Technology, Govt. of India". The start-ups can access a plethora of funding sources including the IAN, which comprises of around 125 investors that provide funding of up to a million dollars. The period of incubation can last anywhere from eighteen to twenty-four months. For the start-up to get selected, one may have to wait for up to 90 days. The sectors that are preferred include cloud computing, alternative energy, gaming and animation, retail technology, media, IT/ITES, telecom, healthcare technology, education technology internet\web, manufacturing products. The entrepreneur can email his\her business plan to incubator@indianangelnetwork.com

2. iCreate

iCreate is an initiative of GFEE (Gujrat Foundation of Entrepreneurial Excellence) and a joint venture (JV) of GMDC (Gujarat Mineral Development Corporation Limited) and GEVPF (Gujrat Entrepreneurship and Venture Promotion Foundation). Potential candidates are groomed via the programs conducted here. The program also assists with mentoring, seed funding, networking, incubation of the idea. It has an advisory board that boasts of many experts from the industry and academia. Various seminars, networking events and reach-out programs are conducted by the centre operating in the GMDC building located in Ahmedabad. These incubation and grooming programs are held for a batch of twenty five candidates for a period of thirteen weeks.

8.12 Understanding Initial Public Offerings and its Relevance in a New Venture

IPO

IPO's can be raised by a young company who is trying to get in some much needed revenue or it could be raised by an established company who wants to go public. Whether a start-up is trying to pay out its debts or is just trying to grow and expand, they can look at IPO's to raise funds. Investments in an IPO can be risky to the investor as no one can foresee whether the stock would be profitable or not as there isn't enough historical data to predict how the new-venture will perform.

Many entrepreneurs have become millionaires and even billionaires after their company went public. But this isn't always the case. The start-up best prepared to go this route should have a good track record and should be a part of the industry that's already getting a lot of hype. Going through an

IPO process is not a cheap step for a start-up nor is it a solution for every new-venture. The new-venture needs to have audited financials for the last few years to be able to think about an IPO. Also the same applies if the industry that the start-up operates in is not on a high growth trajectory.

Raising an IPO is not just about the money. A successful IPO screams out success for the new-venture. A successful IPO can help to generate interest about the start-up and it can signal to the top-talent in that sector that this new-venture has achieved a certain height. It can also act as a boost to the employee's prestige especially after he has stuck to the start-up through both happy and rainy days.

There are downsides to the IPO too. The investors will become part owners of the start-up and will have a say in decision making. Also, as the public takes notice of a new-venture that was successful in raising funds via an IPO, they also notice the start-ups that failed to do so. One needs to consider all these factors before deciding whether the company should go public via the IPO process. Before making any decision about the IPO, it is wise to seek legal and financial counsel specifically for the new venture.

Process of Raising an IPO in India

1. The first step in this process is that of underwriting which is a process of raising funds via equity or debt. As a first step, an investment banker needs to be appointed. Theoretically speaking, a firm can sell its shares by its own abilities but realistically speaking it is important to appoint an investment banker. The underwriters act as middlemen between the general public and the company. A deal has to be negotiated between these two parties.

   A few examples of underwriters are Credit Suisse, Goldman Sachs and Morgan Stanley.

   The various factors which are considered along with the investment bankers comprise the following:

   • The amount of money to be raised by the start-up

   • What type of security is going to be issued

   • Other negotiating details pertaining to the underwriting agreement

2. SEBI

A statement of registration is put together by the investment bank, which is to be filed with SEBI once the deal gets agreed upon. This document comprises of information about the offering and also contains company information like the management background, any legal issues encountered, financial statements and how the funds are going to be used etc. The SEBI then takes a 'cool off period' wherein they investigate and make sure that all material info has been revealed. An effective date is set from when the stock would be offered to the general public after the SEBI has approved the offering.

3. The final stage

The underwriter then puts everything together during this cool off period. An initial prospectus is created that comprises all the information pertaining to the start-up except for the effective date and the offer price. With this in hand, the start-up and the underwriter try to create hype and generate interest around the issue. Efforts are put in to target large institutional investors.

When the effective date comes closer, the start-up and the underwriter come up with a price for the issue. This entirely depends\relies on the start-up company, the conditions prevailing in the current market, the degree of success of the multiple promotional activities. Finally, money is obtained from the investors by selling the securities on the stock market.

8.13 Understanding How Commercial Banks Help Startups

8.13.1 Commercial Banks

Taking out a small business loan from a bank is a prime source of finance for a small business. Small businesses usually turn to a commercial bank for their first loan. Due to the perceived risks, it can be hard to obtain a loan from a commercial bank. Most mature small ventures are able to obtain loans from commercial banks, though access to loans become difficult at the time of recession.

The entrepreneur needs to take a little time to ponder on the below mentioned points before going to a commercial bank to obtain a loan:

1. The entrepreneur should perform a thorough comparison of the banks that operate in the community and find out that provides better services and whether they will be accessible to him\her.

2. The start-up owner should try to get a grasp on the basics of term loans before he\she thinks of applying for one. A few basics like collateral, minimum and maximum amounts etc.

3. A few important factors will be considered when an entrepreneur applies for a bank loan like how much funds would be needed for the assets of the new-venture, the business plan of the new venture, entrepreneur's credit history and the documentation for the loan.

4. When an entrepreneur applies for a business loan, the commercial bank will use a particular protocol to evaluate the application. One of the things that the bank will use is the 4 C's for performing credit analysis to evaluate the loan application.

New-ventures usually have a hard time getting loans from commercial banks mainly because they have a high component of risk associated with their enterprise. So, it is understandable that most banks are hesitant about giving loans to start-ups.

Let's take a quick look at the "4 C's of credit" that most lenders expect the start-up borrowers to have:

Capital: Banks expect start-ups to have business assets (which can be devised to build products\services) and also can be converted to cash in order to pay back the business loans. Most new-ventures, especially service based start-ups have very few assets.

Collateral: Banks prefer business owners who can provide collaterals like cash or personal assets against the loan provided to them. But most start-up owners are low on cash and may not even have a co-signer who has assets to pledge against the loan.

Capacity: A past track record that portrays the ability of the business to generate enough revenue to pay back the loan.

Character: This speaks about having a good credit rating. The entrepreneur may have a good personal\business credit rating but that will not guarantee him\her the approval of a loan. In case one has a poor credit rating, then they can probably bid good bye to their chances of getting a loan.

One can make an attempt at obtaining a loan by following these five steps:

1. Review the costs required to start-up

Ensure that one is clear about how they are going to use the loan amount. The entrepreneur should ask himself\herself why he\she would need that loan.

Does the entrepreneur want to use the loan money to pay for day to day expenses?

Does the entrepreneur need that amount for growing the business?

Does the entrepreneur need that amount to build a safety cushion?

2. Look for the right type of loan

The reason for taking the loan will decide the type of loan being made available to the entrepreneur.

It is almost impossible to procure a loan in the first year of the start-up's business as lenders need to see a cash flow that could support the loan repayment.

3. Find the right type of lender

One may qualify for more than one loan so he\she needs to pick the one with the smallest APR, as long as one is confident about being able to handle the regular payments to be made against the loan. Annual percentage rate (APR) is the interest rate which is stated as a "yearly rate". APR includes the fees that one could be charged like the origination fees. APR is vital as it can give one a picture of how much he\she will be spending to take out the loan. Find the right type of lender who can offer a loan with a low APR.

One should go to a bank for a loan only if he\she is able to provide collateral and have a good credit rating to back them up and when one does not need the cash on an urgent basis. Getting funded by a commercial bank can take a lot longer than expected (roughly 2-6 months).

4. Take a look at the pre requisites to qualify for the loan

- If the entrepreneur's credit score falls beyond a certain threshold, he\she may not be eligible for a loan from a commercial bank.
- The entrepreneur must have been in the business for a minimum of one to two years to qualify for the loan.
- Find the minimum annual revenue that the banks require and check whether one adheres to those minimum pre-requisites.
- Take a close look at the start-up's cash flow statements, and check whether the company will be able to afford the monthly loan repayments.

5. Get the documents in place

When the entrepreneur has chosen what type of loan fits his\her financing needs, one need to start applying for it. One needs to know what is required by the lenders and accordingly get those documents in order.

8.14 Understanding How Leasing Helps New Startups

8.14.1 Leasing for Start-Ups

Leasing is in interesting option for start-ups wherein they can save on entirely purchasing new assets and just lease the assets by reducing capital expenditure. The cash that was saved because of the leasing can be re-invested into R & D, staff and marketing, new technology. Other plus points of leasing as mentioned by most start-ups include an increase in cash flow, avoiding technological obsolescence, tax benefits etc.

The most leased equipment's by start-ups are technology based like computers, servers, database storage, copiers, software, fleet vehicles, printers, telecommunications equipment. Most start-ups have expressed a desire to have more software's to be made available on lease.

Leasing is the way forward for many start-ups and is one of the major ways of procuring equipment's for the business. Most businesses in the growing stage face issues related to cash flow and the requirement for new equipment. The start-up can get equipment without major capital investment and also enjoy benefits from real cash flow by opting to lease.

It is possible to lease most kinds of equipment today and an entrepreneur should exploit these opportunities.

A few tips to keep in mind before any entrepreneur opts to lease out any equipment for his\her new business:

1. Before getting in touch with a provider who provides financing options for leasing equipment, ensure that the entrepreneur is able to understand and comprehend his\her business credit & they are able to organize their financial details.

2. Don't assume that one would be given the best offer by their bank or the finance company of the equipment manufacturer. A major chunk of all equipment leases are organized and supported by providers of equipment on lease.

3. Ensure that one gets into a deal with only those providers of financial solutions that are reliable and established.

4. Describe how acquiring new equipment's will benefit the new business to the finance provider of equipment leasing. Show them a projection of how costs will be saved.

5. Try to bundle up different equipment's from the various vendors under a single lease. This makes sense as smaller transactions usually leads to higher rates. Bundling equipment under a single lease will also help to minimize the processing fee.

Benefits of leasing:

- The money that the entrepreneur will roll out to make monthly lease payments will mostly be lesser than the amount he\she will end up paying via other options of financing.

- The entrepreneur can save cash for other expenses that are unexpected in nature or for working capital when the revenues are kind of low.

- Through leasing, the entrepreneur will encounter minimal costs that have to be incurred up-front and he\she will be able to immediately start using the equipment.

- Bank credit lines will not be impacted by leasing. The entrepreneurs can safe-guard his\her ability to borrow for other important business needs.

- Technology is ever changing and advanced equipment's keep coming into the market very frequently. Leasing helps the entrepreneur get access to the best and latest equipment.
- The entrepreneur will not be subject to fluctuating interest rates as in the case of a bank loan. The payments that the entrepreneur will encounter when he\she leases the equipment are fixed and not subject to fluctuations in the market.
- Lease payments are treated as a pre-tax expense so the entrepreneur may have the added benefit of reduced taxes.

8.15 The Different Sources of Debt Financing

8.15.1 Other Sources of Debt Financing

Does the word 'debt' sound nasty? Most businesses use debts to their advantage and it is one of the top most ways to finance the acquisition of new assets or to fill the gap when cash flows are interrupted. It can also be said that sometimes having debt is better than giving away equity. Let's say, the entrepreneur borrows some amount of cash instead of accepting it from someone who wants to invest in the company, then he\she will not have to give away any decision making power or any ownership. But most new-ventures have lesser financing options than established\big companies.

Loans

This is one of the most common and sought after mode of debt for most companies. Businesses can borrow from lenders like commercial banks by placing some collateral as security. Businesses need to make a regular payment of interest to the bank\other commercial lenders for a fixed period of time. There are long, short and intermediate term loans available to cater to the needs of different businesses.

Trade credit

This is a purchase now and pay later arrangement offered to businesses. In this manner most businesses can avail short term debt financing. This is also a good way for start-ups to avail short-term finance as they may be unable to afford loans wherein they have to place their assets as collaterals.

Instalment Purchase

This type of purchase involves purchasing an asset & making pre-determined instalment payments against the same. This is a different type of fund-raising process through debt. The buyer will mostly have to mortgage the asset until he finishes paying for all the instalments. If the business has a good credit rating, they may not have to undergo the mortgaging process. Finance and bank companies do provide the option of purchasing assets via instalments.

Asset Based Lenders

Some finance companies lend money to purchase assets. The entrepreneur will have to pledge assets like accounts receivables, inventory etc. Businesses which have real estate, account receivables, large inventory or other assets can benefit from this type of financing.

Bonds

New-venture owners usually do not consider bonds as an option to raise money. It can be a good option to raise money in the long-term when the company has established itself. Local governments sell bonds to finance their capital projects and repay them later with the money brought in by those projects. Small companies also raise funds via issuing bonds, but the interest rate is high due to the high amount of risk associated with small new ventures.

Insurance Companies

Insurance companies also help to finance small companies. They provide mortgage loans and loans against policies. The entrepreneur can mortgage an asset to avail a mortgage loan. The person's life insurance policy is placed as collateral and a loan is given against it in a policy loan.

There are many more debt instruments available in the market. The entrepreneur can choose what source fits his financial requirements best and make a decision.

8.16 Understanding how Strategic Partnerships Helps New Ventures

Strategic Partners

To grow in the long-term, the start-up will have to find strategic partners to work with even though it does not seem like a glamorous option. Being strategic partners with a big company will provide the entrepreneur with many advantages. One can expand their reach with the help of their strategic partners and one can build their reputation through such an association. A lot of customers will hear about the entrepreneur from their partners and one can benefit from this if their partner has a good image in the industry. To form a sound partnership with a partner one needs to be honest about the potential and reach of their company and also ensure that their partner is honest about their capabilities. An entrepreneur is more likely to become successful if they have one or more partners as they add more value to the business. A few benefits that arise from such a partnership are as mentioned below:

1. The ability to look out for new customers

The biggest benefit of a partnership is that the entrepreneur will be able to reach out to more customers. The entrepreneur can have access to the customer pool of their partner and can enjoy the benefits that this offers. Suppose a start-up makes eco-friendly shopping bags and is able to tie up with a big retailer like Reliance Retail, they will be able to sell more bags via partnering with this retail giant.

2. The entrepreneur can reach out to a wider location

Most start-ups do not have a national reach. Small businesses mostly operate well in their immediate area and may even be very popular in their niche markets. But, exposure to a wider geographic area would mean getting more customers and generating more revenue. If the start-up wants to expand geographically, they should team up with other businesses who sell products that are compatible with their own line of products.

3. Better access to new resources and technology

The entrepreneur may sometimes face resource constraints because of being a small business. If the entrepreneur can partner with a company that uses the technology that he\she desires, they can overcome their problem and grow in the direction that they had planned. The entrepreneur can also access counsel from their strategic partner in case they encounter some difficulties.

e.g.

Coca Cola has teamed up with co-founders of a start-up to provide an "on demand stocking platform" to deal with the problem of out-of-stocks. Coca Cola sells across more than two hundred countries and hence out-of-stocks was a major concern. Coca Cola formed partnerships with Yong Kim and AJ Brustein to form Wonolo and this has helped Coca Cola to restock their shelves instantly and organize "Right Execution Daily" (RED) surveys.

CASE IN POINT

Caselet Situation 1

Michelle runs a website called sportsware.com that sells sports gear. They sell sports equipment, sportswear, nutrition supplements etc. They have been into the business for roughly eleven months. Her website makes a sale of roughly 25-30 products each day. She has already raised ₹ 1,00,000 from her friends and family. Her monthly revenue is close to ₹ 1,50,000. Her expenses per month are close to ₹ 45,000. She faces issues related to maintaining inventory. She also plans to start manufacturing of sports apparel. She wishes to raise finances to support her growth plan. Suggest whether she should go in for debt from a commercial bank or bring in an investor?

Case 2

*"**Robin Sauve was** growing increasingly anxious. She and her husband, John, had started Barkley Logistics, based in Enfield, Connecticut, last June, shortly after buying the assets of her former employer, Premier Logistics, which had shut down after running out of financial options. Now, four months into the life of the new business, orders were slowly picking up for Barkley, which arranges merchandise shipments and deliveries of time-sensitive materials such as coupons and promotional fliers. Though not nearly as much business as Sauve had hoped for, the flurry of new jobs*

was nonetheless straining her ability to finance operations, and Sauve's financial adviser had told her she would soon need to get a line of credit to finance the company's growth.

But the idea of going deeper into debt put both Robin and John, who heads sales and marketing, into a panic. They had already taken on $40,000 in credit card debt, a tolerable level, they figured. Though Robin believed in the business, she reasoned that if things didn't work out, she could still sell the company's assets, find a new job, and pay off her credit cards. Taking on even more debt with a line of credit—her financial adviser had said she would need at least $75,000—was a leap she felt she just couldn't make, as she would possibly be putting everything at risk, including her house. "In my head, this was huge," Robin says. "I thought, if you do this, there is no turning back."

The Sauves are a pair of unlikely entrepreneurs. Starting Barkley "was unexpected, almost surreal," Robin says. They are the type of people who always seem to hold down a steady job and manage to carefully save. But the bank seized Premier's assets in late May, and within days, the Sauves made their move. As Premier's vice president of business administration, Robin knew how effective the company's software was. And she figured a new company with fewer employees, a solid client list, and less overhead could be a money-maker. Sauve offered the bank a little more than $6,000 for Premier's assets, which consisted mainly of the software. She pulled together the money from savings and credit card advances. The Sauves hired three former Premier employees, who agreed to defer their salaries until the company was on surer footing. The Sauves' Great Dane, Duval Street, was also often in the office, especially when the team worked late into the night.

Buying the business was the easy part. The fallout from Premier's implosion was another matter. Premier contracted with trucking companies to move material for its customers. But when the logistics firm ran into cash-flow problems and couldn't pay those carriers, the carriers turned around and tried to collect from Premier's customers. (Girard Robitaille, Premier's former president, declined to comment except to say, "We were in business for almost 10 years and served our customers well.") And even though Barkley was not affiliated with the former owners of Premier, Sauve knew former Premier clients would be wary of doing business with her. At the same time, she needed to contract with some of the very trucking firms Premier had short-changed. And she feared they might think her firm was just an extension of Premier and refuse to deliver shipments until she covered their losses from Premier. "That would have collapsed us before we got off the ground," she says. "It was nerve-racking."

As she got her start-up off the ground, Sauve realized she needed some help. Though she knew the operations side of the business, Sauve wasn't as strong in finance. An accountant friend introduced her to Robert Perry, a retired partner at her friend's firm. Perry agreed to oversee her books and counsel her on strategy. His very first bit of advice: Sauve would need access to outside capital. But he said a bank would want to see several months of revenue before it would even consider funding the company.

Sauve was having some early success at lining up customers. Dan Boyden, sales manager with former Premier client Mailing Services of Virginia, says that although his company had to scramble to find backup shipping options when Premier shut down, he didn't hold Sauve responsible. "We trust Robin and her team," says Boyden. "So it was natural to give them a shot." By the end of July, Barkley was doing about $20,000 a month in revenue.

Still, Sauve wasn't ready to go hunting for bank capital. For one thing, not all former Premier clients were as trusting as Boyden. Sauve had hoped to win over about 20 percent of Premier's former clients, but by late summer, less than 10 percent had signed on. "Some people still had a bad taste in their mouth about the old company," says John Sauve. "Certain clients want to take baby steps—do a small deal with us and see how it goes before committing." Says Robin: "I thought, If we go for the line of credit too early, we might regret it."

Her doubts were echoed by warnings from family members. John's and Robin's fathers were Navy veterans who left the service and became engineers. Both had earned a steady pay check all their lives and had impressed on their children the importance of financial discipline. Robin remembers John's dad asking a litany of questions, then concluding with a statement: "Just make sure you have your heads screwed on straight."

After months of troubled nights filled with anxious dreams, Robin started gaining more confidence. Barkley completed 30 jobs in October, double the business in September. For the first time, revenue covered operating expenses (though the Sauves still weren't, and aren't, paying themselves or their employees). Sauve was also encouraged that some former clients who had been gun-shy about giving her business seemed to be coming around. One former customer wrote Sauve an e-mail explaining that the fallout from Premier's failure made Barkley "a bit toxic around here," but he didn't see it as "a long lasting problem" and admired her "chutzpah" in starting the new business.

The Decision *In late November, Sauve met with Perry in her office to go over Barkley's finances. Perry pointed out that with business picking up; she was going to have difficulty paying the trucking firms on time if she didn't have some outside financing. He argued she couldn't continue to rely on credit cards—she needed to go for a line of credit backed by a personal guarantee. "Those are the rules of the game," Perry said. "If you want to play, that's what you have to do."*

Given the pace of new contracts, Barkley was on track to hit $100,000 a month in sales by the end of April—a trajectory that gave Sauve confidence that putting her personal assets on the line wasn't as foolhardy as she originally feared. After a conversation with her husband, she decided to move ahead with an application for the line of credit. "I knew this was the make-or-break moment," she says. "We need to either go for it or stop operating the business."

In December, Sauve and Perry applied for a line at the bank from which Sauve had purchased Premier's assets. In mid-January, she received a notice that the bank intended to grant the line. If the line comes through as expected, she plans to pay off about one-quarter of her personal credit card debt, a move that will save her thousands in interest charges. And, assuming the company continues to grow, the Sauves will have enough money to move out of Premier's old office space, which still holds boxes and files from the old company. "We would love to start fresh and have a change of environment," Robin says. And she is growing more comfortable as an entrepreneur. "We had the rug yanked out from under us when Premier closed and had to make some quick decisions," she says. "But every day, we get more accustomed to this new life."

[Source: Article by Amy Barrett (2011) inc.com/magazine/20110301/case-study-small-business-start-up-financing.html.]

Key Terms Discussed

Strategic Partnership, Debt Financing, Personal Financing, Incubators, Angel Investor, Employee Recruitment, Customer Relation, Business Environment

Case Questions

1. Do you think it is a good idea for Sauve to lease her future assets instead of buying them? Why?
2. Do you think bootstrapping is a good idea for start-ups in the beginning?
3. How do you think Sauve can solve her issues with Cash flow?

Review Questions

1. What are the roles of the board of directors, advisors and lenders in building a new venture?
2. Discuss how self financing can be done for a new venture.
3. What steps should a new venture follow in recruiting and selecting employees for a new venture?

Applied Questions

1. Study how Book My Show and Uber have raised finances for their start-ups
2. Define business incubators and find popular business incubators in India.
3. Study the current start-up scene and pick any one popular start-up and study how they have raised finances for their venture?
4. Check for yourself by talking to a bank employee whether their commercial bank offers loans to start-ups and what are their pre-requisites.
5. Study any start-up that has raised finances through an IPO by going public.

Additional Reading

1. 15 Businesses You can Start for $10000 or Less, www.entrepreneur. com.

2. The Best Businesses to Start with 10k, www.businesslaw.com.

3. 50 Best Small Business Ideas to Start with $10k in 2020, www. profitableventure.com.

4. 10 Podcasts that every Indian entrepreneur must listen to, www. startup-mark.com.

5. 7 Lessons that every Entrepreneur must learn from Steve Jobs, https://yourstory.com/2020/06/seven-lessons-every-entrepreneur-learn-steve-jobs.

References

1. Tank, A. (2017, February 15). 9 Ways to Recruit the Best Talent for your Start-up. Retrieved from https://www.entrepreneur.com/article/287574.

2. Kowlesser, A, F. (2018, June 11). The Start-up Guide To Creating A Board Of Directors. Retrieved from https://magazine.startus.cc/the-startup-guide-to-creating-board-of-directors.

3. Forrest, C. (2014, June 3). Start-ups – Demystifying the Board of Directors. Retrieved from https://www.techrepublic.com/article/startups-demystifying-the-board-of-directors.

4. Schoeneberger, S. (2018, June 10). You Grew Your Startup; Now Build Your Advisory Board. Retrieved from https://www.entrepreneur.com/article/314675.

5. Hoey, K. (2017, April 13). Why Your Start-up Needs An Advisory Board. Retrieved fromhttps://www.inc.com/kelly-hoey/why-your-startup-needs-an-advisory-board.html

6. Helman, J. (2016, July 11). The First 5 People to hire for your Tech Start-up. Retrieved from https://www.forbes.com/sites/under30network/2016/07/11/the-first-5-people-youll-hire-for-your-tech-startup/#6a68237618a7.

7. Riley, J. Finance: Personal Sources of Finance for a Startup (GCSE). Retrieved from https://www.tutor2u.net/business/reference/finance-personal-sources-of-finance-for-a-startup.

8. Fundera (2018, August 2). Mixing Equity and Debt: The Lesser-Known Key to Airbnb, Uber, and Sweetgreen's Explosive Growth. Retrieved from https://medium.com/@fundera/mixing-equity-and-debt-the-lesser-known-key-to-airbnb-uber-and-sweetgreens-explosive-growth-616ef62aa38b

9. Lakhani, M. (2018, April 11). A Founder's Guideline to Debt Financing. From https://medium.com/startup-grind/a-founders-guideline-to-debt-finaning-14e99e9d58b6.

10. Cremades A (2018, August 19). Debt vs. Equity Financing: Pros & Cons For Entrepreneurs. Retrieved from https://www.forbes.com/sites/alejandrocremades/2018/08/19/debt-vs-equity-financinpros-and-cons-for-entrepreneurs/#23e17aec6900.

11. Peavler, R. (2018, May 22). What are Angel Investors? Retrieved from https://www.thebalancesmb.com/what-are-angel-investors-392985.

12. Bizztor Editors (2018, December 28). Top Things Angel Investors Look for in Startups before Investing. Retrieved from https://bizztor.com/in/angel-investors-india.

13. Harroch R (2018, March 29). A Guide to Venture Capital Financings for Startups. Retrieved from https://www.forbes.com/sites/allbusiness/2018/03/29/a-guide-to-venture-capital-financings-for-startups/#6f994bfe51c9

14. Team Inc42 (2014, December 22). Top 47 Most Active Venture Capital Firms In India For Startups. Retrieved from https://inc42.com/resources/top-47-active-venture-capital-firms-india-startups/

15. Nicole Willson (2012, May 09). What is a Startup Incubator? Retrieved from https://www.topmba.com/blog/what-startup-incubator.

16. Entrepreneur. Business Incubator. Retrieved from https://www.entrepreneur.com/encyclopedia/business-incubator.

17. The Tech Panda Team (2014). What is an incubator? Retrieved from https://thetechpanda.com/indian-startup-incubators

18. Rocket Lawyer Incorporated (US). How the IPO Process for Start-ups work? Retrieved from https://www.rocketlawyer.com/article/how-the-ipo-process-for-startups-works.rl

19. Jeff Hayden (2018, October 19). Take Your Startup Public? This CFO Says an IPO May Be the Last Thing You Want to Do. Retrieved from https://www.inc.com/jeff-haden/take-your-startup-public-this-cfo-says-an-ipo-may-be-last-thing-you-want-to-do.html.

20. Peavler, R. (2018, May 15). Commercial Bank Loans for Small Businesses. Retrieved from https://www.thebalancesmb.com/business-loans-from-commercial-banks-for-small-businesses-393101.

21. PR Newswire (2000, November 20). High Tech Start-ups Identify Equipment Leasing As Key to Financial Success. Retrieved from https://search.proquest.com/docview/449251311?accountid=185290.

22. Prime Commercial Lending Website. Retrieved from https://primecommerciallending.com/financial-options/equipment-leasing.

23. Borad, S, B,. (2018, December 31). Sources of Debt Financing. Retrieved from   https://efinancemanagement.com/sources-of-finance/sources-of-debt-financing.

24. Merritt, C. Sources of Debt Financing. Retrieved from https://smallbusiness.chron.com/sources-debt-financing-67077.html

25. Resnick, N. (2017, July 10). Why Start-ups Should Strongly Consider Strategic Partnerships. Retrieved from https://www.business2community.com/startups/startups-strongly-consider-strategic-partnerships-01876285

26. Holland, K. (2016, October 20). 3 Powerful Corporate-Startup Partnerships that Paid Off. Retrieved from   https://www.rocketspace.com/corporate-innovation/3-powerful-corporate-startup-partnerships-that-paid-off

27. Barrett. A (2011, March 1) Case Study. Retrieved from https://www.inc.com/magazine/20110301/case-study-small-business-start-up-financing.html

9

Marketing Issues of New Venture

Dr. Sanjeev Malaviya
*(Assistant Professor & Faculty Coordinator, ICFAI Business School,
ICFAI University Dehradun)*

LEARNING OBJECTIVES

After reading this chapter, the reader should be able to:

1. Comprehend ways to divide the total market into consumer groups on needs similarity (Segmentation).

2. Analyze consumer groups (segments) to serve to   degree of effectiveness (Targeting).

3. Analyze and decide on the value proposition for the targeted segment of buyers (Positioning).

4. Apply critical thinking to build and manage brands to maximize the value and create loyalty through effective STP.

9.1 Introduction

Patanjali, an Indian brand of Ayurvedic, herbal and wellness products has been able to establish in the Indian FMCG space through creating strong brands. These are built on the strength of Yoga, Ayurved and Baba Ramdev. The elements of purity and 'swadeshi' developed an emotional connect. The company not only was effective in segmenting but also successful in targeting the ardent supporters of yoga, Ayurved and the followers of Baba Ramdev. The increasing awareness and media exposure contributed in building up a growing affinity towards herbal and natural ingredients in the products.

This provided an opportunity for Patanjali Ayurved to differentiate itself from the competitors in the FMCG sector- some of them being the established HUL, P&G, Colgate Palmolive. With Baba Ramdev taking charge of the promotions the company developed and established a successful positioning based on Ayurved and health benefits that jolted the might of the established players. Patanjali Ayurved, which started out as a small pharmacy, quickly grew to challenge multinational FMCG giants as it expanded into diverse segments.

Dantkanti, a leading toothpaste brand in India from Patanjali Ayurved Ltd., is a case in point apart from the vast portfolio of products that Patanjali has in its FMCG kitty. The muddy-brown toothpaste with a tingling taste serves a wide range of consumers from children and adults to elderly people and those suffering from common dental ailments like pyria, gingivitis, and bad odor. With the oral care industry in India worth INR 5400 crore and almost 60% share coming from toothpaste, the company realized that the solution for expanding the market and achieving growth is by adopting more focused approach through segmentation and targeting, using specially formulated products for different segments. The products that emerged from this strategic thinking in the toothpaste market were DantKanti Junior addressing the dental and oral health problems of children; DantKanti Medicated targeted another segment of consumers that required medicinal benefits from the toothpaste. DantKanti fresh Active Gel targeted the youth, DantKanti Red was aimed at the segment, especially rural, that was migrating from powder to paste.

There are not many successful new brands in the FMCG sector that have tasted success of such magnitude. The high promotional costs for creating awareness to the new brand, cost of establishing a strong network and issues of quality have always been major deterrents. It has been a combination of right strategies for dividing the market into segments, targeting the right segments and developing effective positioning and branding strategies that have helped Patanjali to create value for its target customers.

The company reached ₹ 10,000 crore in revenues in FY16 from less than ₹ 500 crore in FY12 and aims to achieve ₹ 20,000 crore in annual revenues in three to five years. It has also hinted to go public.

Source://economictimes.indiatimes.com/articleshow/67072314.cms?utm_source=contentofinterest&utm_medium=text&utm_campaign=cppst

To compete and succeed, a new venture needs to focus on:

1. Dividing the total market into consumer groups on needs similarity (Segmentation)

2. Selecting – one or more-consumer groups (segments) to serve to a degree of effectiveness (Targeting)

3. Deciding on the value proposition for the targeted segment of buyers (Positioning)

4. Building and managing brands to maximize the value and create loyalty.

9.2 Directing the Marketing Efforts- Mass Marketing versus Micromarketing

The first step in the process of effectively directing the marketing efforts by any company- whether it is a start up venture or an established entity- is to focus on Market Segmentation. A successful marketer, before attempting to segment the market, should understand that a company has a choice to make between Mass Marketing (provided it has sufficient funds to do so!) or to have focused marketing efforts through a well defined Micro marketing approach.

9.2.1 Mass Marketing

If a company can reap strong advantages by serving the entire market why should it focus on a small pie, a natural question for intriguing minds. When Ford launched its Model T- Ford it aimed to serve the market with the approach of Mass Marketing – in which a seller engages in mass production, mass distribution and promotion of a single product for all the buyers. "You can have any color as long as it's black", a famous quote attributed to Henry Ford describes this approach. The advantage of Mass Marketing is creation of largest potential market, the economies of scale resulting in reduction of costs. This in turns may lead to lower price for the product, facilitating deeper penetration, or higher margins for the company, depending on the choice made by the company. Coca Cola with its Coke in the 6.5 ounce bottle was another mass market product. With the obvious advantages there were trends that made mass marketing difficult for companies to practice. The splintering of markets with changing consumer tastes and preferences and a rapid rise in advertising media and distribution channels made it difficult to reach to mass audience. The heterogeneity in the markets led to a shift in companies focus to Micro marketing from the lucrative mass markets.

9.2.2 Micromarketing

Micromarketing involves focusing marketing efforts for marketing product or services to smaller groups of customers and can be done at four levels- Market Segment, Niches, Local Areas and Individual marketing.

Market Segmentation

The heterogeneous markets required companies to fine tune their marketing programs to suit customers needs and counter competitors marketing. Successful product and service brands like Patanjali Dantkanti, Nirma detergent, Indigo Airlines rest their laurels on careful market segmentation- a process that companies use to divide large heterogeneous market into small markets that can be reached and served more effectively. It involves identifying a group of consumers, called market segment, that share a similar set of needs. Suzuki sells cars from Alto, Wagon R, Ignis, Vitara Brezza, etc. to meet the needs diverse consumer groups.

But even in a market segment not everyone may want the same thing, this prompted marketing experts to suggest that marketers should present Flexible marketing offerings comprising of the naked solution- that has product and service elements valued by all segment members- and discretionary options- suiting the preference of a section of segment members but not of all. Suzuki offers its brand Ignis with the basic model, Delta and higher end options as Zeta and Alpha.

Niche Marketing

Mass marketing focuses on producing the 'hits'- the products in the portfolio that bring most sales and occupy the head of the distribution curve and most companies neglect the tail of the curve occupied by the products that cater to the needs of a specialized section within a segment. For instance, one such specialized segment in the detergent market can be consumers looking for a mild liquid detergent for washing delicate woolen clothes at home without having to avail costly services of the dry cleaners. It was served effectively by Godrej through its Ezee brand. Niche Marketing involves combining the preferences of a specialized group of customers in a market segment and offering this narrowly defined sub segment a distinctive set of benefits which this sub segment seeks. Paras Pharmaceuticals with its 'Crack' cream and 'Itch guard' brands has practiced niche marketing with aplomb, successfully capturing niche markets for its brands. The marketing efforts for its 'Crack' brand focused on a specialized segment of women especially the homemakers who faced problems of cracked heels that aggravates in winters and the creams and lotions meant for dry skin are not of much help. A niche market is a small part of the market segment that has sales, profit and growth potential. Niche marketers should aim to understand this sub segment so well that the consumers do not hesitate to pay a premium for the offering that provides a solution to their distinctive needs. Online commerce has paved way for successful niche marketing.

Local Marketing

Meeting the needs of local customer groups through uniquely designed marketing programs constitutes Local Marketing. It has the challenges of increased costs- both manufacturing and marketing, reduced economies, logistic problems and dilution of brand image but still companies are embracing it to reach to the customer as close as possible. Banks, Matrimony sites, Google- providing search options in regional languages or Hollywood Movies released in local languages (with Spiderman mouthing dialogues in Bhojpuri!) are all attempts towards grass root marketing.

Individual Marketing

Taking a step further when companies customize their marketing programs to serve a segment of one, it leads to individual marketing. It involves designing a product or service to meet the needs of individual customer (Customization) to doing it for large number of customers (Mass Customization). Asian Paints follows this strategy in paint retailing, providing its customers options to create their own shade of color. When operationally driven mass customization is combined with customized marketing such that it empowers customers to design their choice of product and services it is called customization.

Market Segmentation Variables

There are two broad groups of variables to segment consumer markets-Descriptive and Behavioral. The marketers look at the descriptive characteristics- geographic, demographic and psychographic of the consumers and the behavioral characteristics i.e., the consumer responses.

Descriptive Variables

Geographic segmentation involves concentrating the product, promotion and sales effort to match the needs of consumers in individual geographic units- regions, states, cities, urban and rural markets. Chic shampoo sachets were focused on the providing small affordable sachets of shampoos for the rural markets.

Demographic Segmentation involves segmenting the market based on demographic variables like age, gender, family size and life cycle, income, occupation, religion, generation, race and nationality. These variables are easier to measure. Brands like Junior Horlicks and Dove have quiet successfully targeted market segments based on age and gender respectively.

Psychographic segmentation involves personality traits, Values and Lifestyle to divide the market into segments with similar needs. Titan watches for their brands Raga, Fastrack, Sonata uses lifestyle segmentation approach. Values and Lifestyles approach is also a powerful segmentation variable.

Behavioral Variables

Behavioral segmentation involves dividing consumers into groups based on their response towards a product or services and understanding the role played in the buying decision process. The key behavioral variables include: Occasions (regular or special for a buyer of Cadbury's chocolate) Segmentation, Benefit segmentation (like quality, service, economy for a buyer of car), User Status (a non user, potential user, first time, regular user for a brand like Lifebuoy soap), Usage rate (categorizing buyers as light, medium or heavy users for a telecom services, say, of Airtel), Buyer Readiness Stage (categorizing buyers into Unaware, Aware, Informed, Interested or Desirous for a service like stem cell banking), Loyalty status (hard core loyal, split loyal, shifting loyal or switcher for Indigo Airlines) and Attitude (Enthusiastic, Positive, indifferent, negative or hostile for a brand say Maggi Noodles).

Besides having knowledge of the above behavioral variables, for a focused marketing, marketers should be able to recognize who is the User, whether she is the same as Buyer, who is the Decider, is she the Initiator too, is there someone who is the Influencer. The understanding of these five roles becomes significant particularly if the product or service carries a high-risk perception like purchasing a sports car or choosing a resort for vacation.

9.3 Choosing the Segment (s) to Target

A company going for a new liquid hand wash may breakdown the target market based on behavioral segmentation as under:

The process for segmentation may start with identifying a group of customers on the basis of need similarity/benefit sought using specific statistical tools, determine the descriptive and behavioral characteristics that give distinct identity to this group or groups of customers, measure the attractiveness (growth, competition intensity etc.) of the group(s) of customers, profitability of the group of customers and decide on the target customer group(s) to serve. This is followed by designing a suitable positioning, marketing mix and branding strategy for each Target customer group identified by the company to be the focus of its marketing efforts.

Market Targeting-Segment(s) selection for directing the Marketing efforts

Segment selection for a focused marketing effort involves a process called Market Targeting in which the company evaluates attractiveness of each customer group (ie., market segments it has identified using segmentation variables) based on certain criteria. The segment(s) that the company selects for focusing its marketing efforts is called the target market. A company can choose more than one segment to serve with distinct positioning and marketing mix strategy. The target markets differ for Pantene, Heads and Shoulders and Rejoice brand of shampoo, which are incidentally the brands offered by the same company- P&G!

Marketing Effort-Deciding the Strategic Mix for Marketing Products or Services

The strategic tools that marketers use to integrate the various marketing activities comprises of four Ps of the marketing also referred to as the marketing mix. The marketing mix comprises of Product, Price, Place and Promotion. The successful marketers integrate various marketing activities to create a mix that focuses on meeting the needs of a target market. The Product element involves working on the product's Variety, Quality, Design, Features, Branding, Packaging, Services, Warranties, Returns etc. The Price element involves working on setting the List Price, Discounts, Allowances, Payment periods and terms of credit etc. The Promotion element focuses on creating an integrated strategy for communicating with the target market by a proper coordination of elements of communication mix that include Sales Promotion, Advertising, Public Relations, Personal Selling and Direct Marketing. Digital Marketing has emerged as powerful marketing tools to develop a direct connect with customers. The Place element deals with creating a distribution strategy to effectively and efficiently reach out to the target market and involves decisions on Channels, Coverage, Locations, Inventory, and Transportation etc.

Marketing of Services is somewhat different from a physical good due to the characteristics of services. Services like a medical checkup, airlines services or a hair cut involve an offer that has Intangibility (cannot be judged by a customer's five senses prior to purchase and sometimes even after the purchase), Inseparability (a service offer is produced and consumed simultaneously therefore requiring consumers presence during its production; you cannot have a hair cut without being physically present at the barbers shop !), Variability (a service offer involves human element resulting in variations in quality of services provided as compared to a physical product, even if the service is provided by the same service provider!) and Perishability (a service offer cannot be stored making return of the service product a challenge, you cannot return a poor haircut instead have to live with it !). These characteristics have resulted in addition to three more elements resulting into a Services Marketing Mix that has seven Ps- 4Ps of marketing mix plus People (includes all human actors in services like service providers, customers and even other customers present during service delivery, like co passengers who may be traveling with you in an Airlines) Process (involves a careful inspection of all the steps that go into service production and delivery) and Physical Evidence (all the tangible evidence of service- bills, brochures, uniforms, equipments, facility etc.).

These additional elements in the services marketing mix need to be carefully planned to effectively manage the challenges involved in services marketing.

9.4 Key Criteria for Choosing a Target Market

The criteria for deciding the attractiveness of a market segment require measuring the size, growth, profitability, scale economies, risks perception and synergies that the market segment has with the existing target market.

The attractiveness of the market in the long run is determined by the degree of threat posed by five forces as identified by Michael Porter. These are Threat of intense segment rivalry (presence of a strong, aggressive competitors in a market segment enhance this threat and make the segment unattractive, markets for Airlines and Telecom services score high on this threat); threat of new entrants (a segment where new entrants can come in easily make it unattractive to serve and even worst is the case for a segment where new entrants find it difficult to leave after an otherwise easy entry); threat of substitutes (higher a segment scores on this threat more unattractive it is for the company desirous to enter it); threat of supplier's bargaining power (a growing bargaining power of suppliers makes a market segment less attractive; Intel commands a strong reputation in its market making it less attractive for its competitors); threat of buyer's bargaining power (a high and growing negotiating strength of buyer's reduces the attractiveness of the market segment, Walmart being a case in point for its hapless vendors)

Kotler identified five key bases for defining utility of a segment or segments that can be target markets for a company. These criteria for choosing a target market are Measurability (a segment should have measurable characteristics, size, and purchasing power); Substantiality (a segment should be substantial both in terms of size and profit); Accessibility (a segment should be reachable with a degree of efficacy); Differentiability (a segment should be distinct from other segments and should provide distinct responses to diverse set of marketing mix elements) and Actionability (a segment should be actionable i.e., marketing programs can be actually be designed to attract the customers and to serve them)

9.4.1 Target Market Selection Designs

The overall attractiveness of the market segments, as identified above, needs to be, mapped with the company's overall objectives and the resources available with it. On the basis of this mapping a company can choose any of the five designs as mentioned below:

Single Segment Concentration: A company targets a single market segment with a suitable marketing mix designed to meets its needs, if done properly it may emerge as a successful *Niche* marketer.

Selective Specialization: A company may target a number of market segments each with a different set of marketing mix uniquely designed for each target market This practice is also called differentiated marketing strategy. If successful, the company may establish a strong position and achieve higher sales. Although it may incur a higher cost on account of increased expenditure involved in designing separate marketing mix for the multiple segments it may choose to target.

Product Specialization: A company, although targets multiple segments as in selective specialization, but offers them a product in which it specializes. An example may be a paper manufacturer that may sell to three different market segments comprising of general printing, office supplies, and point of purchase displays respectively by manufacturing specialized papers meeting the distinct requirements for these three market segments by varying the finish quality and weights of papers.

Market Specialization: A company selects a particular market segment and specializes in meeting its various distinct needs. A company may choose commercial laboratories as a market segment and serve them through a portfolio of products.

Full Market Coverage: A company, if it is large enough, may decide to serve the entire market with the products that the market may require. Model T Ford and Coke in 6.5 oz bottles are an example of products offered by Ford motors and Coca Cola respectively for the entire vehicle and beverage market. The approach that ignores differences in customer needs and tries to serve the entire market with a single product is also called mass market approach. Since segment differences are ignored, the strategy is called undifferentiated marketing. Only big companies like Microsoft, Coca Cola or our own Reliance Industries can think of practicing this strategy but at their own peril!

Although large companies also have an option to cover a market by practicing differentiated marketing strategy – it involves offering distinct products to meet the needs of all distinct market segments- a strategy that involves higher costs but may generate overall more revenue as well, for the company.

9.4.2 Positioning a Market Offering

After careful selection of a target market segment design the next step is deciding the value proposition for the targeted segment of buyers. It requires choosing the value proposition for a product and establishing it such that it has a distinctive place in the target consumers' mental space. This act is called **Positioning.** Market positioning involves designing a product or service and image by the company such that it has a distinct as well as desirable place, relative to competitors, in the minds of target consumers.

Mahindra and Mahindra developed a successful positioning strategy for its SUV brand 'Scorpio' by clarifying the brand essence through its value proposition 'Luxury of a car and thrill of SUV' for its consumers (a segment that required lifestyle products). The value proposition combined the benefits of ruggedness of SUV and comfort and luxury of car. Scorpio brand occupied a distinct and desirable place in the minds of targets consumers.

Creating a distinct and desirable place in the minds of consumers requires identifying attributes in a product or service that are Important to the consumers (example safety may be an important attribute for a product or for a service like Airlines). Important attributes help a company to place their brand along with other competing brands for consideration by a consumer before they make a purchase. These attributes help in establishing the company's brand in the category of other competing brands which may offer to be its substitutes (a concept called Category Membership). This establishes the competitive frame of reference -the context in which company's brand is viewed by the consumers along with other competitive brands- for the company.

Important Attributes may create parity for the company's brand with other competing brands -called Points of Parity- but may not give distinctive identity to a brand. If majority of the Airlines have strong reputation for safety, this Important attribute although desirable but may not offer distinct identity to the company's brand. The company should now look at instilling those attributes in its brands that determine a consumer's choice and are called Determinant Attributes. They create unique associations of consumers with the brands- called Points of Differences. If all Airlines score high on Safety (an important attribute) then 'on time departure' may be a Determinant Attribute that may swing consumer's choice towards the company's brand.

A company can create meaningful differences through a suitable strategy called **Differentiation**. The strategy involves creating meaningful differentiations by a company so as to have an advantage over its competitors in the long run. A differentiation strategy can be based on **Product or Service differentiation** (Southwest Airlines- 'low cost, fun airlines'; **Image differentiation** (Raymonds 'Complete Man' image), **Channel differentiation** ('Nexa' channel of distribution by Suzuki for its certain brands); **Personnel differentiation** (Singapore Airlines differentiates effectively through its well trained employees) or any combination of these elements of product, service, image, channel or personnel. It should be noted that a difference should be established if it is important and distinctive from consumer's perspective; superior and pre-emptive from competitor's context; communicable, affordable and profitable from company's viewpoint.

9.4.3 Positioning Errors

A company should choose its positioning wisely, avoiding errors of **Underpositioning** – when company gives too broad picture of a brand; customers don't find anything distinct; **Overpositioning** – when company creates too narrow picture of a brand; too much focus on a particular position; **Confused or Muddled Positioning-** when company creates a confused image of the brand, consumer is not sure what brand actually offers- happens when company changes its position too often; **Doubtful**

Positioning-happens when company offers hard to believe benefits, like instant cure to baldness!.

9.4.4 Building Brands

A company that has done its homework properly (in terms strategic marketing- creating an effective STP strategy) is set to create an intangible asset for itself- the brand. It can be- Apple, Google, Amazon – a few of the most valuable global brands or Tata, SBI, LIC, Reliance which are a few of the most valuable Indian brands. Brand, an intangible asset, is "a name, term, sign, symbol, or design, or a combination of them, intended to identify the goods or services of one seller or group of sellers and to differentiate them from those of competitors," as has been defined by the American Marketing Association.

A strong brand creates loyal customers and competitive advantage that is sustainable over a period, besides host of other advantages it brings to the company.

Marketing Advantages of Strong Brands

- Improved Perceptions of Product Performance
- Greater Loyalty
- Less Vulnerability to competitive marketing actions
- Less vulnerability to marketing crises
- Larger margins
- More inelastic consumer response to price increases
- More elastic consumer response to price decreases
- Greater trade cooperation and support
- Increased marketing communication effectiveness
- Possible licensing opportunities
- Additional brand extension opportunities
- Improved employee recruiting and retention
- Greater financial marketing returns

Source: *Kotler Philip et al, 2013, 14th Edition, Marketing Management - A South Asian Perspective, Pearson Education*

The value that a brand adds to a product or service is called brand equity. The interplay of brand elements-name, logo, symbol, package design etc.- creates differences in consumer responses towards marketing of a product or service. If the consumer response is favorable, brand is said to create positive brand equity where as an unfavorable consumer response to the marketing of product or service as a brand results in negative brand equity.

This requires a careful application of brand elements to a product or service. The branding strategy may therefore range from choosing new brand elements through marketing research, to applying existing brand elements (if a company already has well established brand) or a use of a combination of new and existing brand elements, for the new product or service that a company plans to launch.

The four general strategies to choose a brand name are:

Individual Brand Name: a company can choose to have a separate brand name in each category of products it is selling (P&G successful brands Ariel and Tide in fabric care category and brands like Pantene, Heads and Shoulders, Rejoice in Hair Care category are case in point).

Blanket Family Name: a company following this strategy uses blanket family name for various products in diverse product categories. (Tata Group successfully ties it reputation to sell from salt to steel -Tata Salt, Tata Steel -using blanket family name).

Separate family Name for all products: Aditya Birla uses this strategy to brand its various products in different product categories using a separate family name like Ultratech for cement and Hindalco for aluminium.

Combination of company name and individual brand name: Sony uses it to brand its various products in different categories by combining company name and individual name like Sony Vaio (laptops), Sony Xperia (smartphones), Sony Bravia (Color televisions).

9.5 Key Terms Discussed/ Summary

Mass Marketing involves a seller engaging in mass production, distribution and promotion of a single product for all the buyers.

Micromarketing involves focusing marketing efforts for marketing product or services to smaller groups of customers and can be done at four levels- **Market Segment, Niches, Local Areas and Individual marketing.**

Descriptive and Behavioural characteristics are two broad groups of variables to segment consumer markets. The marketers look at the descriptive characteristics- geographic, demographic and psychographic of the consumers and the behavioral characteristics ie., the consumer responses.

Market Targeting is the process in which the company **evaluates attractiveness** of each customer group (ie., market segments it has identified using segmentation variables) based on certain criteria.

Marketing Mix comprises of Product, Price, Place and Promotion called the four Ps. The three additional elements –people, Process and Physical Evidence- along with the four Ps make the Services Marketing Mix.

Market positioning involves designing a product or service and image by the company such that it has a distinct as well as desirable place, relative to competitors, in the minds of target consumers.

Differentiation is the strategy by which a company can create meaningful differences in its offering made to the target consumer segment, as compared to the competitors.

Positioning Errors made by a company include Under positioning, Over positioning, Muddled positioning and Doubtful positioning.

Brand, an intangible asset, is "a name, term, sign, symbol, or design, or a combination of them, intended to identify the goods or services of one seller or group of sellers and to differentiate them from those of competitors," as has been defined by the American Marketing Association.

Review Questions

1. Define Micromarketing and explain the levels at which it can be done?

2. What is a Flexible Marketing Offering?

3. Describe the key elements used for segmenting consumer markets.

4. Describe the criteria for deciding the attractiveness of a market segment.

5. Explain how a company can wisely choose the value proposition for its targeted market segment.

Applied Questions

1. For a major Indian brand like Amul, describe the brand portfolio it has created and identify the core brand values for Amul.

2. 'The growth of Internet will fuel micromarketing efforts for companies'. Comment.

3. Discuss how a company should carefully choose a design for selecting a target market after assessing different market segments.

4. Evaluate how Mahindra & Mahindra has positioned its Scorpio brand in the market place.

5. 'A small business due to its resource constraints have to look for some creative ways for positioning and building successful brands without losing the focus and consistency in its marketing efforts'. Discuss

Interesting Facts

'Our entrepreneurs can beat the best from the world: Nandan Nilekani'

Source: www.moneycontrol.com/news/business/our; First Published on Jan 25, 2019 09:26 pm

Amid concerns on how to foster local entrepreneurship in the face of the hyper competition and pitches for safeguarding the local entrepreneurs' interest being made, Nandan Nilekani, said we are the only nation where the local entrepreneurs have to compete with the offerings from the best around the world, particularly those from the US and China. He said it in a Bombay Management Association event on startups. He pointed that India is at an interesting juncture where private innovation is being supported by government through programmes like Aadhar, which he helmed, or the Unified Payment Interface.

"We need innovation more than ever before. We face challenges in every aspect--water, education, healthcare, environment, and infrastructure among others. You name it and we have a challenge," Nilekani said. He warned that "business as usual" will not work given the challenges that we face, and said **innovation with scale** is the only way forward. It is the only way to meet the aspirations of over a billion people exposed to latest developments in the technology, media and entertainment spaces, and "are impatient for improvement their lives", he said.

Nilekani said government is also ushering in innovation through its policies and initiatives, which include Aadhar, GST and UPI. Direct benefit transfers straight into citizens' accounts alone have resulted in savings of over ₹ 90,000 crore in the past few years. The current scenario has set the stage for "us to leapfrog" onto every stage, be it education, healthcare, logistics and transportation, he said.

About Nandan Nilekeni

Source: www.infosys.com/.../Pages/nandan-nilekani.aspx; www.forbes.com/profile/ nandan-nilekani;http://timesofindia.indiatimes.com/articleshow/61732423.cms?utm_ source=contentofinterest&utm_medium=text&utm_campaign=cppst

Nandan Nilekani is listed at 80th position among the India's richest 2018 Forbe's list with a **real time net worth of $2 billion** as of 1/26/19. He is the cofounder of tech giant Infosys and its non-executive chairman since August 2017. He left Infosys in 2009, but was brought back in 2017 after a boardroom shakeup at the company and the sudden departure of its CEO.

Nandan Nilekani is the Co-founder and Chairman of EkStep, a not-for-profit effort to create a learner centric, technology based platform to improve basic literacy and numeracy for millions of children. He was most recently the Chairman of the Unique Identification Authority of India (UIDAI) in the rank of a Cabinet Minister. Nandan Nilekani was previously the co-chairman, Infosys Technologies Limited, which he co-founded in 1981.

Born in Bengaluru, Nilekani received his Bachelor's degree from IIT, Bombay. Fortune Magazine conferred him with "Asia's Businessman of the year 2003". In 2005 he received the prestigious Joseph Schumpeter prize for innovative services in economy, economic sciences and politics. In 2006, he was awarded the Padma Bhushan. He was also named Businessman of the year by Forbes Asia.

Time magazine listed him as one of the 100 most influential people in the world in 2006 & 2009. Foreign Policy magazine listed him as one of the Top 100 Global thinkers in 2010. He won The Economist Social & Economic Innovation Award for his leadership of India's Unique

Identification initiative (Aadhaar). In 2017, he received the Lifetime Achievement Award from E & Y. CNBC- TV 18 conferred India Business leader award for outstanding contributor to the Indian Economy-2017 and he also received the 22nd Nikkei Asia Prize for Economic & Business Innovation 2017. Nandan Nilekani is the author of "Imagining India" and co- authored his second book with Viral Shah, "Rebooting India: Realizing a Billion Aspirations".

Nilekani is credited with building Aadhar, India's mammoth identity card scheme, while chairman of the Unique Identification Authority of India. The tech magnate, who still has shares in Infosys, has been backing startups in recent years. He and wife Rohini signed the Giving Pledge in November 2017- pledging to give half of their wealth for philanthropy. The Giving Pledge was created by Bill and Melinda Gates and Warren Buffett in August 2010. Nilekanis are the fourth Indians to sign up for the network to sign up for the network of the world's wealthiest individuals committing half their wealth to philanthropy.

CASE DISCUSSION

'Small' Dominance- Case of an 'Ace'

(Source: https://commons.wikimedia.org/wiki/File:Tataintroace.jpg#/media/File:Tataintroace.jpg)

The emphatic success of the Tata Ace, a mini-truck with the engine capacity of less than one ton launched by Tata Motors in 2005, was due to deep understanding of the market needs and customer requirements.

The company realized that, as the Indian economy was growing, there would be a demand for smaller vehicles that can navigate through the narrow roads and by lanes of cities, small towns and villages to service the feeder routed. However, in order to compete effectively with the three-wheeler majors who dominated the market for small payload vehicles, the company needed to offer a better solution to the customers. The solution lay in the market, and that is where the engineers went-to talk to the transporters, the small traders and the farmers-to learn what they wanted.

Discussions with potential customers and a detailed market research indicated that potential customers needed vehicles for the last-mile distribution for carrying less than one-ton load over short distances. Such a vehicle should have low maintenance and operating costs, higher driver safety, and better driving comfort. Customers were willing to pay a marginally higher price for such a product. But what came out more strongly was the social status associated with a four-wheel vehicle. Based on customer insight, the company decided to introduce a vehicle positioned as a Tata truck in mini size with a competitive price tag while maintaining high quality standards. The cost reduction was achieved through using and modifying parts already developed for other vehicles in the Tata stable as well as through outsourcing, which constituted as much as 82% of the product.

In order to meet the customer requirement of rapid turnaround time, the company designed the vehicle to achieve higher top speeds than that of the other three-wheelers. The cargo bed was also made bigger. The product was designed with low turning radius to easily navigate the narrow lanes and bylanes of towns and villages. The sporty, car-like features ensured comfort in ride and handling. The overall design, fit and finish differentiated the vehicle from the three wheelers and at the same time, bestowed social prestige of the owner as well as the driver of the vehicle. The vehicle was advertised using the symbol of baby elephant with the tagline "small is big". Tata Ace was launched with a 15% to 20% higher price tag than that of a comparable model of a three-wheeler. As the vehicle operated only within a limited radius, the service points had to be closer to the vehicles operating routes. For this purpose, the company augmented the service network by training automobile garages that where branded as Tata-certified service point. Within 22 months of the launch of the vehicle, the company rolled out the 1,00,000ᵗʰ Ace, surpassing the company's optimistic targets. Besides the Indian market, Tata Ace was also launched in the markets in Sri Lanka and Nepal.

(Source: Kotler et. al, 2009, Marketing Management, 13ᵗʰ Edition, Pearson India Education Services.)

Questions

1. Explain the market positioning strategy of Tata Ace.

2. What are the key elements of the Tata Ace brand that have contributed to its success?

References

1. Kotler Philip, Keller K. L, Koshy A and Jha M, 2013, 14th Edition, Marketing Management – A South Asian Perspective, Pearson Education.

2. Ramasamy V.S. and Namkumari S, 2009, Marketing Management – Global Perspective Indian Context, Fourth Edition, Macmillan Publishers.

3. Baines P, Fill C et al., Marketing, 2013, Asian Edition, Oxford University Press.

4. Lovelock C, Writz J and Chaterjee J, 2018, Services Marketing : People, Technology, Strategy, Pearson India Education Services.

5. Berman B and Evans J.R., Chatterjee P. M., 2018, Retail Management – A Strategic Approach, 13th Edition, Pearson Education.

❑❑❑

10

The Importance of
Intellectual Property

Dr. Amit Kumar Marwah
(Professor, Acropolis Institute of Technology and Research, Indore, MP)
Manisha Gaur
(Assistant Professor, Swami Vivekanand College of Engineering, Indore, MP)

LEARNING OBJECTIVES

After reading this chapter, the reader should be able to:

1. Understand various aspects of Intellectual Property (IP), the stages of an invention cycle and the types of IPs,

2. Explain the process of obtaining a patent, what is patent infringement,

3. Explain trademarks and what is protected under trademark law, the process of obtaining a trademark,

4. Explain copyright, exclusions from copyright protection, how to obtain a copyright, what is copyright infringement, and copyrights & the Internet.

10.1 Introduction

The term Intellectual Property (IP) is not new. Knowingly or unknowingly people are dealing with any one of the Intellectual Property (IP) in their daily lives. Whether it is a novel one reads in the bus, or branded clothes one wears or the latest mobile phone in the market- IP is everywhere! And this makes it so valuable and worth protecting. Specially, in present times, when the world is observing strong waves of innovation, and to ride these waves and to reap the benefits of the innovation and hard work involved in putting ideas to commercial use stage, an innovator or rather anybody should have an idea about the concepts of Patents, Trademarks, Copyrights and other forms of IP. This also ensures that the time, money and energy spent is fruitfully recovered till the benefits become open for use by all.

IP relates to original ideas or results that emanate from brainstorming or research, and generally it includes some critical business information. IP contributes enormously in the development of any nation's economy and society. The range of intellectual property is not limited to any field of engineering, literary artistic and even musical works.

Any thought or idea which is developed by anyone into new or creative work in any field comes under intellectual property. The legal rights with which person or entity protects his/her intellectual work or properties from being used or exploited are broadly termed as "Intellectual Property Rights" or IPR.

One might think that IPR is a recent buzz word but the first recorded reference to IPR dates to 500 BC. On 14th July 1967. World Intellectual Property Organization (WIPO) was established to protect IP throughout the world.

IPRs are recognized globally for the following reason:

- They provide incentive to the individual or an entity for new creations.
- They provide recognition to the creators and inventors behind the IP.
- They ensure the tangible reward for the IP.
- They endure and maintain the availability of the original products.
- They are important for economic growth and advancement in technology sector.

They are important for business growth in the field of technology.

10.2 Stages of an Invention Cycle

It is a general assumption that IP protection is required only when the final product is ready. But this is a common misconception. IPR associated with the product life cycle can be classified into the following stages (as a typical invention cycle):

(*i*) Idea Stage

At the idea stage, an individual or a company can either file a Provisional Patent Application (PPA) or keep it a trade secret to safeguard an idea.

(*ii*) Research & Development Stage

This important stage of the invention cycle demands appropriate IP protection. Patents, trademarks, copyrights of design registration can be applied for.

(*iii*) Testing Stage

Since this the last stage before the product is launched, it is recommended to complete all the IP filings before the end of this stage. This ensures safeguarding

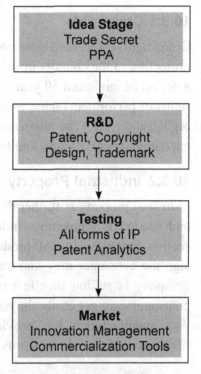

Fig. 10.1: Stages of an Invention Cycle

of the product from the potential infringement before it is launched into the market.

(*iv*) Commercialization Stage

Once the product is available in the market, continuous monitoring of IP is needed. Also, use of innovation management strategies and IP commercialization tools becomes essential to get the best results.

10.3 Types of Intellectual Property (IP)

Intellectual Properties (IPs) are broadly classified into two categories, namely:

1. Copyrights
2. Industrial Property

10.3.1 Copyrights

Copy right is the auto-generated Intellectual Property right. It provides protection to the creators in the field of literary, music or artistic work for a period of minimum 50 years. Rights related to copyright includes all the rights of performers (actor, musicians, and singers), rights of broadcasting organisation etc. The main reason behind protecting such works is to encourage creativity and intellectually stimulate the general public.

10.3.2 Industrial Property

Industrial property is further divided into two sections: one is information and second is innovation. Industrial property dealing with information section includes sign of products and services so that by seeing that sign the consumer may know about the product or services. If a mobile company is selling mobile having the sign of a bitten apple, then the consumer may get easily the name of that company by which the product was manufactured. For providing such protection industrial property 'Trademark' is used to identify and distinguish the product or service of

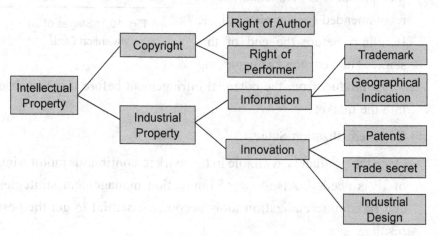

Fig. 10.2: Types of Intellectual Property

an entity from another; 'Geographical Indication 'indicates the particular area from where goods are manufactured or produced (e.g. Alphonso Mango has received Geographical Indication (GI) tag in October 2018).

Another division of Industrial property focuses on Innovation which includes Patents (e.g. a technical invention), Industrial Design (the rectangular design of an iPhone) and Trade Secrets (e.g. manufacturing process of Mc Donald Pizza).

The entire lot of IP can again be divided into 2 categories from business perspective:

(*i*) the limited life IP where the duration is limited after which it comes into the public domain and people can use it and

(*ii*) the unlimited life IP where it is not subjected to renewal, but it can be kept alive forever.

10.3.3 Brief Information about Major forms of IP

Patent is a statutory/legal right granted to a patentee for owning the right which prevents others either to make, use, sell, or import an invention for a limited period of time, usually up to 20 years if it fulfils the criteria of being new and non-obvious to an expert in the technology area, and has a utility or application (for example, any technological invention).

Patents can be of following three types:

(*i*) **Utility patent:** This patent may be granted to anyone who either invents or discovers any new and/or useful process, or a machine, or an article of manufacture, or any composition of matter, or does any new and useful improvement(s);

(*ii*) **Design patent:** This patent may be granted to anyone who invents a new or an original design for an article of manufacture; and

(*iii*) **Plant patent:** This patent may be granted to anyone who either invents or discovers and asexually reproduces any distinct or a new variety of plant.

Trademark is a common law right to protect a unique mark such a name, logo or other form of visual identity which identifies goods or services offered by an entity (for example, the bitten apple logo of Apple Inc®).

Copyright is another form of IP which legally protects the original (either published or unpublished) works of authorship that are fixed in a tangible form. Copyright laws protect paintings, photographs, literary works, live performances, movies, and software (or example, rights over musical compositions, novels, paintings etc.).

A Geographical Indication (GI) is a sign which is used on products that either has a specific geographical origin or possess qualities or has a reputation due to that origin. Essentially, the GI tag provides an assurance of quality and uniqueness, attributed to the place of its origin (for example, Darjeeling tea, Nagpur oranges, Madhubani paintings, Kashmir pashmina, etc. and recently in October 2018 Alphonso Mango has received GI tag for Maharashtra).

Design registration is a legal right to protect a new and innovative design for an existing product. It provides protection to the visual and aesthetic aspect of a product (for example, unique shape of a phone or a car).

10.4 Who can Apply for a Patent?

According to patent law, a person who has invented a new product or design or implemented a new idea may apply/file for a patent, but with certain exceptions. For some of the cases if the inventor may not be able to apply then the application for the patent can still be processed. Following are some of the cases where the inventor is not able to apply for patent but still the application for the patent can be processed:

- if the inventor is deceased or incapacitated then the application for the patent may be processed by the legal administrator or the legal representative (e.g. Guardian).
- if more than two persons have invented a new creation then the application can be processed as joint inventors.

10.5 The Process of Obtaining a Patent

To encourage innovation and scientific research, use of new technology and for industrial progress the patent law is constituted in India. India is a member-state of Word Intellectual Property Organisation *(WIPO). WIPO is* an international organisation which is responsible for the promotion and the protection of IP throughout the world. In respect of patents, India is also a member of the following International Organisations and Treaties:

- World Trade Organization (WTO) (w.e.f. Jan. 1-1995).
- World Intellectual Property Organisation *(WIPO)* (since Jan. 1, 1995).
- Paris Convention for the protection of Industrial Property (w.e.f. Dec. 7, 1998).
- Patent Co-operation Treaty (PCT) (w.e.f. Dec. 7, 1998).
- Budapest Treaty (w.e.f. Dec. 17, 2001).

The various steps involved in obtaining a patent are as follows:

(*i*) Step 1: It is always recommended to conduct Prior Art search to check whether the invention is novel or not. After the search if it is found novel, then the applicant may proceed for filing the patent application. Who can file application is mentioned in article 2. based on the circumstances.

(*ii*) Step 2: The patent application along with provisional specifications or complete specifications may be filed at any of the following offices in India:

(*a*) **Mumbai Patent Office:** For Madhya Pradesh, Goa, Gujarat, Chhattisgarh, Maharashtra, Union territories of Daman, Diu, Dadar & Nagar Haweli.

(*b*) **New Delhi Patent Office:** For Jammu & Kashmir, Punjab, Rajasthan, Haryana, Himachal Pradesh, Uttar Pradesh, Uttaranchal, Delhi, and the union territory of Chandigarh.

(*c*) **Chennai Patent Office:** For Kerala, Andhra Pradesh, Karnataka, Tamil Nadu, and Union Territory of Pondicherry and Lakshadweep.

(*d*) **Kolkata Patent Office:** For Rest of India.

After successful passing through the patent office, an application number will be issued by the patent office. The applicant can track the status of the application using that application number.

(*iii*) Step 3: The patent office publishes the patent application in the official Patents Journal, published every week by the patent office on its website after the 18 months from the date of filling application or the date when the application is recommended to the check the novelty of the invention (whichever is earlier). On publication, the patent specification including drawings and deposits are available in the public domain.

(*iv*) Step 4: The application is then passed through the process of patent examination where it is allotted to the patent examiner who has a specialization in that particular field for which the invention is concerned. For this process the applicant has to fill the formal request with official fee within the 48 months from the date of filling application or the date when the application is recommended to the check the novelty of the invention (whichever is earlier).

(*v*) Presently in patent office there are four broad categories of the technical specification namely; (i) Chemistry and allied subjects (ii) Biotechnology, Microbiology and allied subjects (iii) Electrical & Electronics and related subjects (iv) Mechanical & other subjects.

(*vi*) Step 5: Within 1-3 months the First Examination Report is issued based on the procedural as well as patentability grounds.

(*vii*) Step 6: The application has to pass through the changes and the objections made in the step 5 by the applicant under next 12 month. If all the changes and objections are overcome then a patent is granted for the 20 years. If the required changes and objections are not overcome within the given time frame then the patent application could get rejected. A patent is granted only when the application has not been successfully opposed by the third party.

(*viii*) Step 7: Once the patent is issued, the applicant needs to maintain the patent by paying an annual renewal fee from third year onward till the life of the patent before patent office. It is compulsory to commercialise your patent within 36 months from grant of patent for which you need to submit a status of working of the patent periodically. In case the applicant does not submit the working of the patent as stipulated by the patent office, then the patent can be revoked by the patent office.

10.6 Patent Infringement

Under the Indian Patent Act 1970, there are no defined activities of the patent infringement; however, the act provides the protection rights to a patentee to exclude any other parties from selling, manufacturing, importing, using etc. It is an act of prohibition for the use of patented invention without permission from the patent holder. It can be therefore concluded that violation of the monopoly rights constitutes patent infringement.

As per the section 104(A) of Indian Patent Act (IPA), 1970 in a patent infringement suit, where

- The subject matter or content of a patent is a part of the process of obtaining a new product, or
- There is substantial likelihood that a identical product can be made by the patented process, and
- A patent holder or a person having the interest in the patent from him, has proved that the product is identical to the product that is obtained directly by the process which is patented.

In the above conditions if the patent holder, through the reasonable efforts, could not prove or establish that the infringer has actually use the process then the court may give directions to the defendant so as to prove that the process used by him/her to obtain the product, which is identical to the product obtained by the patented process, is altogether different from the patented process.

As per the section 47 of IPA 1970, there are following exceptions for the infringement and non-infringement activities:

- For government use
- For research work
- For supplying patented drugs to health institutes.
- Use of patented invention on foreign vessels
- Parallel import
- As a ground for defence

10.7 Types of Trademarks

Trademarks are one of the forms of Intellectual Property (IP). It is separately used for product & services. It is named as product trademark and service trademark as per the application. It is represented as ^{TM} with the name of product or services.

Following are the important functions of the trademark:

- It provides the exclusive right to the owner of the mark to use the mark to identify the product and services.
- It provides protection from making fraudulent use of trademarks.
- It provides protection from trademark infringement.
- It protects skills and intellect of any person or company.

A Trademark falls under different class based upon the goods manufactured and services offered. WIPO (World Intellectual Property Organisation) has administered The Nice Classification which is an international classification of goods and services. The 11th edition of the NCL which came into force on January 1, 2018, provides a comprehensive list of different classes of trademarks. There are total 45 classes of trademarks out of which 1 to 34 falls under the category of goods and 35-45 deals with services.

10.7.1 Various Classes of Trademarks

There are 45 different classes of the trademarks and each class categorizes what is protected under each class.

10.7.2 Trademarks Exclusions

One will be unable to obtain registration for trademarks which are not having any distinctive character.

- Trademarks which exclusively consist of signs or indications and which only designate the quality, quantity, kind, desired purpose, value or geographical origin of the goods or services to be traded under the mark will not be registered.
- Such signs will not be registered which exclusively indicate the time of production of goods or that of rendering of services.

- Trademarks which consist exclusively of signs or indications which are customary in the current language or in the bona fide and established trade practices will not be registered.

- Trademarks which exclusively consist of the shape resulting from the nature of the goods, or a shape which is needed to obtain a technical result or a shape which provides substantial value to the goods are also excluded from protection.

- Trademarks which are contrary to public policy or to the principles of morality, applications made in bad faith or trademarks which are to deceive the public with their nature, quality or geographical origin of the goods or service will not be registered.

However, if a trademark has acquired distinctiveness through its use, it will not be refused registration for the reasons in the paragraph above.

10.7.3 The Process of Obtaining a Trademark

Following is the process of obtaining a trademark:

Step 1: Once the mark has been finalized, it is recommended to conduct a trademark search to check availability and strengths of the mark.

Step 2: After a positive result the trademark application is filed before a appropriate trademark registry at the following Trademark offices in / India

(*a*) **Mumbai Registry:** For Maharashtra Madhya Pradesh & Goa.

(*b*) **New Delhi Registry:** For Punjab, Haryana, Uttar Pradesh, Himachal Pradesh, Jammu & Kashmir, Union Territories of Delhi & Chandigarh.

(*c*) **Kolkata Registry:** For Bihar, Orissa, West Bengal, Assam, Arunachal Pradesh, Manipur, Mizoram, Meghalaya, Sikkim, Tripura, Nagaland and Andaman & Nicobar Island.

(*d*) **Ahmedabad Registry:** For Rajasthan, Gujarat and Union Territories of Daman, Diu, Dadra and Nagar Haveli.

(*e*) **Chennai Registry:** For Tamil Nadu, Andhra Pradesh, Kerala, Karnataka, and Union Territory of Pondicherry and Lakshadweep island.

Step 3: Trademark registry office issued an application number and official receipt to applicant. Around 10-12 months will be taken to receive the

Examination Report. The applicant has to make necessary changes and objection suggested in examination report within 30 days of the reception of the examination report.

Step 4: After that the mark is published in the official Gazette of Trademark Registry. This is the opposition period of three month where the third party can oppose the mark from the date of publication.

Step 5: If the third party has no objection on the mark then the Trademark Registry Office will issue a registration certificate.

Trademark registration is valid for a period of 10 years and has to be renewed once the registration phase is over. After receiving the certificate, the applicant is eligible to use the symbol ^{TM}. The applicant has the right to use the symbol ® while processing through the registration process. However, there are certain rules to use the symbol ® such as:

1. It can only be used once the mark is registered and not while the application is pending.

2. It can only be used in connection with the goods and services listed in the trademark application.

3. It can only be used as long as the registration is alive and active.

10.8 Copyrights

Copyright is an auto-generated Intellectual Property (IP) but still it comes under some exceptions. The following three exceptions are allowed for the use of a work without seeking permission from the copyright holder and by paying fees:

- *Fair use:* If any copyrighted material is used by other than the author for the fair purpose then the other person does not need to take permission. A four-factor analysis method must be applied to each use to ascertain whether the use is fair or not.

    (*i*) The first factor caters to the character and purpose of the use of the work.

    (*ii*) The second factor calls for the creativity of the work. Creative works are given more protection than those which are factual in nature.

(*iii*) The third factor considers the amount of the work that is being used. Generally, weightage in favour of fair use is given to a small amount of work where a large amount would be given more weightage in favour of requesting permission.

(*iv*) The fourth factor considers how the intended use of the work would impact the market for the work or the end use. Generally, the more restricted is the use, there will be less impact on the market.

- *Face to Face instructions:* In a traditional classroom with face-to-face teaching, the teacher or the instructor and the students of an (non-profit) educational institution are at the same place and the teaching and learning also takes place at the same time. In this type of arrangements all performances and displays of a work are allowed.

- *Virtual instructions:* Virtual instruction is when a course is delivered either fully online or when some parts of face-to-face instructions are taught online using learning management systems (LMS). Virtual instructions involve transmitting class materials to students via a digital medium.

10.8.1 What is Protected by a Copyright?

All the literary, dramatic, musical and artistic works and producers of cinematographs films and sound recording published or unpublished work are protected by Copyright Protection in India. Registration for copyright is not mandatory rather it is an auto-generated intellectual property right. However, it is advisable to register for the copyright. The copyrighted material is represented by the symbol ©.

The term or tenure of protection granted for copyright work varies and depends upon the work which is to be protected. Literary, musical or artistic works (other than photographs) are granted copyright protection for the period which covers the lifetime of the author and 60 year from the year in which the author dies. In case the work is not published or performed or offered for sale or broadcast to anyone, during the lifetime of the author, even then the copyright protection shall continue for the period of 60 years from the end of the year in which any of these acts are done relating to the works.

10.8.2 How to Obtain a Copyright?

Following are the steps to obtain a copyright:

Step 1: In India the copyright registry office is at New Delhi and applicant must apply in that office. It must contain a 'Statement of Particulars' (SoP) and 'Statement of Further Particulars' (SoFP). The application is processed with signature of the author himself or the advocate who is representing him and provided with the power of attorney.

Step 2: A filing number, a filing date and a receipt will be provided to the applicant by the copyright registry office after the application is accepted.

Step 3: For the period of 30 days the application undergoes through the process of objection by the third party. If there is any objection from the third party then a hearing will take place and the matter will be resolved during this period of 30 days.

Step 4: Next to this period the application is subjected to the examination phase if the there is no objection in step 4. If some corrections or changes are required in the application after the examination phase, then the applicant has given the period of 30 days to resolve it.

Step 5: After resolving the objections and the required changes, the Copyright Registry issues the registration certificate.

10.8.3 Copyright Infringement

Under the copyright Act the copyright owner is allotted with the exclusive right to protect his work and the process of using the copyrighted work without the permission of copyright owner is known as copyright infringement. There are three elements that must be needed in order for the infringement to occur.

1. A valid copyright should be possessed by the copyright holder.

2. The person who is allegedly infringing it must have access to the copyrighted work.

3. The duplication or copying of the copyrighted work should be outside the exceptions.

For copyright infringement the legal penalties are as below:

1. The infringer has to pay the actual amount of damages and profits.

2. A penalty in the range from $200 to $150,000 can be imposed for each work infringed.

3. The infringer has to pay for the attorney's fees and court costs.

4. The Court can issue an injunction to stop the infringing acts.

5. The Court can impound the illegal works.

6. The infringer can be sent to imprisonment.

10.8.4 Copyright & the Internet

Internet technology is developing quite faster than the laws that govern it. The legislation or the courts have established new laws that apply to the internet; copyright laws are among them. A very common myth about the internet is that any content that is posted online can be copied or downloaded. In reality, anything one browses on the internet is of equal potential of being protected by copyright as anything one sees in the library or any book shop.

CASES

Case - 1 (Benz)

Someone, selling undergarments in India, used the Benz Tristar logo. The authorities stopped it because the right holder has the right to use the mark in the way he or she wants. So, even if you are not working in those businesses, you can stop others from using it. You could also prevent people from using it. If it is a reputed mark, the exclusive set of rights on a patent related to the right to make, the right to sell the right to use, the right to offer for sale and the right to import an invention lies with the patentee.

1. Why Benz Tristar logo was prohibited to be used for an undergarments company, even though the businesses were different?

2. Are there any limitations related to the scope of use of logos?

3. What the undergarment company could have done, if it really wanted to use the Benz logo?

4. Can you cite any similar case?

Case - 2 (Apple wins trademark case against Xiaomi)

Apple Inc has successfully prevented the Chinese smart phone maker Xiaomi, Inc from registering its "Mi Pad" tablet computer as a trademark in European Union on the grounds that the name was too similar to Apple's "iPad". The European Union's General Court, had given the decision that Mi Pad was not to be registered as a trademark because the similarity of the signs would confuse the consumers. Even though the iPads of both Xiaomi's Mi and Apple are both tablet computers, the court said that is not sufficient to consider the dissimilarity between the signs, resulting from the presence of the additional letter 'M' at the beginning of Mi Pad, and a high degree of visual and phonetic similarity between the two signs still remains.

In 2014, Xiaomi filed an application with the Intellectual Property Office of the European Union (EUIPO) to register Mi Pad under an EU trademark. Subsequently, Apple lodged a complaint which was upheld by EUIPO in 2016 on the basis that consumers might think Mi Pad was a variation on Apple's iPad trademark. The court agreed with the decision of EUIPO and conveyed that English-speaking consumers would most likely understand the prefix "Mi" as meaning "my" and therefore could pronounce the "i" of Mi Pad and iPad in the same manner.

(Source: https://telecom.economictimes.indiatimes.com/news/apple-wins-trademark-case-against-xiaomi/61941109)

(a) Can two similar sounding signs be registered in different countries?

(b) Suggest your views against the act by Xiaomi.

(c) If you were a patent attorney representing Xiaomi, what would be your strong points?

(d) Can you discuss any similar case?

Questions for Self Assessment

1. What is the term of a Patent in India?

(*i*) 5 years   (*ii*) 10 years

(*ii*) 15 years   (*iv*) 20 years

2. Which one of the following cannot be protected by Intellectual Property Rights?

(*i*) A book on mathematics   (*ii*) A program code in C++

(*iii*) Lyrics of a song   (*iv*) A new product

3. A patent can be granted if the invention is

(*i*) Novel   (*ii*) Non-obvious

(*iii*) Capable of industrial applicability

(*iv*) All of the above

4. Patent Amendments Acts were carried out in the following year

(*i*) 1996   (*ii*) 2000

(*iii*) 2002   (*iv*) 2008

5. Which of the following inventions can be patented as per Section 3 of the Patents Act, 1970?

(*i*) A method of treating human beings from diabetes

(*ii*) A topography of integrated circuits

(*iii*) A human made microorganism

(*iv*) A perpetual motion machine

6. Which among the following form is used for application for grant of patent

(*i*) Form 1   (*ii*) Form 2

(*iii*) Form 3   (*iv*) Form 4

7. In the case of application where the complete specification is filed directly, the priority date for such applications

(*i*) Date on which the provisional application was filed

(*ii*) Date on which the patent application for a divisional application was filed

(*iii*) Date on which the complete specification was filed

(*iv*) All of the above

8. Once the Controller publishes the notice of a surrender of patent, any person interested may, within _____ give notice of opposition to the Controller

   (*i*) 1 month   (*ii*) 2 months

   (*iii*) 3 months   (*iv*) 4 months

9. An invention capable of industrial application means that the invention is capable of

   (*i*) Being assembled in an industry

   (*ii*) Being imported by the industry

   (*iii*) Being exported by the industry

   (*iv*) Being used in the industry

10. An applicant, originally a resident from Mumbai, now residing in USA and runs his Business in USA, files an application in India through a law firm based in Delhi. The applicant's appropriate office for submitting the application is

    (*i*) USA   (*ii*) Mumbai

    (*iii*) Delhi   (*iv*) Chennai

References

1. Gupta N. Malakar Sreemoyee. (2015). *Intellectual Property Portfolio.* Berlin: Small industrial development Bank of India (SIDBI).

2. Indian IP Law. Retrieved from URL http://www.ssrana.in/Intellectual%20 Property/Patents/Patent-Infringement-in-India.aspx.

3. The Patents ACT, 1970 (April 23, 2017). Retrieved from URL http://ipindia. nic.in/writereaddata/Portal/ev/sections-index.html.

4. Access the nice classification. (January 1, 2019). Retrieved from URL https://www.wipo.int/classifications/nice/en/

5. Nice classification (trademarks). (February, 24, 2018). Retrieved from URL https://euipo.europa.eu/ohimportal/en/nice-classification

6. Inclusion and Exclusion of Trademark. (Sep 01, 2017). Retrieved from URL https://enterslice.com/learning/inclusion-exclusion-trademark/

7. Who can apply for a patent? (April, 2016). Retrieved from URL https:// www.prv.se/en/patents/applying-for-a-patent/before-the-application/who-can-apply-for-a-patent/

8. Procedure to obtain patents in India (October, 2018). Retrieved from URL https://www.pharmatutor.org/articles/procedure-obtain-patent-india.

9. Copyrights exceptions. (June, 2019). Retrieved from URL https://www.lib. purdue.edu/uco/CopyrightBasics/exceptions.html

10. Stim, R. (2018) *Patents Copyright & Trademarks: An Intellectual Property Desk Reference.* USA.

11. Lanning G. Bryer, Scott J. Lebson, Matthew D. Asbell (2011) Intellectual Property Operations and *Implementation in the 21st Century Corporation.* John Wiley & Sons.

12. Alexander I. Poltorak, Paul J. Lerner. (2002). *Essentials of Intellectual Property.* New York : Wiley.

13. Gupta. N   Malakar.Sreemoyee. (2015). *Intellectual Property Portfolio.* Berlin: Small industrial development Bank of India (SIDBI).

14. Retrieved from URL on (Sep, 2018) http://ipindia.nic.in/ipr/patents.htm

15. Retrieved from URL on   (Oct, 2018) http://ipindia .nic.in/tmr_new/default. htm

16. Retrieved from URL on (Nov, 2018) http://copyright.gov.in/

Additional Reading

1. Gallié, E.P., & Legros, D. (2012). French firms' strategies for protecting their intellectual property. Research Policy, 41(4), 780-794.

2. Grossman, G.M., Lai, E.L.-C., 2004. International protection of intellectual property. Am. Econ. Rev. 94 (5), 1635–1653.

3. Park, W., 2008. International patent protection: 1960–2005. Res. Policy 37 (4), 761–766.

4. Cohen, W.M., et. al. (2000). Protecting their intellectual assets: Appropriability conditions and why U.S. manufacturing firms patent (or not), National Bureau of Economic Research Working Paper 7552.

5. http://ipindiaservices.gov.in/agentregister/agentlisttest.aspx

6. http://paai.org.in/paa/resources/innovators/list-registered-patent-agents-india/

7. http://ipindiaservices.gov.in/GirPublic/DetailsGIR.aspx

8. http://ipindia services.gov.in/patentsearch/index.aspx

9. http://ipindia services.gov.in/eregister/eregister.aspx

10. http://ipindia services.gov.in/designapplicationstatus/designstatus.aspx

❑❑❑

11

Challenges of Business Growth: Preparation and Evaluation

Dr. Himani Singhal
(Assistant Professor, DPGITM, Sector 34, Gurugram)

LEARNING OBJECTIVES

After reading this chapter, the reader should be able to:

1. Understand the meaning of sustained growth.
2. Explain how a firm may adequately prepare for its growth.
3. Discuss the reasons firms pursue growth.
4. Understand the significance of knowing about the stages of growth.

A Story Full of Inspiration

A winner's smile brings positivity around; an encouraging smile wore by Mr. Vijay Shekhar Sharma. A man who dreamt of Silicon Valley and become a entrepreneur. He tasted victory the hard way. There was time when he had only ₹ 10 in his pocket and now the current value of his company is more than $3 billion in the market. This achievement was not easy at all. Vijay was not very good in English, but he mastered it with the help of books, secondhand magazines and his friends. He stopped attending college and decided to make internet his playground and started building his own content management *system with his college mates. The content was so good that they were used by the biggest news publications including The Indian Express. But again, dark time entered his life and his own friends left him bankrupted. Big eureka moment came in 2011 when he pitched the idea of entering the payment ecosystem. He put 1% of his equity on the table and tried to convince the board members. As a result, the first face of Paytm, Pay Through Mobile, came into picture. The trust he builds with customer lead this company to shinning sky.*

11.1 Appreciating the Nature of Business Growth

Entrepreneurs most of the time are represented as Heroes as they are the risk takers, innovators with full confidence. Entrepreneurial venture is associated with the expression of individualism where, strategies are initiated and made by one prominent individual (entrepreneur) and the focus is on opportunities rather than problems. Decision making is always guided by the founder's vision and epitomized by large bold decisions. The primary and the important goal for any organization is growth. Though an individual is perceived to be leading the entrepreneurial activity, others involvement is also very important – who often occupy crucial roles within the organization. Before diving deep into the nature of business growth let's discuss some important terminologies which will help us to understand the concept clearly.

- **Vision–** Vision is dreamt of more than it is articulated. Entrepreneurs envision the position that their firm or company would like to attain in distant future. Sometimes in the starting it is not even evident to the entrepreneur who usually thinks of a vision but gradually becomes clear as they took actions to materialize their dreams. Vision also provide a roadmap to firm's future.

- **Mission** – Mission primarily reflects what business we are in and what we do? A mission broadly describes firm present capabilities, customer focus and business activities. Directly or indirectly mission statements talks about moving on track, growth and achieving new dimensions which is possible by following the path laid by the management of the organization.

Just to have a clearer picture, Vision and mission statements of TATA International are stated below

> **TATA International**
>
> **Vision-** To be globally significant in each of our chosen business by 2025.
>
> **Mission -** To be the most reliable global network for customers and suppliers, that delivers value through products and services. To be a responsible value creator for all our stakeholders

- **Business** – 'What is business' is almost same as asking what mission of the organization is and in simple statement, it is a declaration of an organizations life cell. Therefore, it is very important that the mission statement should be clear and can be easily understood by the people working for that organization.
- **Profit** – For any business, enterprise or organization the primary goal is to make profit.
- **Growth** – Growing business into new directions is also important and the graph for any business should be moving upward.
- **Power** – Every business needs vast resources for its operations. With resources gaining power is also an important goal as command on vast resources lead enterprise toward holding of economic and political power.
- **Employee satisfaction and development** – Without people there is no business. A satisfied employee is always a boon to the organization. So, caring well for the employee's satisfaction and providing them with development features help the organization grow faster.
- **Quality Products and Services** – Customer is the king of the market, it is vital to keep them by proving better and improved goods and services.
- **Market Leadership** – Organization enjoys leadership only and only if it has succeeded and earned a niche for oneself in the market for which innovation is the key. Keep innovating and keep leading.
- **Challenges** – To explore opportunities one should be able to accept challenges and achieve success.

- **Joy of creation** – When the entrepreneur experiences the transition phase where his/her idea gets converted into a product or service, he/she celebrates the joy, "the joy of creation".

- **Service to society** – Being an indispensable part of the society, every entrepreneur wants to and should serve the society by contributing towards several activities.

Business Growth is that crucial phenomenon which keeps the business/enterprise alive. This liveliness can be explained beautifully with the help of a wrist watch. Everyone knows that traditionally the basic and only function of a wristwatch considered was to display time. But, with the changing scenario and time, its utility is also changing converting a wristwatch into a fashion accessory; fitness tool moreover a style statement, focusing that you need to have more than one watch. It is true that one's personality is reflected through his/her appearance where accessories play an important role. Likewise, high value and antique watches reflects one's personality and status. And these antique watches are also used as pieces of art, depending on the bearer wish.

How to Analyze Growth?

It is always arguable that one factor measures growth for one organization and that same factor may not serve the other organization(e.g., increase in employment). Let's have a brief description on some of the common factors:

- **Motivation:** Growth is not universally desired or sought by small business owners. Though growth motivation is not considered to be the single determining factor in explaining whether or not a firm in fact achieves growth, it can be expected to significantly influence the strategic choices made by those that seek it.

- **Education:** Level of education earned by the entrepreneur may not really be an end, but rather it can upgrade the business visionary's inspiration and capacity to utilize various abilities that are helpful in overseeing endeavors. It can likewise give certain control on particular points of interest to business visionaries who start a new business in territories in which they have been formally educated (e.g., bio-innovation or visual communication) and it might additionally set the proprietor's desires for their endeavor profit in a situation that is best met with regards to a growing business.

- **Ownership/management experience:** Entrepreneurs having previous experience of owning or managing other business may be naturally more cautious than those who are the new ones.

- **Number of founders:** There one school of thoughts, one saying that growth orientation in small businesses that are established with multiple founders may get distracted by conflict amongst the founders , but there are empirical studies saying that businesses managed by multiple owners are likelier to grow faster at better speed than those managed by individuals acting alone.

- **Sector:** This factor shows that the sector in which that organization is operating is also very important in determining the growth rate of any organization.

- **Location:** Location in which the organization will operate is also very important. This factor should be taken care of very seriously as selection of wrong location may lead to unfair situation.

- **Size:** Here, "size" relates to the number of employees in the firm. For the most part, smaller firms tend to be developing more quickly than bigger firms, except for non-business sole proprietorships, huge numbers of which are not built up with a view to giving work to anybody separated from the proprietor.

- **Business management practices/strategies:** The ability of a business to plan its development, take right decision at required time supports and pushes the firm' stability to survive and grow.

- **Workforce training:** Trained work force is always a boon the organization.

- **Technical resources:** It is essential to walk with the world and for that, organization needs timely up gradation of all the resources.

- **Planning:** Existence of step by step planning, gives a clear path to create success stories.

- **External advice and support:** Taking advice for the betterment of the organization can never go is usually beneficial and if that support is taken from experts outside the organization may turn the bar graph in upward direction.

• **Financial resources:** External financers may open up financial resources but dilute ownership. Entrepreneurs are not comfortable in sharing their ownership easily resulting in minimum help from the external financers and banks become wary of lending to such firms, often demanding safety-net collateral that many small business owners are unable to produce.

11.2 Staying Committed to a Core Strategy

It is believed that if one wants to achieve growth then try hands on new things as introduction of new product, new technology, expansion of business, diversifications and many more. But many firms are seeking success by focusing on their core business for example offering the core product in new formats or versions. They tend to make the core of the brand as distinctive as possible as Galaxy chocolates has successfully competed with Cadbury by positioning itself as "your partner in chocolate indulgence" and featuring smoother products shapes, more refined taste, and sleeker packaging. They drive distribution through both existing and new channels – Costa coffee the ranked one coffee shop in United Kingdom's, has established new distribution routes using drive-through outlets, vending machines at service stations and in school coffee shops.

Entrepreneurs are good at foreseeing opportunities but under this strategy it is not necessary to chase every growth opportunity presented. If not taken care off may lead to competitive disadvantage and too many distractions. Entrepreneurs follow typical growth with commitment to core strategy where they start selling a product and service that is consistent with their core strategy; this can be explained with the help of stability strategy - an attempt by an organization at incremental improvement of functional performance. The strategy is relevant for organizations operating in a reasonably certain and predictable environment is a mindful decision to not attempt anything new and to move ahead with the present business definition.

A stability strategy could be of three types.

- **No change strategy** – as the term indicates, this stability strategy is a conscious decision to do nothing new, i.e., to continue with the present business definition. This could be characterized as an absence of strategy, though in reality, it is not so. Taking no decisions sometimes is a decision too. The organization did not find any significant opportunities or threats operating in the external environments. There are no major strengths and weaknesses identified within the organization.

- **Profit Strategy** – An organization cannot run for longer period with a no change strategy. Things do change and the organization faces with a situation where it has to do something. An organization may assess the situation and assume that its problem are short-lived and will go away with time. Till then, the organization tries to sustain its profitability by adopting measures like reducing investment, cost cutting, raising price etc.

- **Pause / Proceed with caution strategy** – A tactic which is employed by organization that wish to test the ground before moving ahead with a fill fledged corporate strategy. It is adopted by organizations that have had a blistering pace of expansion and wish to rest awhile before moving ahead.

11.3 Planning for Growth

Planning is a roadmap to any business throughout its survival. For each activity we need planning as it serves as a blueprint from starting to its ending note. Planning is then a key to run a business and maintain that pace throughout its existence. For that planning every business should regularly review its plan and ensure that it is serving the needs without any discontinuation, so that the correct and appropriate strategy is applied at the right time. For targeting that area of key growth firstly there is need to identify all the growth areas, now focusing on the key growth area that an entrepreneur wants to target it's time to revisit the business plan and make it a roadmap to the next stage for your business.

Converting your business from papers to a running one, guidance from a lot many strategies is required. The following points will guide in achieving the same:

- The importance of ongoing business planning
- What should your business plan include?
- Sketching a more sophisticated business plan
- Effective resources planning and allocation
- Use targets to implement your business plan
- When and how to review your business plan?

The Importance of Ongoing Business Planning

A good business plan should set the course of business over its life span. It is usually seen that this business plan is to attract the potential investors so that they can help in funding of the business. Continuous active business plan tells that whether entrepreneurs are achieving their business goals or not. An effective business plan can be used as a tool to check the status elaborating where entrepreneur is at present and may direct him to focus on the direction he wants his business to grow. A business plan will also ensure that entrepreneur cracks the key targets and manage the priorities for the business. Some business chose to assess progress every 3 or 6 months.

The chance of the success can be maximized by adopting a continuous and regular business planning cycle that helps in keeping the process up to date. This can be attained by regular business meetings with the key people.

These types of assessment helps entrepreneur to be on track. Regular monitoring is a good vehicle for showing direction and commitment to employees, customers and suppliers.

Defining your business purpose in your business plan keeps you focused, inspires your employees and attracts customers.

What Your Business Plan Should Include?

A proper business plan accommodates each and everything which may be required during processing of business. A good business plan should include brief of what business is, how it has reached this level and what entrepreneur wishes its future to be. Particularly it explains the strategy helpful to your business in improving the existing sales and process to achieve the desired growth.

There is need to set a time frame to make it clear that up to how much time, this plan is used. Like this plan will be for 4 months or 9 months or 12 months.

Broadly the requirements of plan are as follows:

- **Marketing information** – Its aims and objectives, for example number of new customers you want to gain and the anticipated size of your customer base at the end of the planned period.

- **Operational information** – such as where your business is based, complete information about your business, its supplies and equipments needed

- **Financial information** – It includes forecasting of profit & loss, cash flow sales

- **Summary** – A summary of the business objectives, together with targets and important dates.

- **Exit Plan** – At the end an exit plan is also very necessary as it includes the planned time of your departure and the circumstances for example: -family successor, sale of the business, floating your business or closing it down etc.

In case the owner intends to present the business plan to an external audience such as investors or banks, following points may be included:

- Detailed history of the business with aim and objectives focusing each area as-
    - Financial records from the last three years or detail of trading till date.

- Information about the skills and qualifications possessed by management involved in the business.

- Information about the product or service of the business with their distinctiveness and how it is best fit for the market.

Drawing up a More Sophisticated Business Plan

It is often seen that every business grows and keep on adding departments or divisions to its business having separate targets and objectives. You may need a more sophisticated plan for the business correlating the individual departments plan with the overall business plan. These separately made plans of different department/divisions are weaved into a single thread with the purpose of having an integrated business plan. This will prove to be a guiding tool for the whole business.

It is not necessary that only large organizations have separate departments/ divisions, many small firms do have separate business units following individual strategies.

To weave plans together from different departments/ division it is important to check that each department should be in coordination and following the same planning path. Précising the objectives, it's time to study individual departments/divisions.

Objectives of individual departments

It is important for each department to feel that they are a stakeholder in the plan. So, it is their duty to draft the unit's business plan and then agree on its final form in combination with other departments.

To achieve that overall business plan for the organization, each unit's budget and preferences must be predefined so that individual plan fits best to the final plan. Generally, there are some key points for preparation of the department's/divisions plan these are as follows:

- Individual unit's plan is required to be more precise and specific as compared to the overall business plan.
- It is very important that the objectives of the business plan should be realistic and deliverable.
- The individual units plan should be easily understood by the employees of the organization.
- There should be clarity in the mind of the employees about the best fitting of the plan.

Plan and Allocate Resources Effectively

To achieve the objectives set in the plan it is crucial to prepare and allocate resources effectively, which is done with the help of good business plan.

Once you've assessed your advancement to date and recognized your strategy for growth, your current business plan for success may look dated and may never again mirror your business' position and future bearing.

When the reviewing process is active and you want to go the next stage, it is always good to have a clear picture that how allocation of resources will take place. So that the strategy implementation is fruitful for the organization.

For example: a business unit has a target to achieve. In this case business plan should have allocated required resources to achieve the set target. Now, it is also necessary to check whether these resources are available or need to be generated. Once you have a clear picture on that next step is to have a check on number of employees available are sufficient or need to recruit more people. Now funds will be needed then you may want funds through current cash flow generation or external funding is opted.

In any case, you ought to do some exact planning to choose the correct level of resourcing for a specific unit or division. It's critical that assets are organized, with the goal that zones of a business which are vital to deliver the targets are satisfactorily financed.

Simply it is always better to plan for future growth through revenue generation.

Use Targets to Implement your Business Plan

For a plan to be a business plan it should integrate a proper set of objectives and targets. As it is known that business plan has its strategic goals which can be achieved effectively by using SMART objectives or targets. Here SMART means:

S – Specific

M – Measurable

A – Achievable

R – Realistic

T – Timely

Target gives a clear picture to understand why and when they need to be achieved.

There are certain indicators which help in monitoring and evaluating the performance of the employees. These are as follows:

- Sales/profit numbers for a given period
- Benchmarking in development of a new product.
- Productivity targets for individual team members
- Market share data

With the help of a target, it is easy and clear for an employee to know their best fit zone in an organization and what is required to meet the business objectives. Observing the targets and objectives closely and tracking the delivery can help the business development more effective.

When and How to Review your Business Plan?

There is a need to monitor the plan on continuous basis just to make sure that all the objectives are being achieved. The review process must be made as it follows the update of the progress and finding ways to develop the business in most promising ways.

Some business follows a plan where they monitor the plan regularly and always updated. On the other hand, most business follows an annual plan where the plan is broken into quarterly operating plans. However, when the business experience heavy sales then quarterly operating plan is not suggested, in that case business should opt for monthly operating plan.

Beside this cycle, it is important to keep an eye on the major events in the business target marketplace comprising competitor consolidation, acquisition of a major customer on the business environment as new laws laid by government should be on critical review every time.

Apart from all the plans whether of short intervals or long intervals, business must follow a process where the ball is always in a rolling state with regular assessment of performance against the plan and agreement of a revised forecast if necessary.

11.4 Knowing and Managing the Stages of Growth

As we human beings pass through different stages of life from birth to death. Likewise, businesses also pass through different stages; this is called in Business terminology 'Enterprise Life Cycle (ELC)'. Enterprise life cycle is broadly classified into five stages: Start Up, Growth, Expansion, Maturity, and Decline. Though it is not necessary that every enterprise follow this path, but most of the enterprise pass through similar phases during their growth stages.

It is very important to understand each stage of the process to enable entrepreneurs to adopt the right strategies for growth. As you will study that each stage has distinct characteristics as enterprises develop and grow in course of time.

A brief description of each of the five stages is as follows:

- **Introduction Stage:**

   The introduction stage starts with the launching of new product. Therefore, this stage is also known as 'start-up stage.' Introduction stage is time taking as production is limited with slow sale that too limited to a small area and as a result profits are negative or low with low sales and high distribution and promotion expenses. No existence of competition at all because the product is in introductory stage. The main concern of entrepreneur in this stage is to try to get more and more customers for the product. Therefore, more and more money is spent in promotional activities like sales promotion and advertising. Also, much money is required to attract distributors to one's product and build inventories.

   Special measures are planned particularly to advise the forthcoming customers and influence them to give that new product a try. There is no pressure to refine the product as the product is in introductory stage. Entrepreneurs are more focused on the buyers who have shown interest in the product. As it is the first stage of the product's entire life cycle, entrepreneurs should take this stage very seriously following the famous saying "well begun is considered half success".

   Entrepreneur should keep in mind that launch strategy is not to make money overnight but however some of the entrepreneur likely to sacrifice long-run revenue for the sake of short-run gain. The entrepreneur also needs to design different marketing strategies at different stages of product life cycle. The marketing strategy at the introduction stage is characterized as "try my product."

• **Growth Stage:**

If the new product satisfies the requirement of the market, then the product enters the next stage called 'growth stage.' During this stage, the enterprise is known to and accepted by the market. The early adopters keep continuing to buy the product and the prospective buyers start following their lead, especially if they hear favorable word of mouth from the existing buyers. As a result, production increases and sales start climbing quickly but supply falls far short of demand for the product produced by the entrepreneur. More production provides the benefit of economies of scale by reducing per unit cost of the product. As a result, profits increase.

Attracted by the opportunities for profit, the new competitors enter the market. In order to survive and thrive in the competitive market, the competitors will introduce the product with new features. This will lead to market expansion and increase in the number of distribution outlets. Sales jump almost with the same price where it was or falls slightly. Promotional expenses remain almost at the same level or a slightly higher level. Educating the market remains still a major goal, but now the entrepreneur also needs to meet the competition in the market. Therefore, the entrepreneur at this stage tries to change its business strategy 'buy my product to try my product'.

The entrepreneur uses several strategies like improving product quality, adding new product features and models, and shifting advertising focus from building product awareness to building product conviction and purchase. By following above strategies, the entrepreneur can capture a dominant position in the product market and earns the maximum profits

• **Expansion Stage:**

This is the stage in which the entrepreneur makes efforts to expand his / her business by way of opening its branches and introducing new product lines. The enterprise is transformed from a single-line enterprise operating in a limited market to a multi-line company penetrating new markets with new products and services. Product and service lines are broadened through innovation and development.

Business activities at this stage are diversified to reap the maximum benefits from the business opportunities available in the market. Delegation of authority ensues during the expansion stage. Entrepreneur needs to be able to accept leadership roles quite different from their founding roles. One such role requires leadership vision evidenced through a higher level of aggressiveness.

• **Maturity Stage:**

At some point of product life cycle, the product's sale starts slowing down mainly due to increasing competition. As a result, profits tend to decline. Such a stage is called 'maturity stage.' The maturity stage normally lasts longer than the previous stages. As such, majority of enterprises are found in maturity stage.

In such stage, marginal enterprises which find difficult to withstand the competition start dropping out and finally leave the market. Different enterprises adopt different marketing strategies to overcome the challenges posed by the maturity stage. Some enterprises adopt methods such as 'trading in' to survive for some more time in the market. Enterprises can try to redesign their marketing mix-improving. Sales can be improved by changing some elements of marketing mix. They can also slash down the prices of their products to magnetize new customers and competitors' customers. They may change the style of advertising by developing a better advertising drive or may use aggressive sales promotions. The enterprises need to understand that if their business is growing, they can move into larger market channels by using mass merchandisers. As a result, enterprises can offer new or improved services to their buyers compared to what the competitors have been offering. Although many products in the maturity stage usually appear to remain same for long period, but decision should be taken to make some changes in the existing product, market and marketing mix. Product can be modified by making changes in quality, features, or style to attract new. It may result into improved quality of the product with better performance.

Entrepreneurship in India   240

It can also improve the product's styling and attractiveness. For example, Hyundai a car manufacturing company restyles its i10 car to attract buyers who wanted a new look. Similarly, the producers of consumer food and household products introduce new flavors, colors, ingredients, or packages to revitalize consumer buying.

- **Decline Stage:**

This is the final/last stage of product life cycle of an enterprise. At this stage, the enterprises find it difficult to survive either due to the gradual replacement of enterprise product or due to some new innovations on account of change in customer behavior. The sales of most of the products abruptly falls and brands eventually dip. The decline may be slow, sales may plunge to zero, or they may drop to such a low level where they continue for many years. There can be any reason like technological advances, shifts in consumer tastes, and increased competition. Enterprises start incurring losses at an increasing rate.

In such situations, some entrepreneurs prefer to withdraw from the market and close their shutters. This is characterized as the 'decline stage.' Some remaining entrepreneurs may initiate pruning their product offerings. They may also opt for cut in promotional measures and reduce the prices of their products to remain in the market.

There may be entrepreneurs who decide to maintain their product brands without change in the hope that some of the competitors will leave the market. As Procter & Gamble presents one such example which made good profits by remaining in the declining liquid soap business as some of the competitors withdrew them from the market. Most of the entrepreneurs drop the products reached to their weak position, i.e. decline in sale. The reason is that carrying a weak product over the period may cause one type or other costs to the entrepreneur. While decline or negative cost is open and easily perceptible, there are hidden costs as well.

These may include too much of management's time, frequent price and inventory adjustments, more attention to sales promotion, and most importantly a product's failing reputation can cause customer concerns about the enterprise and its offerings. Thus, carrying on a weak product's biggest cost may well lie in the future. Besides, keeping weak products also delays the replacements of products, creates a lopsided product mix, impinges upon the current profits, and weakens the enterprise's foothold to stand in the market in future.

It is not necessary that all products will pass through the above life cycle stages and will remain for the same period at each stage. It is found that most of enterprises dissolve in the initial stages of the first and second stages.

It is reported that like human infant mortality, small enterprises also experience a high infant mortality rate. Some pass through some stage within a short period of time while other stays at the stage for a quite longer period. It is also not necessary that all enterprises exactly follow the life cycle stages in the sequence as discussed above.

11.5 Challenges of Growth

Entrepreneurs try hard to attain growth in their businesses and for that they optimize the business systems. This helps them to ensure that they could adequately meet customer demand and maintain the ongoing standard of their brand and customer services.

Below are listed six challenges that you may face as your business grows, alongside advice that will help you successfully manage these changes.

- **Cash flow management**

  Entrepreneurs may face problem of cash flow as they need to invest funds to make more money as required in growth stage, but quickly this concept may not help the entrepreneur and goes out of control leaving in a unsteady position. So, it is very important to manage cash during this time. Focus on channels that have the potential to produce regular sales and work to maximize their contributions to the base line. Good negotiation skills for payment terms with partners and vendors may help entrepreneurs in overcoming this challenge.

- **Responding to Competition**

  When your business achieves good success rate an interesting thing happens. People identify the opportunity and try to enter in the market for that business as a result they become the competitors. Many budding entrepreneurs are not completely ready to face the fierce competition and responds the competition so late that they failed to move further in that business. This is the time to focus on your strongest side and at what you are best and should step forward in communicating the same to the customer.

- **Nurturing a great company culture**

  The company culture is very much helpful in keeping all the stakeholders on same track. As business grows, more people get attached to the company; it is always difficult to put pressure on the culture you are following because you will be on the risk of having it derail. To handle this, value system of the company must be strong then let your company values guide all of your decisions and hire great people who will embrace their role as champions of the organizational culture. With allies on your side at all levels of the business your culture will be allowed to grow and flourish.

- **Learning when to delegate and when to get involved**

  There are situations when entrepreneur's personal involvement is necessary such as future strategic planning and recruiting important person for key. Then there are situations where it is required to delegate and trust that your managers will make the best decision for their team and the company. Every business owner must learn to get a feel for these situations and step in when needed without burdening their leadership team.

- **Keeping up with market changes**

  There is no such sector that does not go through tough phase, ups and downs are very common in some sector and they take place very frequent, if your company experiences the same you have to be prepared well in advance to tackle the fluctuations. And it is necessary to internalize the idea that disruption is the latest standard and that there is need to prepare the employees well in advance to face and fight the uncertainty.

- **Deciding when to abandon a strategy**

  It happens some time when the pre decided marketing channels does not perform the way they were drafted. For instance, new product line introduced in the market failed to catch attention of the customers now this is a lesson to learn from this failure. Failure can teach us how to identify problem area, become compatible to cope up the failure and find solutions.

11.6 Strategies for Firm Growth (Internal and External)

In simple term 'strategy' is used in almost daily activities whether personal or professional. Strategy is a well-planned course of actions devised to achieve an objective. Accordingly, growth strategy is a well-designed system to develop business function. Practically the types of growth strategies vary between the organizations. Broadly growth strategies are classified in two categories:

- **Internal Growth Strategies** – When the enterprise strives by itself without joining hands with the outside enterprise is known as internal growth strategies. An internal growth strategy includes expansion, modernization and diversification strategies.

- **External Growth Strategies** – enterprise attains the growth by joining hand with other enterprise. An external strategy includes joint venture, mergers, acquisition and strategic alliance.

  Let us understand the internal and external growth strategies in detail.

- **Internal Growth Strategies**

  Several actions are performed under internal growth strategy including new product service their designing and development, exploring new opportunities for existing product/service, push market sales of existing product's sale by tapping new market, add more to existing product line or service, open boundaries for foreign market as well.

These ways are mentioned in Ansoff model, a model which is used to find out the growth direction for their business.

Ansoff's product matrix is a combination of four strategies-

- Market Penetration
- Product Development
- Market Development
- Diversification

Let us discuss these strategies one by one

- **Market Penetration** – The objective of this strategy is to enhance your market share by increasing the sales of existing product/ service to the present market. So, the main objective is using a market penetration type of concentration strategy. This strategy is also used to maintain or increase market share of present product, restructuring a mature market by driving out competitors and gain advancement in growing market.

- **Market Development** – Market development basically involves selling the product/service in the new market. So, to expand the market entrepreneur must find out different ways. These different ways can help organization to offer present product and services to unexplored market. This can also be done by segmenting the customers and where it is not necessary that new market is segmented based on geographical area but in term of demography.

- **Product Development** – This strategy directly hits the product and involves selling of new product to the existing market. New offers are made to the existing customer with the aim of better sales turnover. Changed and better products may be achieved by investing in some areas as research and development, acquiring rights to deal in some other products etc.

  For example – Indian tourism industry is focusing on product developing with an objective of attracting more tourists and for this, pressure is laid on selling India as an ayurvedic based medical treatment or any other distinct quality.

- **Diversification Strategy** – Diversification strategy is a single strategy but a set of strategies that involves all the dimensions of strategic alternatives. These strategies are generally adopted to minimize risk by balancing it over several businesses. That is the reason an organization opt to diversify from one business to another businesses. There are two basic form of diversification.

- Concentric or Related Diversification
- Conglomerate or Unrelated Diversification

When new products are made for new markets this formula is called diversification or in simple terms the notion of diversifying is related to the newness of product or market or both.

Let us discuss the further form of diversification strategy.

- **Concentric or Related Diversification** - When the activity taken by the organization is related to the current business definition is known concentric diversification. This relatedness can be in the form of 3 dimensions as customer group, customer function or alternative technologies. There are three types of concentric diversification, these are as follows:

    • **Marketing related concentric diversification** – A related type of product is offered with the help of unrelated technology, e.g. a company in the sewing machine business diversifies into kitchenware and household appliances, which are sold through a chain of retail stores to family consumers. the market relatedness here is in terms of the common distribution channel for sewing machines, kitchenware and household appliances. relatedness in terms of common distribution channel for both the range.

    • **Technology related concentric diversification** – When with the help of related technology, a new type of product is offered to the customers. For example- A leasing firm originally offers hire purchase services to the institutional customers only but now started the services for individual customers also.

    • **Marketing & Technology related concentric diversification** – with the help of related technology, a similar type of product is offered to the customer. For example – a company offering bed sheets starts offering sofa covers also. Here the technology and marketing both are related.

Related diversification strategy offers the finest of both world as it helps in diversification of the organization from its actual business and keep it near in terms of relatedness.

- **Conglomerate Diversification** – When the activity taken by the organization is not anywhere related with the present business definition is known as unrelated diversification. This diversification is with the new product/ service those don't have technical or commercial relatedness with existing product, customer function or technology.

  Conglomerate diversification is offering a new product manufactured through unrelated technology for a new group of customers which involves a substantial risk.

  This diversification is made when the organization has excess capital, here excess capital is explained as surplus cash over and this surplus cash is reinvested into new ventures to generate more value for the shareholders.

There are few more growth strategies that can be used to ensure the growth . So, let's discuss them and these are as follows

- **Expansion strategy** – An organization follows expansion strategy when its objective is to attain high growth by broadening the scope of business. Expansion is adopted in term of their respective customer group, technology or customer function to improve the performance of the business. This strategy is helpful in increasing the size of the business in the market which ultimately leads to control the market and competitors better.

- **Expansion through Concentration** – It is also known as "stick to knitting" strategy. Excellent firms tend to rely on doing what they know are best at doing. Practically it can be said that expansion through concentration involves an investment of funds and resources in a product line for an existing market, with the support of previously used technology. This is often the most preferred strategy for an organization. It is better to invest the time and resources in the known business rather than unknown area.

- **Expansion through Integration** – In an organization when the activities related to present activity are combined is known as expansion through integration. Here the concept of value chain comes into picture, where the value chain is a set of interconnected activities operated in the organization which includes arranging the basic raw material and moving that to finished products and finally to the customer/consumer. An organization taking integration as an expansion strategy ensures that it moves to its adjacent businesses only.

  Expansion through integration strategy is further divided into 2 types of strategy as follows:

  - **Horizontal Integration** – When the organization stays in the same industry, where it serves the same market and customers with the existing product range using the same technology is known as horizontal integration. For example – a company offering toothbrush adds hair color brush to its products range.

  - **Vertical Integration** – When the organization starts producing new product that meet their own requirement is called vertical integration. For example – toothbrush company starts making plastics wires used for brush making.

- **External Growth Strategies**
  - **Strategic Alliances** – When two or more firms come together for a project and enjoys the freedom of being independent is known as strategic alliances. The relationship between the independent entities is to give and take as each partner remains active and strength for each other. A pooling of resources takes place and investment take place for mutual gain.
  - **Merger & Acquisition** – When two or more companies come together to form a single organization and for this, they adopt any of the following points:
    - one company acquires assets and liabilities of the other in exchange for shares and cash.
    - both the companies are dissolved, and a new company arrives with new issued stock.

- **Joint Ventures** – A partnership which creates a new independent firm for which partners contributes personnel, cash, equipments and intellectual property is known as joint venture. A common governance structure is agreed upon to manage the venture and a significant formula is shared for its revenue, costs and profits.

11.7 Exit Strategy

Exist strategy is also known as harvest strategy, where an entrepreneur harvests or extracts the money from the business achieving success. Exit strategy includes a detail plan of the strategy used and predicts the gain he expects from the business. There are certain steps to be followed for the exit strategy. The very first step is to frame business plan with a course of action to initiate a business and keep it in running form. This means that the form of exit strategy is already mentioned in the business plan which was designed at the time of starting a business. An appropriate exit strategy is one which proves to harvest the best possible return at that given point of time. The purpose of an apt harvest strategy in a detailed business plan is to get the maximum worth of the business well before starting the process of transforming the business's investment or ownership interests into cash or equivalent.

Enterprises should cautiously harvest or divest tired old business to release resources for other uses and cost reduction.

There are certain options available for small business owners to close the present business. These are as follows:

- **Sell to existing partner** – Some businesses opt for selling their stake to the remaining partner (s). When this option is taken then detail of the entire process including the buyout prices is already established. The advantage of taking this option in exit strategy is that the business remains with minimum alteration which generally does not affect the working of the business.
- **Sell to family member(s)** – This option of selling the business to family member(s) is often anticipated in advance. For smooth transition consultation of attorneys, accountants and family successors takes place. However, it provides the flexibility in determining future involvement in the business operations and creates easy transition for the stake holders.

- **Sell to a key employee** – This option takes place when a capable employee with available financial resources has the desire to take over the business. To design a partnership and buy sell agreement, consult an attorney.

- **Sell to an individual in an arm's length transaction** – It is good option for a person who keeps the desire of becoming an entrepreneur but wants to avoid the risk of starting a business from the scratch. There are many advantages for the buyer under this option as he or she gets the existing stream of sales and cash flow with tried and tested system, existing clients and brand name.

- **Sell to a competitor or another business** – This is also an option but for this your business should be in the hot market. Acquisition allows the business owner to hold a position with the newly merged organization. This option is an attractive option for those who want to stay in the market but without the ownership as they enjoy the exchange of ownership for financial payoff. Make yourself comfortable if offered to perform a new role in the newly merged firm. Try to understand the culture and other working of the merged firm.

- **Sell to employees** – This option involves a tax qualified, defined employee benefit plan as "Employee Stock Ownership Plan". Depending on the transition structure some employees of the organization buy share. This buying of shares takes place in two modes. In first mode the employees buy shares immediately upon owner's exit. In second mode the employees buy shares over a period. This option requires proper legal planning and a set of business factors that are rare in small businesses.

- **Liquidate** – The most common one is liquidation option as it allows quickest and easiest exit. This option allows owners to recover some value while avoiding investment of additional resources before exiting the business. Proper procedure is followed which includes selling assets, collecting outstanding receivables paying off debts, addressing contractual commitments, releasing employees, and finalizing legal and financial obligations before closing the business

11.8 Franchising

Franchising system is basically a group which is knitted firmly with individuals firms known as franchises. Operations of these franchisees are planned, directed and controlled by the operation designer, known as franchiser. Following are the three distinguished characteristics of the franchises-

- The trademark or service mark which is owned by the franchiser is licensed to franchisees in exchange of royalty payments.

- As franchisee make the payments to become the part of the system. Generally, startup costs comprise of rent and lease for the equipments and fixtures and a license fee.

- After this the franchisees are provided with a proper system for doing business.

Franchisees of Mc. Donald's invested $1.5 million in the total startup cost and fees. Payment expected from franchisee was some percentage of sales during that month and monthly rent. To make franchisees as a part of system they were required to attend "hamburger" university in Oak Brook, Illinois, for a couple of weeks so that they can understand and learn to manage business. Franchisees were asked to follow certain procedure in buying materials.

Franchising is a system that gives benefits to both the parties as franchisor gets highly motivated and enthusiastic employees who are not employees but are entrepreneurs. The thing which turns in the favor of business is the familiarity of franchisees with the local communities and circumstances. Now let us discuss some benefits of having a franchisee as business

- **Capital investment is low** – Franchisor requires some capital to expand network which is invested by the franchises. So, capital investment by the franchisor is low.

- **Attain Expansion** – Franchisor uses the franchisee's capital and establishes a good number of outlets quickly. This rapid expansion is achieved without incurring the overheads and costs associated with opening company owned outlets.

- **Easy recognition by the consumer** – The outlets are made in same design with same color and all so that it helps the consumer to recognize the brand more easily

- **Motivated employees cum entrepreneur** – Franchisor attains expansion of the business by franchising it and handing over the system to motivated people who are energetic to make it work.

- **Higher return on investment** – The return on investment is much higher for businesses that expand through franchising. Because there is less capital employed, the franchisor's profits are generated on a much lower capital investment. Although the revenue from franchised units is less than that received from company owned outlets, a higher percentage of the revenue is profit.

- **Less management required** – Franchising also allows the business to expand without spreading managerial resources across too many business units. A business owner may wish to keep his/her own operation small and tightly run. Operating more than a few outlets can drain business resources. A franchise system requires less management than a company owned chain of outlets. Hiring, training, motivating and retaining competent staffing are all functions handled by the franchisee, not the franchisor.

- **Owner manager v/s salaried manager** – Businesses choose franchising as a means of expanding their enterprise because of the ambition and energy of owner operators and sometimes especially in the case of small, one-person enterprises because the service provided by the franchise is very demanding and needs the extra attention of an owner manager. The owner manager is usually more motivated and effective than a salaried manager because he or she has a vested interest in the business.

Although there are so many advantages of having a franchising business, it has some disadvantages as well. Some of the disadvantages are as follows:

- **Lack of Control** – The franchisee is not completely independent. Franchisees are required to operate their businesses according to the procedure and restrictions set forth by the franchiser in the agreement.

- **Additional fees** – In addition to the initial franchise fee, franchisees must pay ongoing royalties and advertising fees.

- **Others' fault is your loss** – A damaged, system-wide image can result if other franchisees are performing poorly or the franchiser runs into and unforeseen problem.

Successful businesses with suitable concepts have failed to successfully franchise. Companies must meet certain criteria before embarking on the franchise route. Even when they have met those criteria, prospective franchisors must be ready to invest both money and time in the development of the franchise system. While it has its advantages, it is not a simple means to expansion.

Review Question

1. What are the different goals of an enterprise? Give a brief description.

2. Business Growth is that crucial phenomenon which keeps the business/enterprise alive? Explain.

3. Many firms are making profit by staying committed to their core strategy. How?

4. State the importance of ongoing business planning.

5. When and How to Review your Business Plan?

6. What are the stages of Growth? Explain all the stages.

7. Entrepreneurs may face challenges when attaining growth. Explain any 4.

8. Discuss some external growth strategies.

9. What is franchising system? Discuss its characteristics.

Applied Question

1. Select a FMCG company. Identify the major competitors and analyze the type of internal growth strategy used by the firm.

2. What are the benefits of becoming a fully integrated firm?

3. List a few recent instances of Indian companies that adopted diversification strategy and make observations on the type of diversification used.

4. Explain Harvest strategy and discuss at what point does an organization decide it need a harvest strategy?

5. Give an example of working Franchise in India. Explain its franchising system?

References

1. Burns, P. (2016). *Entrepreneurship and small business: Start-up, growth and maturity.* New York: Palgrave Macmillan.

2. Drucker, P.F.(2011). *Innovation and Entrepreneurship: Practice and principles.* Harper & Row, Publishers, Inc.

3. *Franchising as a means of business expansion* (2017, June14). Retrieved from https://www.franchisedirect.com/information/franchising your independ entbusiness/franchisingasameans of business expansion/10/105/

4. Kazmi,A.(2009). *Strategic management and business policy.*NewDelhi:Tata McGraw Hill.

5. Kittaneh, F. (2018, January 30). *6 Growth challenges your business will face (and how to overcome them).*Retrieved from https://www.inc.com/ firas-kittaneh/6-growth-challenges-your-business-will-face-and-how-to-overcome-them.html.

6. Kotler,P.,&Keller, K.L.(2009). *Marketing management.* Upper SaddleRiver, N.J: Pearson Prentice Hall.

7. Lax,D.A.&Sebenius, J.K.(2006). *3-D negotiation: Powerful tools to change the game in most important deals.* Boston, Mass: Harvard Business School Press.

8. Matthew Dobbs, R.T. Hamilton, (2007) *"Small business growth: recent evidence and new directions", International Journal of Entrepreneurial Behavior & esearch,* Vol. 13 Issue: 5, pp.296-322, https://doi.org/10.1108/ 13552550710780885

9. Morris, M., N. et. al., (2006). *The dilemma of growth: Understanding the venture size choices of women entrepreneurs. J. Small Bus. Manage.,.* DOI: 10.1111/j.1540-627X.2006.00165.x

10. Mullins, J. W. (2006). *The new business road test: What entrepreneurs and executives should do before writing a business plan.* Harlow, England: Prentice Hall/Financial Times.

11. Pillai,R.(2012). *Corporate Chanakya on leadership.* New Delhi: Jaico Publication House.

12. Puranam,P.&Vanneste,B.(2016).*Corporate strategy:Tools for analysis and decision making.* Cambridge: Cambridge University Press.

13. Robinson, S. and J. Finley, 2007. *Rural women's self employment: A look at Pennsylvania. Acad. Entrepreneurship* J., 13: 21-30.

14. Sinha, D.K. *5 Stages of growth strategies used in business-discussed.* Retrieved on 17-August-2018 from http://www.yourarticlelibrary.com/business/5-stages-of-growth-strategies-used-in-business-discussed/41202.

15. Storey, D. J. (1994). *Understanding the Small Business Sector : Reflections and Confessions. In Understanding the Small Business Sector* (pp. 21 – 33). London: Routledge.

16. *Tata mission.* Retrieved on 13-09-2020 from https://tatainternational.com/about-us/vision-mission-values.

17. Zwiling, M. (2011, January 11) *Growth Strategies- Five mart exit strategies.* Retrieved from https://www.entrepreneur.com/article/217842.

❏❏❏

12

Social Entrepreneurship

Dr. Kumar Abhishek
(Assistant Professor (MBA Dept.) & Assistant Registrar (Academic),
Dr. Abdul Kalam Technical University, Lucknow)

LEARNING OBJECTIVES

After reading this chapter, the reader should be able to:

1. Discuss what social entrepreneurship is and how it differs from business entrepreneurship
2. Identify areas of economy/society where social entrepreneurs work
3. Understand the Impact of social entrepreneurs on society

12.1 Introduction

Social entrepreneurship is an attempt to draw upon business techniques to find solutions to social problems. This concept may be applied to a variety of organizations with different sizes, aims, and beliefs. Social entrepreneurship is concerned with using the exclusive research to define a certain social issue, then causing a change with the help of establishing a social venture.

The social entrepreneur is a mission-driven individual who uses a set of entrepreneurial behaviors to deliver a social value to the less privileged, all through an entrepreneurial oriented entity that is financially independent, self-sufficient, or sustainable.

Bornstein Define: "A social entrepreneur is a path breaker with a powerful new idea who combines vision and real- world problem solving, creativity, has a strong ethical fiber, and is totally possessed by his or her vision for change".

Social entrepreneurs play the role of change agents in the social sector, by:

- Adopting a mission to create and sustain social value (not just private value),
- Recognizing and relentlessly pursuing new opportunities to serve that mission,
- Engaging in a process of continuous innovation, adaptation, and learning,
- Acting boldly without being limited by resources currently in hand, and
- Exhibiting a heightened sense of accountability to the constituencies served and for the   outcomes created.

The conceptual aspect of social entrepreneurship is very old, only the language used is new. The scope of social entrepreneurship can be extended with the help of this new language. This type of entrepreneurship not only includes the innovative non-profit making organization but also a number of social purpose organizations, like profit making community development banks, many hybrid organizations which combine both non-profit and profit-making organization.

Example: Shelter for homeless focusing mainly on their training and employment.

The term social entrepreneurship is developed with the help of three elements which are sociality, market orientation, and innovation. These elements are examined not to provide a constrained or an exclusive definition of social entrepreneurship but to provide a framework to this concept so that its prominent characteristics can be isolated, examined and understood. In fact, a wide variety of questions related to the nature of these enterprises and their relation to their operating situations can be explained by focusing on the differentiating features between social organization and other organizations.

12.2 Characteristics of Social Entrepreneur

- The usual ideologies and principles do not holdback social Entrepreneurs. They are always looking at breaking them.
- Social Entrepreneurs are impatient. They do not go well with the bureaucracy around them.
- Social Entrepreneurs have the patience, energy and enthusiasm to teach others.
- Social Entrepreneurs combine Innovation, Resources and Opportunity to derive solutions to Social problems.
- Social Entrepreneurs DO NOT lose their FOCUS anytime.
- Social Entrepreneurs always jump in before having their resources in place. They are not traditional.
- Social Entrepreneurs ALWAYS believe that everyone can Perform and have the capacity to do so.
- Social Entrepreneurs ALWAYS display DETERMINATION
- Social Entrepreneurs can ALWAYS measure and monitor their results.

12.3 Brief Description of Social Enterprise, Social Entrepreneurship and Social Entrepreneurs

At the present literature, the three terms-social enterprise, social entrepreneurship, and social entrepreneurs are indescribable. As per the sociological research, the ability or quality of a person to adopt a suitable management approach to deal with certain social problems is referred as "social entrepreneur".

(a) Social Entrepreneur and Social Entrepreneurship

Social entrepreneur is an individual or a group of individuals who initiate or lead an organization which is involved in social entrepreneurship. They are also termed as "civic entrepreneur", social innovators or "public entrepreneurs".

Arthur C. Brooks describes the social entrepreneur as:

- Having a mission to develop and maintain social value (apart from personal value),

- Acknowledgement and persistent hunt for opportunities of social value,
- Commitment towards nonstop learning and innovation,
- Performing more than the available limited resources, and
- Intensified accountability.

Basically, doing business for the welfare of the society is called social entrepreneurship. It is the environment where social entrepreneur design actions and procedures to fulfil their social goals. Just like other entrepreneurs, innovation has been the motive for social entrepreneurs. They are determined towards the innovation like new production methods, new sources of supply, new technologies, new distribution outlets, etc. Initiating new ventures or new products or services can also be innovative.

Social Entrepreneurs find out the origin of social problems and come up with path-breaking ideas to generate large-scale changes. They also convince others to adopt those changes. Such changes are transformative in nature and can be implemented at both national and global levels. However, these can be concentrated to a certain location and have similar power to impact.

12.4 Social Enterprise and Social Entrepreneurship

The enterprise engaged in fulfilling the social objective of the social entrepreneur through the act of social entrepreneurship is called 'social enterprise'. It is very difficult to determine if any enterprise is social or not because many times the social causes may be personal to an individual. In such situations, it becomes very difficult to differentiate between a social cause and a personal cause.

It is a common understanding that a social goal (benefiting the society anyhow) is the main driving force for social entrepreneur and their enterprises. The focus of social entrepreneur remains on improving the social values, i.e. to help in the social welfare or wellbeing of community. But still, there are some conflicts related to the position and the objectives of these social objectives. It is the social mission rather than wealth creation, which is the most critical aspect of social entrepreneurship. In his opinion, wealth should be used to achieve a certain aim by social entrepreneurs. It indicates that the personal profits to an entrepreneur have no significance in the objectives of the enterprise.

12.5 Types of Social Entrepreneurship

The different types of social entrepreneurs are stated below:

1. The Leveraged Non-Profit

This business model leverages resources in order to respond to social needs. Leveraged non-profits make innovative use of available funds, in order to impact a need. These leveraged non-profits are more traditional ways of dealing with issues, though are distinguished by their innovative approaches.

The entrepreneur sets up a non-profit organization to drive the adoption of an innovation that addresses a market or government failure. In doing so, the entrepreneur engages a cross section of society, including private and public organizations, to drive forward the innovation through a multiplier effect. Leveraged non-profit ventures continuously depend on outside philanthropic funding, but their longer-term sustainability is often enhanced given that the partners have a vested interest in the continuation of the venture.

2. The Hybrid Non-Profit

This organizational structure can take on a variety of forms but is distinctive because the hybrid non-profit is willing to use profit to sustain its operations. Hybrid non-profits are often created to deal with government or market failures, as they generate revenue to sustain the operation outside of loans, grants, and other forms of traditional funding.

The entrepreneur sets up a non-profit organization, but the model includes some degree of cost-recovery through the sale of goods and services to a cross section of institutions, public and private, as well as to target population groups. Often, the entrepreneur sets up several legal entities to accommodate the earning of an income and the charitable expenditures in an optimal structure. To be able to sustain the transformation activities in full and address the needs of clients, who are often poor or marginalized from society, the entrepreneur must mobilize other sources of funding from the public and/or philanthropic sectors. Such funds can be in the form of grants or loans, and even quasi-equity.

3. The Social Business Venture

These models are set up as businesses designed to create change through social means. Social business ventures evolved through a lack of funding—social entrepreneurs in this situation were forced to become for-profit ventures.

The entrepreneur sets up a for-profit entity or business to provide a social or ecological product or service. While profits are ideally generated, the main aim is not to maximize financial returns for shareholders but to grow the social venture and reach more people in need. Wealth accumulation is not a priority and profits are reinvested in the enterprise to fund expansion. The entrepreneur of a social business venture seeks investors who are interested in combining financial and social returns on their investments.

4. Activists

Those social entrepreneurs who are more inclined towards the society, very vocal and freely share their social values with other individuals, so that they can also be involved in the process of social welfare. In comparison to other types of social entrepreneurs, activities, select their suppliers on basis of social factors rather than looking at their financial aspects. They also advocate their values with their workforce.

Example: They might establish their enterprise in area of low income or target the minority population for their products.

5. Change Agent

The creation of social value will be done either with the help of donation towards the various causes or giving donation to others. The focus in this social entrepreneurship is to upgrade the life of customers by delivering better products that facilitate pollution control, organic products and cleaner energy. The different types of services which are offered by change agents are financial counselling to individuals and businesses and assisting them in financial selection as per their values and choice.

6. Market Pioneers

The social entrepreneurs who are termed as market pioneers are very forward about their intentions of social values creation and market change effect to their customers. In fact, they are also forward about their financial objectives. They make their agenda very clear with whom they are interacting. They mainly focus on impacting the system and co-workers to initiate changes in the society. They also make use of statistics and facts to their advantage.

7. Market Influencer

Focus of a market influencer remains on the financial aspects of the venture. They also look for creating social values but do not make it very clear to their target customers. They have the opinion that the customer might get distracted if the mission of the firm is shared with them which can lead to confusion, thereby hampering the financial success of the venture. Internal business strategies can be used by such entrepreneurs as main techniques of social value creation.

Example: Such entrepreneurs may choose to locate their business in the interior of the cities or employ disabled person. During the selection of suppliers, the focus of the market influencer will be on financial aspect rather than the environmental or social aspects.

12.6 Importance of Social Entrepreneurship

The main importance of social entrepreneurship can be understood by the following points:

1. Employment Development

Establishment of job and employment is the first and foremost economic value which is created by social entrepreneur as it is mutually shared by both the businesses and entrepreneurs. Approx. 1-7 % of individuals are having the employment opportunities in the social entrepreneurship sector. Apart from this, the social enterprises are also involved in providing the job and training opportunities to those individuals who belong to rare segments of the society.

Example: Homeless, disabled, gender-discriminated women, long-term unemployed and at-risk youth.

2. Innovation/New Goods and Services

Besides the production of new goods and services, the innovations which are critical for the social and economic development are implemented and promoted by social enterprises. Innovative methods are employed to tackle issues such as mental ill-health, illiteracy, crime, HIV, and drug abuse. These are among the most critical problems of the society.

3. Social Capital

Social capital is among the critical values which are generated by social enterprises. It can be commonly understood as network of relationships among people which include mutual recognition and acquaintance. The success of Japanese and German economies can be seen as the typical example of social capital.

4. Equity Promotion

An equitable society is created with the help of social entrepreneurship. This could be done by addressing the different social issues and accomplishing the continuous sustainable development by using the social mission instead of focusing only on maximizing profit.

The policy makers and academicians should pay a greater attention towards it. This becomes even more significant in those welfare states and developing economies which face the issues of finances.

12.7 Limitations of Social Entrepreneurship

Limitations of social entrepreneurship are stated below.

1. Funding

Social enterprises are neither pure corporations nor charitable organization. They can be placed somewhere in the middle. Therefore, they can also be operated either for making profit and not making profit. While some enterprises can generate enough profit by selling products that benefit the society, many enterprises cannot. In fact, corporate investment, donations and funds form government can be the other forms of funding for such enterprises. However, it will be difficult to attract investors if the enterprises seem to be less oriented towards profit. This is because the investor cannot expect an equitable return on their investment. At the same time, most of the investors do not trust social enterprises that focus more on generating profits.

2. Communicating Value Objectives

Social enterprises are not just focused towards creating commercial values; in fact, the social entrepreneurs are really motivated by the additional social values that are created in the process. Since these social values are difficult to be evaluated, therefore, it is not easy to communicate these value objectives to the donors, investors and community. Thus, for the progress of enterprise, it is important to take the correct decisions and stay neutral towards convincing the investors and donors.

3. Strategy and Long-Term Focus

The social enterprises face a lot of trouble due to their primary purpose of creating social benefits and values. In most of the cases, different types of social benefits can require different goals and it is vital to determine the cost of all the goals for guaranteeing true creation of values. A strong values proposition can be determined with the help of strong strategy which also defines the activities that the enterprise will not engage in.

4. Remaining True to the Mission

Dealing with problems at hand and avoiding long-term goals of the enterprise often seem easier. However, this could divert the enterprise from creating the desired social value. A regular review of the strategy and working towards it are pursued by the successful enterprises. However, the effectiveness of the enterprise may get reduced if changes are incorporated in the mission of the enterprise.

12.8 Recent Trends in Social Entrepreneurship

Latest trends in social entrepreneurship are as follows:

1. Social Media and the Role of Technology:

It plays a major role in the funding of the social entrepreneurial ventures. Entrepreneurs now have supreme access to fund and capital for their ventures due to an increase in the connectivity all over the world.

Example: Social entrepreneurs are now using Facebook, WhatsApp, Twitter and Instagram etc. not only to connect with their supporters but also to facilitate fund from donors.

2. Crowdfunding

It is a practice of collecting and raising money using the internet. The project or entrepreneurial idea is posted on several websites by the entrepreneur so that potential investor for the campaign can be found. The post gives a detailed description regarding the monetary goals of the campaign, method of utilization of funds and the expiry of the social campaign. The method of working of crowdfunding is like equity investment whereby investors do not want to get their investment back along with interest but instead expect a share of the company future profits.

3. Impact Investing

A group of investors assembled at the Rockefeller Foundation in 2007 coined the term *impact investing*. It covers a wide range of investment strategies seeking high profits and returns which are then used for the welfare of the environment and society. Impact investing is gaining popularity due to the amount of opportunities that it offers. Several entities interested in this emerging concept are financial institutions, banks, and different foundations.

4. Millennials are Reshaping the Global Economy

The path of social entrepreneurship is now led by a generation (known as millennials) that has a greater concern for the society and prevailing issues. Many enterprises are now being established by the millennials with the intention of the welfare of the people, environment and society at large. As per the research of Goldman Sachs, millennials form the largest group to enter the field of social entrepreneurship in the last 50 years. Given their different priorities and attitude, they are believed to revolutionize the business operations.

5. Venture Philanthropy

Venture philanthropy is a broader term that originated in the 1990s. The concept of philanthropy when applied to venture capital model gives rise to venture philanthropy. However, philanthropy is regarded as an investment where a philanthropist expects to get his/her investment back in some form. Social entrepreneur may join hands with philanthropists to achieve the objectives of their enterprise.

6. Hybrid Models

The combination of both profit making and non-profit making business models gives rise to hybrid models. According to this approach, an entrepreneur may be an owner of a profit making venture but at the same time create a social impact by way of an associated non-profit making charitable foundation or trust. It is possible that the activities of both the profit making and non-profit making enterprises vary. Therefore, this issue can be tackled by hybrid models. With the help of hybrid models, an entrepreneur can maintain ownership over the firm as a profit making enterprise and also gain tax benefits and philanthropic funds as a non-profit making enterprise.

7. More Resources are Becoming Available

Availability of increased amount of resources for the entrepreneurs is another major trend in social entrepreneurship. Improvements can be seen in the resources and various academic methods of those organizations and professionals that support the concept of social entrepreneurship. In fact, various programs and courses in social entrepreneurship are now being offered at graduate level due to its gaining popularity.

8. Social Platforms for Social Entrepreneurs are Multiplying

Various organizations and institutions are providing platforms for social entrepreneurs so that they could connect with other entrepreneurs and similar minded individuals. This also enables them to cooperate with each other and brainstorm ideas for setting up a social enterprise. Social entrepreneurship is no longer an unconventional concept and is widely gaining popularity. This is because people and customers have started thinking about the individuals and processes behind the development of their products.

12.9 Social Responsibilities of Entrepreneurs

The fundamental job of the business vision is to maintain the business easily and effectively. By maintaining an effective business, the business will help the nearby network by preparing the neighborhood economy, preferably with neighborhood dollars and neighborhood occupations. For most hesitant and fruitful businesspeople, it isn't enough to just invigorate the economy. Most businesspeople are individuals since they need to be their own cook when they eat food, and this incorporates the way they maintain their businesses and how to have any kind of effect on the neighborhood network. The point of view permits a fruitful businessperson to work in a way of thinking that he trusts in, and rouse in what he does.

The responsibility of the entrepreneurs towards society follows as:

1. **Socioeconomic Objective:** These objectives to a great extent incorporate social and financial prosperity of the oppressed. It is the obligation of each organization or firm to utilize its assets to meet the monetary objectives of the general public where it works. It is

likewise important for each organization not to demoralize financial and unjustifiable conduct.

2. **Improvement of Local Environment:** Mindful administration ought to guarantee that (A) its activity doesn't contaminate nature (B) it assists with making a solid situation (C) it improves the personal satisfaction of its workers, gardens for the overall population, Creates recreational offices, play areas and so forth.

3. **Employment Opportunities:** Employment creation is an essential social duty everything being equal. This diminishes joblessness and wrongdoing.

4. **Ethical Behavior:** It is the social obligation of each business to guarantee that the ethical canvas of the general public where it works isn't harmed by its exercises. It ought to be carefully guaranteed that all individuals related with it receive a good and agreeable mentality.

12.10 Arguments against Social Responsibilities of Entrepreneurs

Arguments against social responsibilities of entrepreneurs are as follows:

1. **Profit the Sole Motive:** Some state that augmenting profits is the sole reason for business, while social work and generosity is best for the administration, NGOs and social specialists. It is said that steady, beneficial organizations balance out the economy, cover more assessments, make more occupations, lower costs through large scale manufacturing, procure remote trade for the country, and so forth. All these business impacts in a roundabout way advantage the normal man.

2. **Managers Lack Social-Work Skills:** Business supervisor has his own abilities, that is, to build up the business. He has professional aptitudes however, no social work abilities. Offices straightforwardly identified with business capacities have administrators, for example, specialized and regulatory offices, yet he is likewise talented in his work as it were. So, requesting him engage in social work is a misuse of ability.

3. **Social Overhead Cost:** There are social expenses and social advantages to finish CSR. In any case, these advantages are long

haul. Moreover, the accomplishment of such advantages relies upon a few variable elements, making the outcomes questionable. For example, farmers can be given an intrigue free advance to purchase current hardware, yet the after effect of downpour can be shallow and may not yield the ideal advantages in a specific season. In this manner, social overhead expenses end up being an overwhelming weight on organizations, particularly the open segment.

12.11 Examples of Social Enterprises

1. Aravind Eye Hospital & Aurolab

Social Entrepreneur: Dr. Govindappa Venkata Swamy (Dr. V) & David Green

Type of Organization: Trust

Location: Madurai, India

Website: http://www.aravind.org

Mission: Making medical technology and health care services accessible, affordable and financially self-sustaining

Established in 1976 by Dr. G. Venkata Swamy, Aravind Eye Care System today is the biggest and most beneficial eye care office on the planet. From April 2007 to March 2008, about 2.4 million people have got the outpatient eye care and more than 285,000 have experienced eye medical procedures at the Aravind Eye Hospitals in Madurai, Theni, Tirunelveli, Coimbatore and Puducherry. Mixing conventional neighborliness with cutting edge ophthalmic consideration, Aravind offers extensive eye care in the most efficient manner, pulling in patients from all around the globe.

2. SKS India

Social Entrepreneur: Vikram Akula

Type of Organization: For-profit

Website: http://www.sksindia.com

Mission: Empowering the poor to become self-reliant through affordable loans

SKS accepts that entrance to fundamental money related administrations can essentially increment financial open doors for helpless families and thusly help improve their lives. Since origin, SKS has conveyed a full arrangement of microfinance to the poor in India and are glad for their present effort.

3. AMUL (Anand Milk Union Limited)

Social Entrepreneur: Dr. Verghese Kurien

Type of Organization: Co-operative

Website: http://www.amul.com

Amul has been a real case of a co-usable association's achievement in the long haul. It is probably the best case of co-usable accomplishment in the creating economy. The Amul Pattern has built itself up as an exceptionally fitting model for provincial turn of events. Amul has prodded the White Revolution of India, which has made India the biggest maker of milk and milk items on the planet.

4. Grameen Bank

Social Entrepreneur: Muhammad Yunus

Type of Organization: Body Corporate

Website: http://www.grameen-info.org

Grameen Bank (GB) has turned around ordinary financial practice by evacuating the requirement for insurance and made a financial framework dependent on shared trust, responsibility, support and imagination. GB gives credit to the least fortunate of the poor in rustic Bangladesh, with no security. At GB, credit is a financially savvy weapon to battle neediness and it fills in as an impetus in the overall advancement of financial states of the helpless who have been kept outside the financial circle on the ground that they are poor and thus not bankable. Educator Muhammad Yunus, the organizer of "Grameen Bank" and its Managing Director, contemplated that if money related assets can be made accessible to the destitute individuals on terms and conditions that are proper and sensible, "these a huge number of little individuals with their a huge number of little interests can indicate make the greatest improvement wonder."

As of May 2009, it has 7.86 million borrowers, 97 percent of whom are ladies. With 2,556 branches, GB offers types of assistance in 84,388 towns, covering in excess of 100 percent of the complete towns in Bangladesh.

5. Shri Mahila Griha Udyog Lijjat Papad

Type of Organization: Society

Website: http://www.lijjat.com

Shri Mahila Griha Udyog Lijjat Papad is a Women's association fabricating different items from Papad, Khakhra, Appalam, Masala, Vadi, Gehu Atta, Bakery Products, Chapati, SASA Detergent Powder, SASA Detergent Cake (Tikia), SASA Nilam Detergent Powder, SASA Liquid Detergent. The association is widespread, with its Central Office in Mumbai and its 67 Branches and 35 Divisions in various expresses all over India.

The association began off with an amount of ₹ 80 and has accomplished deals of over ₹ 300 crores with trades itself surpassing ₹ 12 crores. Participation has likewise extended from an underlying number of 7 sisters from one structure to more than 40,000 sisters all through India. The accomplishment of the association originates from the endeavors of it's part sisters who have withstood a few difficulties with steadfast confidence in 'the quality of a lady'.

Particularly since Muhammad Yunus, organizer of the Grameen Bank and a prestigious case of a social endeavor, won the Nobel Peace Prize in 2006 there is expanding enthusiasm for social business for improvement yet the current scholarly writing doesn't give is an adequate connection between social enterprise and monetary advancement strategies. How significant are social business visionaries for the monetary turn of events? What worth is made by social enterprise?

The social businessperson division is progressively significant for financial and social improvement since it makes social and monetary qualities.

Aside from the above mentioned, one can likewise take the case of numerous social business people working at the grassroots in provincial regions with much separation and reasonable habits.

Key Terms Discussed

Social Entrepreneur, Entrepreneurship, Enterprises, Recent Trends in entrepreneurship, Goods & Services, Venture Capital, Sociality, Innovation, Market Orientation.

Review Questions

Review question based on chapter:

1. What is social entrepreneurship?

2. Enumerate social responsibility of entrepreneurs towards society?

3. Explain the concept of social enterprise?

4. What are the different types of problem faced by social entrepreneurs?

5. Give details notes on changing role of entrepreneur?

References

1. www.scholar.google.com

Index

❑❑❑

Printed in the United States
by Baker & Taylor Publisher Services

Printed in the United States
by Baker & Taylor Publisher Services